To Gerry

Love

from

S. T.

April 1997

Edinburgh Law and Society Series

Rationality, Social Action and Moral Judgment

STUART TODDINGTON

EDINBURGH UNIVERSITY PRESS

Edinburgh University Press Ltd
22 George Square, Edinburgh

Typeset in Linotron Plantin
by Koinonia Limited, Bury and
printed in Great Britain
by Page Bros Ltd, Norwich and bound
by Hunter & Foulis Ltd, Edinburgh

A CIP record for this book is available from the British Library.

ISBN 0 7486 0432 4

Contents

Acknowledgements

This book draws together some of the issues which have been the focus of my studies for several years. During this time I have been lucky enough to receive help and encouragement in many ways from many sources. My debts of gratitude are numerous and longstanding, however, I think first and foremost, I must express my thanks to four of my former teachers, who, as friends and colleagues, have been and continue to be extremely generous in their support.

To Deryck Beyleveld I must extend my profound thanks for his central contribution to this work. Theoretically, his influence is extensive and obvious in the structure of argumentation which underpins the critique here presented. In a very direct sense this work can be seen as a continuation of some of the fundamental themes first explored in his co-authored *Law as a Moral Judgment*. I am indebted to him for his many hours of supervision from 1986 to 1989, and in much discussion since, which clarified a host of epistemological problems, especially the relationship between the Kantian reduction and the dialectical procedures in Gewirth's argument to the Principle of Generic Consistency. Without his sustained assistance this book could not have been completed.

To Roger Brownsword, similarly, I owe a great intellectual debt. As co-author of *Law as a Moral Judgment*, he, like Deryck, has been a central influence. I am particularly indebted to him for the time he has devoted to discussion of the main themes of this book and for reading the manuscript and offering some valuable suggestions for its improvement. In the closing stages of the project he was able to offer tremendous help, which is sincerely appreciated.

I am particularly pleased to be able publicly to record my thanks to two great friends and two fine teachers, Ron Phillips and John Schofield. Ron Phillips encouraged and attempted to refine my interest in philosophical matters on my return to full-time education as a mature student more than a few years ago. It was an invaluable experience to be able to argue (constantly, it seemed) with someone who had read almost everything but was disposed to believe very little of it. I am deeply indebted to him for his example, support and generosity.

John Schofield taught me Sociology, and taught me how to teach it. Learning from him and later working with him was a memorable and rewarding experience. For his continuing support, his valuable friendship and his kindness I am very grateful. I owe him a great deal.

In the short space I have left I must record my thanks to William Outhwaite, who, with Roger Brownsword, made valuable contributions to this work during discussion and examination of my Ph.D thesis. William Lucy offered much sound advice and insightful criticism, as did Gerry Johnstone and Siobhan Mullally. I am very grateful to them for their enthusiastic and skilful contributions. And finally, although they all deserve a much grander tribute, I am proud to acknowledge the varied assistance of the following people: the now celebrated John ('Harry') Denham – for an enormous amount of help and support – Howard Toddington, Val and Rachel, RDL, GL and Lucy, the Tinkers, Gareth, Sue, Louise and Paul, our sadly missed uncle Raymond Taylor, J. W. H. Anderton, Alan Walsh, Roger Lloyd, Dave Matthews, Bill Green, Michael Vasey, John Hughes, Michael Fleming-Cooney, Phil Jeffries and Kevin and Fiona Carter.

S. W. T.

Introduction

I hope that the title of this book and the title of the series in which it appears might save a lot of explanation and give a strong hint of its central preoccupations and its anticipated audience. But I am also aware that it might not. For those who half-expected it, I can confirm that this work explores the integral interdependency of the disciplines of philosophy, sociology and law. More precisely, it aims to show that in synthesis, the central problems of the methodology of social science require for their resolution the resources of an objective moral theory, *that such a theory is available*, and that a social science built upon these ethical foundations must serve as the basis of any rational legal praxis. However, in respect of those whose expectations are not so specific, I am fairly confident that I will be forgiven for offering some elaboration. With long-suffering students of law and social theory in mind, I think it unwise to pass up the opportunity to preface the rather brisk technicality of Chapter 1 with a more relaxed explanation of why I think that social scientists must become moral philosophers, and why lawyers must become social scientists.

To begin with I must admit that references to 'social science' and 'social scientists' are too often comfortably ambiguous. I shall attend to this issue presently. But there is a more radical objection to social science than ambiguity. For, if we are to understand by this phrase any activity more ambitious than that of simply recording the assorted attitudes and stated preferences of the general public, it is curious that anyone should think that it is even possible. Leaving aside the problems of the natural sciences, it seems that there has always been a great scepticism about the explanatory power of the social sciences. It is certainly the case that 'positivistic', 'naturalistic' or 'Newtonian' visions of the sociological enterprise have been criticised for naively attempting to employ the observational and experimental methods of the natural sciences. Understandably, this approach attracted the objection that, technically speaking, these methods were inappropriate to the investigation of practical or purposive ('meaningful') phenomena. There are those, like Max Weber, who have argued convincingly for a *verstehende* or interpretive, rather than a naturalistic methodology, but have remained in full accord with the view that such an approach to explanation must remain value-neutral or value-free. But there have been more recent and more complex criticisms of the aspirations of the value-neutral approach. These analyses have rejected both naturalistic and interpretive value-neutrality, and have suggested that it is political or ideological cynicism, not merely methodological confusion, which lies at the core of the social-scientific enterprise.

There have been some important results of this prolonged inspection of the status of science in general and social science in particular. One general result has been to highlight the problems of 'pure' observation in *all* scientific inquiry and to show conclusively that no explanation of phenomena is possible without prior theoretical orientation: a 'fact' is not *given*, it is the *product* of a framework of assumptions comprising an explanatory or interpretive scheme. This has undermined the notion of 'empirical proof'; quite obviously, the 'proof' is a product of non-empirical assumptions which themselves stand in need of justification. The criticism is a general one, but in social science the problem is acute. The suggestion has been that interpretive schemes appropriate to the apprehension of purposive phenomena cannot avoid implicit assumptions of value, or political or personal morality. These reflections have been extremely helpful in that they have sharpened our eye for the hidden presuppositions of social theory. But the widespread acceptance of the view that social science must *interpret* and, hence, must at some point *judge* or morally evaluate the phenomena, has been accompanied by another long-standing and similarly widespread view, namely, that judgments of value or morality are subjectively arbitrary in that they admit of no possible scientific demonstration or objective rational justification.

Logically, the issue is clear: either social science can be value-neutral or it cannot. We can discuss the issue presently in great detail, but it is not particularly contentious to suggest that faith in the possibility of a politically and morally neutral explanation of culture, economy and society is, to say the least, in serious decline. Thus we have in the current debate two well-subscribed theses: (a) that of the anti-value-neutral conception, which holds that social science (for methodological reasons) cannot avoid moral judgments at some point in its attempt to produce knowledge of social phenomena; and (b) that judgments of value, ethics or morality are beyond the scope of science and rationality. If both are true this means that social science or any analogue of it is an absurdity. Objectivity and justification in our attempts to explain social phenomena are logical impossibilities, and so, therefore, is any attempt to invoke 'social theory' or the 'social sciences' in argument or to purport to practise them. One might say that if (a) and (b) were both true, there would be no reason to prefer 'enlightened social and cultural analysis' to the 'simple prejudices' of the tabloid press. But if (a) and (b) were both true, this distinction, in any relevant sense, would be meaningless. To retain the distinction would be equivalent to suggesting that all values are equal but some are more equal than others. Disturbingly, (a) is true. It is clear then, that both methodologically and politically, the absence of a moral epistemology for social science is a grave embarrassment. However, I think it is possible to show that (b) is false. I examine these general points more closely in Chapter 1 and go on in Chapters 2 and 3 to show why social science must adopt a Weberian-like interpretive or *verstehende* approach, but that in so doing must reconsider its pretence to value-freedom or value-neutrality. In Chapters 4 and 5 I show in detail precisely why social phenomena can neither be 'simply' described nor adequately explained without objective moral criteria.

The remainder of the book turns to the search for solutions to these problems. I want to present the task of providing a moral epistemology for social science as essentially one and the same project as the search for an ethical theory of law and legal obligation – a Natural Law theory. That the two projects are indeed identical becomes obvious a soon as we are able to transcend the perspective which is a product of what Unger calls the 'Substantive, institutional, methodological and occupational autonomy' of law.[1] This notion of the autonomy of modern law refers to the set of arrangements which remove legal thinking and legal practice from everyday interaction and transfers it exclusively to

> A special group, the legal profession, defined by its activities, prerogatives, and training and which ... manipulates the rules, staffs the legal institutions, and engages in the practice of legal argument.[2]

The integration of law and social theory turns upon the rejection of this narrow institutional preoccupation. To regard these professional arrangements as somehow essentially constitutive of law is to mistake the organisational contingencies of a particular phase of the division of labour for the *practical point*, the *goal* or the *end* of that labour. If we are to cut through the camouflage of contingency and lay bare the essential components of the legal enterprise, we must be prepared to reflect upon the nature of its ubiquitous societal functions. Unger says:

> In the broadest sense, law is simply any recurring mode of interaction among individuals and groups, together with the more or less explicit acknowledgement by these groups and individuals that such patterns of interaction produce reciprocal expectations of conduct that ought to be satisfied.[3]

This is an impressive formulation. It can be refined slightly, I will argue, by placing 'legitimate' in front of 'reciprocal', but, crucially, does not this description of order expressed through normative arrangements also serve as the unavoidable point of departure for the social theorist attempting to grasp the very notion of society itself? That it does becomes clear if we consider that these 'patterned interactions' and 'reciprocal expectations' imply theoretically, and constitute as a matter of fact, a behaviour-shaping structure or system – i.e. the traditional focus of sociological inquiry. Admittedly, there is more to legal and social theory than the acknowledgement of structured normative relations, but what Unger calls law, Durkheim, with considerable justification, called society. The words, of course, are not important, but our conception of the nature of the objects is, and for present purposes it is clear that we are talking about the same object.

Given this, let us finally consider the respective roles of the Natural Lawyer and the social theorist. Natural Lawyers make it clear that they are not disposed to accord all norms and expectations within a normative or regulatory structure the status of law. Disregarding professional or formal criteria, they openly search for a moral principle by which to judge the validity of norms. Assuming that one is available, and applying it accordingly, the Natural Lawyer is concerned to determine whether or not there is a moral justification for the existence of a particular norm. If so, then there is in turn a reason for its promulgation and a justification of the expectation that it ought to persist and be observed. This, essentially, is the Natural Lawyer's understanding of the moral basis of legal authority and legal obligation. The social theorist, of whatever school, similarly seeks a reason, an explanation or theoretical justification for the existence of norms. Now there need not be the overt admission that the purpose of the investigation is to make any form of critical judgment upon the phenomena, perhaps the stated aim is mere description. Perhaps, on the other hand, some form of critique is intended, but on the basis of non-moral criteria. It is difficult to think of any interesting third option for the social theorist who does not wish to join the ranks of the openly judgmental. But I think I can show quite conclusively in the next few chapters that neither of these alternatives is logically possible. Thus, just as the disciplines of law and social theory share, fundamentally, the same subject-matter, we should not be surprised to find that they share, fundamentally, the same methodological problem: the justification of moral principles. We have already discussed the miserable consequences of failure in this regard. But, if the arguments presented in the concluding chapter are sound, then we have good reason to be optimistic.

1

Social Science, Objectivity and Values

The claim that social science is irreducibly evaluative is true. But how are we to take this? If it is meant as a condemnation of the enterprise in respect of a failure to meet scientific requirements, then the assumption must be that any pronouncements premised upon value-judgments or, less coyly, moral judgments,[1] have no claim to the status of universality or objectivity. There have been a number of responses to this in the past one hundred years or so. One response has been to accept the criticism and attempt to model social science on the methodology of the natural sciences.[2] Another has been to argue for a divergence from the naturalistic approach to explanation but to outlaw value-judgments in constructing such explanations.[3] More recently there has been a resurgence of the Nietzschean idea that *all* claims to theoretical justification are based on some kind of value-judgment – a will to power – and that we should dispense with science, truth and objectivity altogether.[4] I want to argue, in opposition to these views, that although it is true that social science must depart from the methods of natural science in attempting to explain social phenomena,[5] and that it cannot dispense with moral judgment in formulating its basic explanatory concepts, it has no need to abandon its aspirations to objectivity.

To say this is to suggest that it is possible to integrate our conceptions of methodological reasoning and moral reasoning. The method of moral reasoning which I think is appropriate to the task is one which attempts to discover the tacit presuppositions – and hence, the rational obligations – which attend the reflexive awareness of our constitution as purposive beings. This means that we must attempt to show that moral reason is a necessary implication of purposivity, and not merely an optional aspect of it. If philosophical analysis can succeed in this endeavour, then it can enable us to make sense of that complex set of phenomena which is the outward and visible sign of practical reason – namely, the social world.

My approach to this problem has been to try to draw together some of the fundamental concerns of philosophy, sociology and legal theory. My understanding of the nature of this potential integration is shaped by the recognition that the theoretical struggle for the concept of law is a struggle for the concept of society itself, and that this is a philosophical enterprise. This formulation may find more resonance with a sociological readership, pointing as it does to the insights of Durkheim, and, more recently, Unger,[6] than my original formulation which held that a sociological attempt to clarify the debate between Legal Positivists and Natural Lawyers leads to the realisation that sociology requires a theory of natural law – a moral theory – from the outset.[7] By this I mean the following: for the purposes of social science we are obliged to conceive of society as a normative structure. This focus on structure or system is necessary even if we are rightly concerned to accord full recognition to the 'individual' in sociological explanation.[8] To give an account of the nature of the normative (regulatory) arrangements which comprise this structure is to offer an explanation of the *rationality* the *normalcy* or the *pathology* of normative institutions. And whether this explanation is couched in terms of function or power and class, a 'will to power' or even a supposedly 'value-free' conception of calculation and control, it is in effect a claim to have achieved, directly or indirectly, what the Natural Lawyer strives for. That is, to ground the normative structure of a society in reason – to *explain it* – is to allude to a notion of *human interests*. Depending upon which conception of human interests is invoked, these allusions attempt either to legitimise implicitly the forces which maintain and perpetuate the form of regulation intrinsic to the structure , or to provide a reason why it should be modified or even abandoned. The normative arrangements or institutions of which we speak are not only economic-instrumental but interpersonal and thus normative-moral issues. For anyone who can manage to grasp the concept of law as something more than a purely formal, purely professional, politically and morally neutral *procedure*, the solution to the problem of the sociological *explanation* of norms is, quite clearly, the solution to the Natural Law problem of the *justification* of norms.

The attempt to individuate disciplines within this essentially philosophical enterprise is not really necessary or particularly useful. Our concerns are to be metatheoretical and at this foundational level all disciplines are distilled into epistemology. All that needs to be said is that the overall system of investigation into social phenomena requires the resolution of certain conceptual problems, some of which are logically more fundamental than others. Bearing in mind this aspect of unity, we may begin, for the sake of convenience, by making some specific points about what, in terms of degrees of emphasis and generality, may be presented as discrete components of the attempted synthesis.

PHILOSOPHY

In the disciplines of the philosophy of science and especially in social science and ethics, proponents of objectivity and universal truth are not now, and probably never have been, received with much enthusiasm. Relativism has always been an attractive option to the layman – especially when it is conveniently selective in its subject-matter. Developments in professional relativistic thought, however, are brought about by arguments which attempt to out-relativise previous relativisms. Vulgar lay relativisms and doctrines which propounded the fact/value distinction at least made some concessions to the potential determinacy of logic and maths and the odd low-level empirical observation.[9] However, it is now a commonplace to note that the debate concerning the existence or otherwise of rationally determinable foundations for knowledge has been radically reorientated by developments in hermeneutic analysis. In the form of Post-Modernism this relativism is thoroughgoing and impinges strongly on the issue of the relationship between practical reason and cognition. Although this is not a book about Post-Modernism, it *is* about practical reason and cognition, and no attempt to argue the case for any form of objectivism can reasonably avoid it.

Rorty, in his book *Consequences of Pragmatism*, has suggested, I think accurately, that we can trace a line of thought from Conceptual Pragmatists such as Dewey and Peirce, through Quine, to Foucault, Derrida and the corpus of thought which has taken the name Post-Modernism.[10] In naming their roots, neo-structuralist or Post-Modern writers have placed Nietzsche's identification of Knowledge with Power, and Heidegger's struggle to free us from the metaphysics of Being, firmly at the centre of modern philosophical debate. Rorty welcomes these developments and wishes to proselytise on behalf of their proponents. I do not, but I do wish to say something about the relationship between Conceptual Pragmatism and Post-Modernism, and their conception of the role of human interests and practical-reason in the theoretical representation of phenomena.

The two central themes which characterise these developments are the emphasis on the complex pragmatics of cognition and the rejection of the logocentric prejudice which informs our understanding of the relationship between language and the world.[11] With the rejection of the possibility of theory divorced from practical desire, and with the alleged dissolution of the sphere of the signified and its ground in the transcendental subject, we can no longer, so we are told, speak of foundations for knowledge. In opposition to this I want to argue a defence of Rationalism which I think *can* provide such foundations. In saying this I am, of course, suggesting a return to the conception of subject-centred rationality of Cartesian and Kantian provenance. These thinkers suggested that our reflective capacities, properly employed, can discover principles of cognition which *must* condition our practical and theoretical reasoning. For Descartes, it was the programme of systematic doubt and the application of clear and distinct ideas. For Kant, rationality consisted in, first, the identification of cognitive categories through reflection upon the conditions of possible experience; and secondly, their application to theoretical and practical problems *within the limits* of possible experience. Criticisms of the Cartesian programme of systematic doubt, and of the claims to universality of the Kantian categories, are not difficult to find, and it would be foolish to pretend that these claims are not contentious. But I think that the approach which views the epistemological enterprise as the attempt to combine phenomenological reflexivity with universal necessity is one which offers the only hope of a solution to the curious problem of grounding epistemological claims. That is, we know that if anything is true, it is true because something else is true. To end this regress seems to be as difficult as *actually* lifting ourselves up by our bootstraps. But the problem of knowledge is at least intelligible to us, and reflection upon the conditions and limits of this intelligibility as a starting point for a synthesis I take to be the essential message of Enlightenment Rationalism.

It is true, of course, that in epistemology, and especially moral epistemology, and in the attempts to construct theoretical models of social phenomena, the gap between the rational and the 'real' (actual thinking, actual behaviour) is uncomfortably large. Acknowledgement of the fact that it is necessary to work within the confines of reason does not, of itself, dampen our curiosity about what may lie beyond its grasp. Neither does it bring about a harmonious balance between our potential for reason and our psychological, physical and emotional appetites. No one can ignore the claim that reason's grasp on the world of our natural experience appears to be spiritually unsatisfying. In admitting this we can at least empathise with the view that apprehends the readily acknowledged limits of reason as the prison of the soul. But whether or not an unmediated communion with Being is possible or desirable, and whether or not this state of existence is taken to be synonymous with human freedom, a commitment to rational discourse must hold that this attempt to transcend the bounds of reason is impossible. This position is, of course, perfectly circular – but not viciously so: if proper reasoning leads us to an unavoidable conclusion it is not to be dismissed *because* it is unavoidable.[12] This would be to miss the point of the Rationalist project, at least in respect of Descartes' and Kant's intentions. For the aim of Descartes; meditations and Kant's transcendental critique was to demonstrate that there is little point in asking whether or not what must be *rationally* held to be the case, *really* is the case.[13] We may say that *assertorically*, fundamental claims concerning the constitution of the natural or social world or even mathematics and logic cannot be substantiated by any procedures available to us. However, *dialectically*, from the basis of claims which, as presuppositions of our experience, must be made, we can at least identify certain epistemological principles which must be accepted on pain of contradiction – especially by those who seek to deny them.[14]

However, the *pain* of contradiction has been anaesthetised, at least to the satisfaction of many modern philosophers. Empiricism in various forms has acknowledged the phenomenon of 'necessity', but has characterised it as vacuous: tautological, definitional, conventional, purely linguistic.[15] Such arguments fail miserably for the simple reason that the notions of definition and convention presuppose the intelligibility of substitution instances which themselves rest upon the *extra-logical* phenomenon of the *necessity* of the Law of Identity.[16] Post-Modernism has duplicated this mistake and taken it further in suggesting that the notion of necessity, far from being a mere embarrassment to the empiricist theory of the *a priori*, is and always was a pernicious myth.[17] In any event, the power of necessity in its analytical application is denied, and any responsibilities it imposed are abrogated. But to reject the efficacy of reason to settle our theoretical and practical disputes is to defend an alternative to it. In the absence of a defence it is to say nothing of any interest whatsoever.[18] An intelligible solution to theoretical-descriptive or practical-moral problems, therefore, it is only possible *within reason*; and only if reason contains necessary, that is, rationally undeniable, theoretical and practical principles. Thus, in offering some thoughts on the possibility of necessary foundations for moral knowledge, I have been drawn to the work of theorists who suggest that we may discover the necessity of normative-moral or deontic principles as entailments of the reflexively undeniable facts of our constitution as practical beings.

Curiously, this focus on our essentially practical nature has led proponents of early forms of instrumentalism and subsequent forms of Pragmatism and neo-structuralism to deny the existence of rational foundations for knowledge. We have noted that traditional (Humean) and Logical Empiricism have characterised the appearance of necessity as merely conventional. So too with Pragmatism, a radical empiricism. Pragmatism speaks of the naturalisation of epistemology.[19] It claims that there are no universal truths or laws of thought.[20] Instead, rationality is alleged to consist in the recognition that our practical interests shape our cognitive interests, and that this fact obliges us to adapt our theory to the task in hand. There will be beliefs which we adopt under particular circumstances and perhaps expect to abandon to make life more simple, and beliefs whose tenure seems fairly secure – like the principles of logic – unless there is a serious programme of reorganisation of our knowledge. But the difference is one of degree and not one of kind. Hence, we are to accept relativity at the ontological level, and consequently epistemology becomes synonymous with whatever suitably classical abbreviation can be found to designate the study of optimally convenient explanation. I think that these doctrines are false and can be shown to be false. But there is a sense, and I intend no paradox, in which Pragmatism is perfectly valid. That is, as a body of doctrine, viewed from the perspective of the history of ideas, it gives us an acute insight into the pathology of the *actual* institutional development of the philosophy of science.

It is the replacement of epistemological principles by practical criteria, and the redefinition of rational theory choice as a *practical* affair, which characterises the Pragmatist enterprise as a firmly socially located doctrine. It is the philosophy of the technological age; and it is at once ironic and yet perfectly obvious why we find its instrumental view of rationality originating in the attempt to reconcile Divine Revelation with the discoveries of Renaissance science. Popper reminds us of the well-known story of Galileo's dispute with the Inquisition.[21] The moral of the story is more subtle than is often appreciated: the Catholic Church pointed out to Galileo that his disturbing proof concerning the mere appearance, as opposed to the fact, of the diurnal motion of the sun based on his observations of Jupiter and its moons could not be a claim to truth, for the truth was to be found in Joshua 10:12. However, the assumption of a rotating earth did simplify the mathematics and the Gregorian calendar, and as long as Galileo realised that science was confined to simplifying theory, and left truth to the church, there would be no need for any unpleasantness. Faced with this Galileo can truly be said to have seen the sense of Pragmatism. Bishop Berkeley made the same point in respect of Newton's contribution to the science of simple 'explanation'. Thus, whilst I would not deny that the issue of the relationship between human interests and knowledge is central to our discussions of the epistemology of the social sciences, this tale should make some of us uncomfortable about being included in the 'we' when Pragmatists speak of 'our' scientific interests. If this is too cryptic, the point is that *epistemologically* Pragmatist 'explanations' are, at best, either simple descriptions of how we actually do muddle through life, or, at worst, ideologically arbitrary (power-backed) justifications of expediency trading on notions of universal interest. What, then, are the real consequences of Pragmatism?

Twentieth-century Pragmatism does not, of course, hold to the doctrine of revelation. Rather, it dispenses with a notion of absolute truth altogether. However, it envisages the same role for the scientist as enunciated by Cardinal Bellarmino. In the absence of revelation we are not, according to Pragmatist philosophy, to import another notion of truth into the picture to explain the success of technology. The success of technology is explained by its success, for success is its goal. Pragmatism has no revealed truth to fill the void left by the Inquisition's instrumentalist conception of science. It must redefine the scope and nature of our knowledge as being entirely conditioned by our practical interests. It must substitute a pragmatically relative conception of success for truth. When some of the recalcitrant 'we's question the criteria for success, this raises the question of what counts as a 'successful' theory of success. An absolute (non-pragmatic!) criterion of success to settle the matter entails a transcendental conception of truth. Pragmatism, by definition, cannot entertain this possibility. In other words, we end up with an *a priori* rejection of the notions of objectivity and truth, *pragmatism notwithstanding.*

In view of this, what must be investigated carefully is why we are all urged to abandon our quest for truth because *some* consider themselves successful on their own terms. Even more disquieting is the fact that this exhortation to relinquish our aspirations has been widely heeded. The co-operative response from Post-Modernism in this regard cannot, I assume, be interpreted as an endorsement of the instrumentalist-cum-pragmatist-cum-technologist's case. This triumph of the Will to Power of 'technology', and its debasement of modern culture, is apparently well understood by proponents of Post-Modern critique.[22] But this triumph should be understood as 'technology's' contribution to the assault upon reason. If Post-Modernism can speak of the damage to human freedom occasioned by this assault, as it always implicitly and sometimes explicitly claims to do,[23] it can only draw comfort from the demise of Reason by conflating reason with the meagre scraps of instrumental rationality upon which the 'technological' mind is content to subsist. In which case, whose foundations do Post-Modernists wish to demolish, and why? Failure to consider this question carefully, and to answer it clearly, is but a short step away from a grotesque alliance of fatally incompatible 'anti-foundationalisms'.

Post-Modernism, in various forms, has attacked the Enlightenment vision of an all-encompassing reason. I have suggested that mistakes may have been made in the identification of the target by the Post-Modern critique. The *quid pro quo* is to say what I mean by Post-Modernism. Conveniently, I have in mind what Thomas McCarthy says in his introduction to a recent work of Jurgen Habermas:[24]

> The critique of subject-centred reason is ... a prologue to the critique of a bankrupt culture.
>
> To the necessity that characterizes reason in the Cartesian–

> Kantian view, the radical critics typically oppose the contingency and conventionality of the rules, criteria, and products of what counts as rational speech and action at any given time and place; to its universality, they oppose an irreducible plurality of incommensurable lifeworlds and forms of life, the irremediably 'local' character of all truth, argument and validity; to the a priori, the empirical; to certainty, fallibility; to unity, heterogeneity; to homogeneity, the fragmentary; to self-evident givenness ('presence'), universal mediation by differential systems of signs (Saussure); to the unconditioned, a rejection of ultimate foundations in any form. Interwoven with this critique of reason is a critique of the sovereign rational subject – atomistic and autonomous, disengaged and disembodied, potentially and ideally self-transparent. It is no longer possible, the critics argue, to overlook the influence of the unconscious on the conscious, the role of the preconceptual and nonconceptual in the conceptual, the presence of the irrational – the economy of desire, the will to power – at the very core of the rational.

I am specifically concerned with this undeniably normative-moral or, as Habermas says, crypto-normative[25] aspect of Post-Modernism which, like Conceptual Pragmatism, seeks to introduce practical criteria into the epistemological equation. But the seemingly innocuous introduction of practical criteria as epistemological criteria in, for example, the work of Quine, appears to be worlds removed from the sophisticated cultural critiques of Post-Modernism. The epistemology, however, shares an essentially similar premise: knowledge (or 'knowledge') is conditioned by human interests.

Depending upon one's point of view as to whose and which interests are at stake in this analysis of culture, human actions and prescriptions can be interpreted in a variety of ways. Where reason is interpreted as an oppressive and cognitively imperialistic world view, then the Post-Modern vision employs these terms from a perspective which, whether acknowledged or not, presupposes a conception of a higher form of human freedom which Reason cannot comprehend and which, it is constantly alleged, Reason threatens. Thus, what unites the various aspects of Post-Modern critique is the suspicion that behind the discourses of truth, falsity, validity, justification, in fact the whole enterprise of objectivity, lurks a quest for the gratification of less noble appetites than the thirst for disinterested knowledge.[26] Post-Modern thought has explored this hypothesis by way of analyses of diverse media of human communication, notably in the discourses of politics, ethics, literature, gender, sexuality, psychoanalysis and even, as with Foucault, the whole project of the human sciences as a job lot. From Nietzsche to Foucault and beyond there is an organising category of critical interpretation. This common theme can be understood as a constant allusion to a lack of authenticity in the interpretation and representation of real experience. It points to the ulterior motive in thought and deed, and this ulterior motive is always born of a quest for power. Reason and its offspring, objectivity and truth, are, it is alleged, the most fundamental of the ideologies of the ulterior motive. Nietzsche's exposition of Reason's Will to Power has yet to be bettered. He too, like Descartes and Kant, offered a *universal* message: there is an infinity of interpretations of the world. Our needs condition our perspectives of interpretation. As subject-centred hermeneutic products, all perspectives subscribe to the myth of objectivity. Once the myth is acknowledged as myth, all is myth: none true, none false; none worthy, none base; only power elevates one interpretation above the other. Power is the imprimatur which admits one myth to the corpus of knowledge at the expense of another.[27]

This is perfectly plain. Because it is plain we can see that it is contradictory. Of course, interpreted loosely, there can be no quarrel with the claim that we are continually subject to the propaganda of the self-seeking; even if the self-seeking are meek and mild, and even if it is we who seek to delude ourselves. The acknowledgement of this unfortunate state of affairs is a precondition of any critical purchase on the politics of social life. But, equally clearly, we are obliged to pay our epistemological dues for the privilege of this insight. Quite apart from the fact that talk of alleged ulterior motives implies an understanding of rational motives and real interests, a pedant might ask whether or not the demythologisation of the myth was not itself a claim to truth. This question can be formulated with as much pretension to profundity as one wishes – but even if it is the only truth, and we accept it as such, might we not still be mocked by our own words? Perhaps as has been suggested, we should not take words as tokens of something more than words. They are, after all, only jumbles of signs. But if this claim has any significance it is precisely because jumbles of signs are significant.[28] However one asks or answers these questions, it appears that we must propound our liberation from the tyranny of Reason whilst still locked tightly within its structures, and still employing its foundational categories.

Whatever may be said about my pedestrian analysis of the Nietzschean vision there is no doubt that there are, and inevitably must be, contradictions contained in any attempt to present a totalising critique of Reason. To take this *in itself* as a justification for the rejection of reason is just another contradiction.[29] It is not simply that an attempt to furnish a critique of reason ends in inconsistency – this much is perfectly obvious to anyone from the outset of the enterprise. It is the delusion that there can be intelligibility *beyond* inconsistency which at once destroys Post-Modernism from the inside as critique, and yet insulates it from external criticism and thus preserves it as an institution. In the absence of a commitment to consistency, the Post-Modern critique of Reason amounts to the request to abandon Reason for no reason.

There is no mystery in the origins of this unreason if we acknowledge the consequences of Post-Modernism's attempts to introduce aspects of practical-interest criteria into the critique of cognitive foundations. Quite simply, this approach involves the introduction of concepts such as needs, motives, purposes, power, interests, domination, rhetoric and irony.[30] Far from being suitable components of a framework which could direct itself to an analysis of cognitive foundations, these complex practical concepts are *themselves* in urgent need of epistemological analysis. In other words, any intelligible employment of them presupposes foundational commitments. Quite clearly their employment presupposes commitments to legitimate inference and thus logical principles. But, more importantly, and less obviously, they presuppose a commitment to some conception of moral foundational principles. Thus it must be at least acknowledged that the debate cannot be about whether or not there are foundations for our knowledge. Rather it must be about just what these foundations are. I hope to show that a genuinely epistemological approach to the analysis of practical reason – rather than simply characterising it as arbitrary desire – can lead us to firmer ground in these matters.

SOCIAL SCIENCE

I want to show that practical reason is the organising category of social theory, in that social phenomena are practical phenomena and must be essentially apprehended as such.

To define, describe, delineate or 'concentrate upon' a particular aspect of social phenomena must be, in all cases, to offer an ideal-typical model of the relationship between particular norms, conceived as *means*, conditioned by *ends* which are constituted by values. Durkheim's understanding of the family or Marks's analysis of capital rely as heavily upon this notion of the ideal-type as does Weber's conception of the Protestant Ethic. All three of these notables claimed that their analyses of social phenomena were free from the intrusion of value-judgments. although they were judgments about values. More precisely, all three would have rejected the claim that their analyses rested upon moral judgments. All three have been roundly criticised for failing to practise what they preached. Thus if we cannot dispense with the ideal-type, then the crucial question is whether or not we can have the ideal-type without the moral judgment. Before answering the question, or perhaps in order to answer it, we may ask ourselves why we so fear the intrusion of moral judgment in our attempts to explain social phenomena.

The stock answer is that moral judgment precludes the possibility of objectivity; and objectivity is the definitive attribute of science. Consequently we must either abandon moral judgment or relinquish our aspirations for a science of society. But this is, of course, to assume that moral judgment and objectivity are mutually exclusive. If the claims of a general emotivism, which takes many forms, are to be believed, then this exclusivity is apparently obvious. But the claims of a general emotivism are based upon the premise of this exclusivity; they do not explain it.[31] Two points need to be made.

First let us imagine what our theoretical discourse would look like if we could not draw upon the doctrines of logical positivism. These doctrines restrict the scope of genuine science to empirically verifiable claims and, at a push, maths and logic. Let us then also remember that the theoretical basis of any sociological scheme of explanation consists exclusively of non-empirical assumptions. Secondly, let us remember that our acknowledgement of the vast plurality of conflicting moral views, whether those of remote tribal communities or those of our next door neighbours, does not, in principle, provide any argument whatsoever against the possible truth of any particular moral view. What, then, would be our argument against the impossibility of an objective ethics? I make these points merely to suggest that (a) Logical Positivist conceptions of the scope of the a priori and its consequences for moral theory abound in literature which purports to denounce such traditional empiricism,[32] and (b) that the presentation of an a priori objection – of universal scope – to the possibility of moral objectivity, requires much more epistemological effort than is involved in its mere assertion.

If objectivity and moral judgment cannot be reconciled then we face some difficult problems in the attempt to claim a critical intent for social theory. For, if the description of a social institution is to take the form of an ideal-typical model of a means-ends enterprise, how do we resolve disputes, at the level of theory, between conflicting interpretations of particular *ends* to be described? Is, for example, the *end* or goal of the nuclear family either to provide a stabilising environment for its adult members, perfectly integrated with a complex division of labour,[33] whilst simultaneously functioning as a basic socialisation course for the young; or is it to be conceived as the optimal social unit for the maximisation of profit, control and reproduction of the conditions conducive to capitalist accumulation regardless of the material and psychological well-being of its members?[34] Any 'neutral' alternative to this notorious example of theoretical conflict may be substituted; my point does not rest upon the absurd assumption that these blatant ideologies of social theory exhaust our choices. I merely wish to argue that, depending upon our initial conception of the end or goal of the institution, we make corresponding judgments on the component and related phenomena of the institution. Thus the same set of empirical 'data' lends itself to conflicting interpretations at a simple descriptive level. Of course, there are no *data* to be found, but, rather, conflicting interpretations of phenomena. This is neither a novel nor a profound discovery. It amounts to saying that it is possible to interpret the world in different ways. What is more important is the similarly inescapable conclusion that unless a non-arbitrary conception of the practical end or goal of a social institution can be formulated, social theory cannot achieve objectivity. In our example the theoretical problem is engendered by a dispute over whether to characterise the family as a socially integrative unit, or as an institution which perpetuates the source of the exploitation of those bound up in it. We are unsure from *which* perspective of interest it should be viewed, and, even if this could be agreed, *whose* interests are served. These are moral disputes. If such disputes cannot be resolved one way or the other, then social institutions cannot be *described* one way or the other. To rule them both out, and others like them, because they raise moral questions, is simply to assert that moral questions cannot be answered. This claim if true, would still fail to give us a clue as to how we can apprehend social phenomena 'neutrally', without raising such questions.

LEGAL THEORY

Extending these considerations to the sphere of social theory which seeks to conceptualise specifically legal phenomena raises this curiosity: what appears to be an insular dispute within the confines of orthodox jurisprudence is in fact a particular instance of the general sociological problem outlined above. The debate between Natural Lawyers and Legal Positivists seeks to establish whether or not there is a necessary connection between the concept of law and moral reason.[35] But one may well ask whether or not there is a necessary connection between the concept of the family and moral reason, or indeed the concept of any social institution and moral reason. It is vital that we attend to what is meant by 'necessary' here.

Any attempt to distinguish one object of investigation from another requires the formulation of a classificatory concept which, in effect, stipulates the necessary and sufficient conditions under which a particular object is to be correctly distinguished as just that object. Here, and in relation to the empirical significance of conceptualisations of phenomena, there is no formal difference between the natural and social sciences, except that natural science must posit nomological or law-like properties as the identifying features of its objects. Thus to say that there is a necessary connection between law and morality is to say that it is necessary to include the property of moral validity as a necessary, though not sufficient, condition of its identifying criteria. This is the Natural

Lawyer's contention. By contrast, the Legal Positivist opts for a classificatory concept of law which permits the omission of the criterion of moral validity.

I have used the word 'stipulate', which suggests an essential arbitrariness at the level of theoretical definition. If this arbitrariness is unavoidable then the problem at the heart of the dispute between Natural Law and Legal Positivism is as inconsequential as it is insoluble. Thus the necessity, or otherwise, of the inclusion of particular criteria in classificatory concepts appears as a problem at the fundamental levels of concept formation. The possibility of objective explanation, therefore, appears as the problem of which set of identifying criteria we are to opt for in terms of theory choice. In the case of physical theory this problem appears, broadly, as the dispute between intrumentalism and realism. Disputes concerning the concept of law or the concept of any social phenomenon, likewise, can be resolved only at the most general level of social theory. In other words, all disputes concerning the validity of concept formation are epistemological disputes. By virtue of the *fact* of our theoretical disagreement at this most basic level, we are, as natural or social scientists, instrumentalists or realists, Natural Lawyers or positivists, deconstructionists or rationalists, at least united in the epistemological enterprise. In affirming or denying epistemological foundations we are at least concentrating on foundations. How,then, are we to proceed epistemologically?

SOCIAL SCIENCE AS MORAL CRITIQUE

Social science must acknowledge as its point of departure the validity of the distinction between natural and social phenomena. This acknowledgement must be the product of analysis and not of an appeal to common sense or self-evidence; for upon the clear understanding of the nature of this cleavage of subject-matter, and hence, method, rests the possibility of objectivity.

Social phenomena are characterised by their essential purposivity. The subject-matter of social science is social action. To be a social scientist is to subscribe to an ontology of systematically cognisable structures of social action. To individuate aspects of social action, whether in respect of individuals or of institutions, is first to assume the existence of discrete ends, and secondly to identify the essential features of these ends. To select these essential features from the immensely complex and densely interwoven flux of normative phenomena is to force our capacity for abstraction to the very boundaries of intelligibility. It is to imagine an *ideally* rational world. It is the immediate consequence of the assumption of the *possibility* of social science that we are deprived of the hope of finding our idealisations instantiated in actuality.[36] It is at this point that we lose our innocence in employing the term 'description. For, in the attempt merely to describe the social world we arrogate to ourselves the competence to judge what is practically rational and what is not.

Weber clung to his humility by cleaving to his notion of 'value-freedom' in this regard. He claimed to confine himself to the innocuous reconstruction of the purely formal relations between means and *given* ends. He claimed merely to describe but not to judge the institutional goals which characterised a particular epoch. But we have said enough to realise that this is not so humble a claim. For there are, in principle, an infinity of conceptions of the ends or goals of capitalism, Protestantism, or law. Is it the wealth and freedom of nations or the enslavement and poverty of the majority? To select the features of calculation and control as the defining features of bourgeois modernity, as did Weber, is admittedly to attempt to steer clear of the clichéd factionalism of party politics; but, in the absence of a criterion by which we are to judge what is a defining feature and what is not, it is no more objective, no more value-free and no less arbitrary than to select exploitation and inequality, or a rise in consumption and consumer choice as the essentials of the phenomenon. However, to characterise Weber as an ideologist by default, as some have done, is not the issue.[37] For one ideologist to accuse another of the same shortcomings *vis à vis* objectivity is not to further the cause of science. Such bickering does, however, point up a fundamental problem: which point of view should we adopt?

From the point of view of social science we are committed to the interpretation of each aspect of our subject-matter as an aspect of practical reason. John Finnis has been bold enough to draw the simple conclusion that therefore the point of view of social science is 'the practically reasonable point of view'.[38] The next question is not difficult to predict: what do we mean by *the* practically reasonable point of view?

Whatever the right answer may be, we can be sure that this is the right question. We require an analysis of the conceptual structure of practical reason. Pending the results of such an inquiry we can infer the following conditional conclusions.

1. If practical reason reduces to instrumental reason and no more, then our conceptions of practical rationality and, hence, practical phenomena, are doomed to arbitrariness. This follows because instrumental reason may be characterised as formally rational in relation to an infinity of contingent ends. Judgments concerning the rationality of ends in themselves would make no sense. Practical rationality would inhere in the internal relationship between means and ends.
2. If an analysis of practical reason, initially conceived in its bare instrumentality, can reveal a deep structure of presuppositions which

place rational limits upon the range of possible ends, and imply certain obligatory ends, then an ideal type of practical rationality can inform our concept formation in a logically necessary, non-arbitrary way.

3. If (1), then social science is impossible, and even a notion of 'critical' social commentary is logically incoherent.
4. If (2), then we can establish epistemological foundations for social science which can but function to establish social science as moral critique, thus exploding the myth of the mutual exclusivity of objectivity and moral judgment.

This is the rational and critical import of the claim that social science is irreducibly evaluative.

2

The Logic of Verstehen

The thesis that social phenomena must be appropriated through some form of interpretative or hermeneutic exercise is broadly accepted. However, it is the precise nature of this exercise which is in question, rather than the blunt claim that we must acknowledge a divergence of method in our approaches to the spheres of *Natur* and *Geist*. In a work with an epistemological intent it would not be wise, therefore, to present this initial claim as a hostage to fortune.

In offering some thoughts on the matter I have chosen to work towards what I hope may be a clarification of the issue, by looking at Weber's contribution to the late nineteenth-century German methodological controversy or *Methodenstreit*.[1] It is this debate which led Weber to the synthesis of *Verstehen* propounded in the three essays which comprise his *Methodology of the Social Sciences*[2] However, the metatheoretical spadework which underpinned these essays is to be found in the protracted and often difficult volume which appeared as his excursus on his former masters at Heidelberg, *Roscher and Knies: the Logical Problems of Historical Economics*[3] It is here that Weber introduces the notion of the ideal-type. It is through a fuller understanding of the implications of this heuristic device that I hope to be able to make my point concerning the need to integrate moral philosophy and the methodology of social science.

At the most general level the presentation of the problem can be seen as a debate between Weber and Mill.[4] These two notables have been the focus of much biographical discussion but I hope that this does not prove to be a distraction from the purely theoretical point of the exercise. The logical question centres on the problem of whether or not our theoretical interest in the explanation of cultural phenomena can be served by the conceptual operations which appear appropriate to inquiry into natural phenomena. Mill answered at great length in the affirmative, and his explicit epistemological pronouncements illuminate much that is implicit in the work of German theorists whom Weber saw fit to criticise.[5] This is as far as a plausible thesis in the history of ideas needs to go for my purposes. The important thing is that Weber devoted much time and effort to repudiating the naturalistic or *nomological* prejudices in various trends of thought which he referred to as 'emanatism'.[6] Stripped of its pretensions, Weber saw emanatism as the perverse result of the attempt to demarcate the realm of history and culture from the natural world, whilst persisting with the notion that all scientific explanation must be nomological. Nomological or covering-law explanation is the touchstone of positivism in that it seeks to subsume all particular events as instances of general regularities, or empirical laws, which in turn are held to be explainable by reference to universal laws.[7] In *Roscher and Knies* Weber describes how, in the work of his German contemporaries and predecessors, this project leads to the development of cyclical theories of history and culture founded upon the hypostatisation of an ineffable ground or essence of the empirical manifestations of cultural phenomena: the *Volksgeist*.[8]

In the more sober British fashion, minus the support of the *Volksgeist*, and untroubled by the intuitively disturbing distinction between the natural and the socio-cultural, Mill presents the logical gap between the apparent 'empirical laws' of phenomena and the (assuredly nonempirical) universal laws alleged to underpin (explain) them, as the problem of induction.[9] Mill's solution to this twofold problem appear as the positivistic canon of the The Unity of Scientific Method. Weber's methodological writings are a response to this confusion, and his notion of the ideal-type the proffered solution.

In the next few pages I will try to summarise what I take to be the core of Weber's methodological objections to this project of methodological unification. Such compression rarely makes for good reading, but I hope these preliminary reflections may prove to be rewarding at a later stage. This expository task is made easier by Guy Oakes's thoughtful introduction to the 1975 edition, and his commentary is an invaluable guide to this dense work.[10] I will present the summary in two sections. The first concentrates upon Roscher and the problem of achieving a level of generality in the explanation of historical and cultural phenomena without losing purchase on its 'unique' or 'concrete' character. The second looks at Knies and the confusion which surrounds the alleged essential 'freedom' – conceived of as 'unpredictability' – of human action.

ROSCHER: THE ABSTRACT AND THE CONCRETE

Where Mill conceived of a unified scientific method utilising only the basic notions of inductive generalisation which he held to support the assumption of a universal causal regularity, the writings of Roscher, Knies, Rickert, Windelband and others insist on the recognition of the qualitatively distinct nature of the historical or socio-cultural disciplines. This broad German school felt a deep dissatisfaction with the Newtonian inspired thirst for ever increasing generality of explanatory concepts.[11] This generality, they held, was seen to be inversely proportional to the 'richness of content' of these concepts; a richness or 'concreteness' which they felt was required to appropriate the 'uniqueness; of cultural phenomena. The poet and the historian, said Roscher, 'wish to understand the fullness of life.'[12]

Given this antipathy to the generalising tendencies of the natural sciences, we could reasonably expect to find the wholesale rejection of the nomological scheme. It is understandable, therefore, that Weber was 'astonished' by Roscher's claims to the effect that he regarded his (Roscher's) work as being close to that of Adam Smith, Malthus and Rau; that the work of the natural scientist and the historian are 'similar'; that politics is described as the theory of the evolutionary *laws* of the state; that there is in Roscher's works constant reference to the 'natural laws of the economy'; and, importantly, that knowledge of '*lawlike relations* which obtain among a mass of phenomena is described as knowledge of *essential properties*'.[13] Weber says:[14]

> But genuine natural laws of the behaviour of phenomena can only be formulated on the basis of analytical abstractions which eliminate the 'historically contingent'. Therefore, it must follow that the ultimate goal of economics is the formation of a system of abstract concepts and analytical laws, a system of maximal logical completeness in which concrete *contingencies* have been, as much as possible, stripped away. But this appears to be precisely the goal that Roscher has rejected in principle.

In other words, Roscher's distinction between the generality and vacuity, on the one hand, of the explanatory concepts of the natural sciences, and the 'uniqueness' and 'richness' of the concepts of the historical or cultural sciences on the other, either disappears or seems to involve itself in confusion and contradiction.

Roscher's response to this criticism, as we initially noted, is to espouse a philosophy which Weber terms 'emanatism'.[15] Weber uses this term to describe the approach characteristic of the German Historical School of Jurisprudence, (notably Savigny), Hegelianism, and the historical economics of Roscher. That is, the apparent impasse of combining generality with concrete content (and, as we shall note presently, the attempt generally to comprehend the essential 'irrationality' or 'freedom' of the human personality) is overcome by the introduction of a putatively concrete concept, namely, the *Volksgeist*.[16] In Roscher's work, this entity is held to be the essentially irrational and unique source of the cultural capital of a people. However, this is not held to be a provisional classificatory concept intended to subsume a multiplicity of as yet unanalysed, diverse phenomena – as are the concepts of, for example, force and motion in Newtonian physics – but rather, the concept of *Volksgeist* is hypostatised as the 'actual ground of all the individual cultural manifestations of a *Volk*'.[17] Individual historical phenomena emanate, therefore, from this 'essence of history'. Roscher says of the concept of *Volk*:[18] ... it is an intuitable totality, the cultural bearer of a meaningful total essence. This is probably the kind of language which inspired a later generation of Logical Empiricists to work towards its elimination. Yet this poetry does suggest a logical as well as a spiritual feeling of inadequacy concerning our attempts to confront history and culture with a scientific intent. We may interpret this *Angst* as follows: where we are content to mathematicise the realm of natural phenomena, indeed to experience much gratification in this enterprise, the intuitive repugnance we feel for employing such abstraction and remoteness of explanation in human affairs prevents us from accepting this limitation to our understanding. Our thirst for generalisation cannot, it seems, be reconciled with our intuitive respect for the significance of the particular in history and culture. The important point which Weber makes in criticising the drift into mysticism of the emanatist tendencies of German social theory is that if we insist on the antipathy of comprehensiveness of extension of explanatory concepts on the one hand, and a corresponding dearth of content on the other, we face an insurmountable methodological problem.

But Weber shows, albeit at great length, that comprehensiveness of extension *per se* is not the inadequacy which social theory needs to remedy. Rather, it is the fact that nomological explanation must always strive for maximisation of extension of its general theoretical terms and this can be achieved only by taking the *generic* features of phenomena as the *essential* features.[19] Roscher, in the attempt to endow his subject-matter with the requisite profundity, succeeds only in reproducing this central tenet of nomological explanation in his own analyses of the generic recurrences of the history of peoples. He thereby fails to avoid the spiritually unsatisfying abstractions of the natural scientific method. This emphasis on the primacy of generic features of phenomena precludes the possibility of any debate about the distinctive characteristics of social science in contrast to natural science. This problem is not overcome by introducing a poetic or spiritual tone into the arbitrary formation of general terms and insisting that there is some special form of understanding which allows us to 'intuit' or 'empathise' with the 'meaningful' or 'essentially human' aspects of history. A poetic rhetoric does not magically endow general concepts with 'concrete content' as opposed to the vacuity of abstraction. *Volk* is as far removed from the complexity and concreteness of human existence as is 'physical object' from the perceptible qualities of a diamond. Weber's important observation is that the validity of the concept of 'physical object' lies in a domain of scientific interest satisfied by equations which deal with causal relations between generic aspects of phenomena which have a significance for the physicist. It follows, therefore, that the validity of the concept of *Volk* is similarly confined to a particular domain of theoretical interest.[20] Clearly, our interest in the social world extends beyond the enumeration of arbitrarily contrived recurrent features, even though certain factual correlations may be validly reported on the basis of plausible and heuristically useful classificatory schemes. That empirical observations from a particular perspective may yield extensive or even universally valid correlations does not, however, demonstrate the coincidence of the *generic* with the *essential* in explicating a methodology of the socio-cultural.[21]

KNIES: FREEDOM AND IRRATIONALITY

In the second half of his monograph Weber turns to a critical commentary on the work of Knies in the attempt to purge our methodological reasoning from the distractions of the problem of the alleged intrinsic 'irrationality' of the subject-matter of social science. Weber tells us that 'irrational' here means nothing more nor less than that which *resists* nomological explanation.[22] It is in this section that the notion of *Verstehen* and the ideal-type emerge more clearly, in that social action, or action which is meaningful to the individual in terms of the practical employment of means in pursuit of ends, is proposed as the essential focus of sociological investigation.

Knies believed that economics was concerned with the study of human action. Human action is a product of two influences – natural necessity, including simple biological needs and contingently applicable geographical, climatic, technological etc. conditions; and, secondly, 'freedom of will'. We have, therefore, two modes of determination in the historical sciences: the first comprises the blind necessity of the natural environment and the specifically historical forces of what Knies refers to as collective or general complexes. The second is simply the capacity of the individual to make choices of action and thereby determine future events in a specific way. Knies automatically classifies the effects of natural and general complexes as nomological. Causality, again, is regarded as being synonymous with *nomological regularity*. Purposive action, on the other hand, does not, according to Knies, share this nomologically explainable structure – this element of 'freedom' in the sphere of economic processes he designates as the 'irrational-concrete'.[23] Weber presents Knies's position thus:[24]

> If we consider only the effects of 'nature' upon economic phenomena, then, according to Knies, the latter must be conceived as

> nomological consequences of the former. In fact, laws of nature do obtain *in* the human economy. However, they are not laws *of* the human economy. In Knies's view, this is because the freedom of the human *will* – in the form of 'personal' action – is embedded in the human economy.

Weber points to two logical errors here immediately: namely (a) the conflation of necessitation and nomological regularity and (b) the conflation of 'free' and 'concrete' action, this latter being conceived of as the contrary of 'typical' or 'structured' action. This is, as Weber notes, a common error in much historiographical literature where explicit or implicit reference is made to the 'unpredictability' of personal conduct.[25] The 'dignity' of the human individual is a consequence of this 'freedom' from determinism and, hence, the characteristic which puts the individual biography beyond the scope of systematic explanation in a manner appropriate to the study of the natural world. Ironically, says Weber, it is this factor which leads some historians to arrive at the conclusion that it is just this 'unpredictability' which constitutes the proper subject-matter of historical investigation.[26] The distinction which is drawn, therefore, is that between the 'creative' significance of the acting personality and the 'mechanical' causality of natural events.[27]

In considering this notion of the 'creative' properties of human action (particularly in Wundt's psychological theory), Weber points out that there is no special feature of the 'unique' personality in a purely objective consideration of the causal status of actions which 'produces' or causally relates to other historical events.[28] In other words, there is no logical difference between the causal status of individual action and that of geographical, or natural factors. One cannot be said to be more 'creative' than the other – unless we have a specific interest in the role of individual action in our attempts to gain a particular form of historical knowledge. Weber says:[29]

> From a logical point of view, the physical and chemical processes which produce a seam of coal or a diamond constitute a 'creative synthesis' in the same sense as the chain of motives which links the intuitions of a prophet to the formation of a new religion. The two sorts of 'creative synthesis' can be substantively differentiated only by reference to differences in the predominant values in terms of which we conceive them.

Weber's point is this: in the infinity of events of history, conceived as a temporal succession, we may, depending upon our particular interests, isolate certain series of events. Because of our conferral of significance or importance upon one member of the series, all members of the series are not conceived as having the same causal status. Weber says:[30]

> Because of the value relevance[31] in question, the difference in causal

> status is viewed as a difference in *axiological* status. Such a difference in causal status is an intrinsic property of every change in concrete reality that is conceived from a qualitative point of view. This is why reflection concerning value relevance is the ultimate *basis* of the historical interest.

Weber holds that there is no reason to assume that there is some objective pre-eminence of the psychophysical processes over nomological processes as the determinants of historical events. It is simply that when human action becomes an object of scientific investigation it then becomes logically impossible to view the establishment of nomologically conceived equations of causal relations as the goal of the investigation. This is because the interplay of our values in which our historical interest is bound confers triviality or importance on certain events. If we wish to view the causes of these events as being the results of human action, then those events to which we ascribe historical significance are seen as the product of 'creative' action. But, as Weber points out, this status could be similarly applied to natural processes. However, if we consider an action on its intrinsic merits, it is clear that no evaluation of its causal significance can be made without knowledge of its consequences. Clearly, it is whether or not these consequences arouse our historical interest that will determine whether or not actions are deemed 'creative'. The point is that history is not the study of 'creative' action, but rather the *axiology* of action:[32]

> The conception of *differences* in causal status as differences in *axiological* status is the definitive category of the cultural sciences. This is the only possible meaning of the claim that 'creative synthesis' is a phenomenon peculiar to the domain of the cultural sciences – a domain which may include specific mental events, cultural relations, or both.

In exploding the myth of the objective (i.e. intrinsic, non-value oriented) significance of the 'creative' aspects of historical events, Weber turns to a brief examination of the error of conceiving of the role of 'personality' as an essentially 'irrational' factor in the course of events. This 'irrationality' is conceived of in the vulgar sense of 'incalculability'[33] – in that 'freedom of the will' is the characteristic mark of the human condition which stamps a peculiar dignity on the socio-cultural sciences. Weber is unimpressed by this claim because such incalculability is in no sense a feature of our ordinary social experience. Our discourse and actions in an interpersonal sense, or at the level of military or legal policy-making etc., all rely upon assumptions of the calculability of the effects and impressions of our actions on others.[34] From a logical point of view, says Weber, these calculations are no different from the calculations of engineers or chemists or farmers. They do not depend upon absolute unambiguity but are framed within a set of assumptions and inferences which give a guarantee of calculability 'sufficient *for the purposes* which the command, the law, and the concrete utterance are intended to serve'. Weber says:[35]

> There is no *logical* difference between these cases and 'natural processes'. The calculability of 'natural processes' in the domain of 'weather forecasting', for example, is far from being as 'certain' as the 'calculation' of the conduct of a person with whom we are acquainted.

This mundane point is perfectly true. Clearly, the issue centres on *a priori* assumptions about the nature of the subject-matter which we seek to explain or understand. What is it then that may lead us to assume that natural phenomena are inherently more 'rational' than human actions? Weber's answer is extremely illuminating.

Weber asks us to consider a commonplace event in the natural world: that of a boulder being dislodged from a cliff and crashing to the ground, splintering into thousands of fragments.[36] We could explain the causal sequence of the general, overt event, but we could not reconstruct the causal sequence which explained the minutiae of the splintering, the number of splinters, the direction of every crack and fissure, or the cause of every serration. The simple point is that we are perfectly satisfied with a general causal equation which encompasses the infinitely complex nature of individual concrete phenomena because of the absence of any empirical intrusion upon the validity of our assumptions of determinism operating in this domain of phenomena.[37]

Similarly, Weber notes that sciences like biology have recourse to providing explanations of individual phenomena which are, in principle, no more elaborate than the general explanations offered for the infinitely complex splintering of the boulder:[38]

> '... it is no longer necessary to emphasize the infinite distance between, e.g., the biological concept of "adaptation" and any "exact" account of established (or conjectured) phylogenetic processes'.

In moving on to the final, synthesising section of his monograph, Weber tells us in a few pages what social science is *not* about and what, in essence, it *is* about. Furthermore, we are told, once and for all, that the distinction between socio-cultural and natural science bears no relation to intrinsic properties of the object of these investigations, but to the *mode of theoretical interest* in which such objects are conceived. Weber says:[39]

> Physical and psychical 'reality', or an aspect of 'reality' comprehending both physical and psychical components, constitutes an 'historical entity' because and insofar as it can 'mean' something to us. 'Meaningfully' interpretable human conduct ('action') is identifiable by reference to 'valuations' and 'meanings.' For this reason,

> our criteria for *causal* explanation have a unique kind of satisfaction in the 'historical' explanation of such an 'entity'.

In the case of human conduct which we assume to be conditioned by values, there is, says Weber, a peculiar sense in which our understanding of this conduct is 'self-evident'. It is here that Weber introduces the notion of an ideal-type for the first time in his methodological writings. Here we are presented with the relationship between a causal explanation of action, and the empirically verifiable ground of determining the rationality of an action or series of actions, by reference to the ideal-type of instrumental rationality. It is understandable that much confusion has been caused by Weber's remark that these ideal-typical constructs have no pretence to universal empirical validity, yet that they are derived from empirical experience and can be checked – in respect of their strict rationality – against empirical experience. Weber is perfectly clear on the issue and there should be no problem expounding it here as long as it is first acknowledged that the ideal-type is not meant to be an empirical generalisation of typical or statistically frequent aspects of actual practices. Neither is it meant to be prescriptive in any normative-moral sense. An ideal-type, for Weber, can and must be constructed in terms of the optimum *instrumental efficacy* of certain means employed to achieve ends – ends which are *unambiguously given* or which we unambiguously postulate. Thus, because we know that[40]

> There is no rational action independent of the causal rationalization of certain aspects of reality which are conceived as objects and instruments that can be manipulated ... [and that] ... without the belief in the reliability of empirical generalizations, there could be no action based upon an estimation of the means required for an intended result. ... [Thus] given an unambiguous purpose, there is a sense in which the selection of means is 'determined'. ... The selection of means is 'determined' by a disjunction of a plurality of possible means, the differences between which are a consequence of the circumstances of the action. Rational interpretation [ideal-type construction] can, therefore, assume the form of a conditional judgment of necessity ... (Its logic is as follows: ... given a certain intention *x*, and in view of established empirical generalizations, it is '*necessary*' for the actor to select the means *y* – e.g. one of the means *y*, *y*', *y*'' – for its attainment.)

This judgment, says Weber, can also serve as a teleological 'evaluation' of an *empirically* verifiable action in that we can demonstrate that[41]

> ... according to established empirical generalizations, selection of the means *y*, as opposed to *y*' or *y*'', makes the attainment of the purpose *x* most likely, or attains this purpose with the least sacrifices ... This is a purely 'technical' evaluation ... confirmed solely by

> observation. ... [T]here is no sense in which this proposition leaves the ground of an analysis of the empirically given. And within the domain of knowledge of *real* events, rational 'evaluation' functions *exclusively* as an hypothesis or as an ideal-typical construct.

How then are we to employ these constructs?[42]

> We compare the actual action with the action which is, from a 'teleological' point of view and on the basis of ... causal generalizations, rational.

What will this achieve?[43]

> The purpose of this comparison is to establish one of the following. *Either* there was a rational motive which would have guided the actor and which we could employ in order to establish that his actual actions qualify as a means appropriate to a purpose which he 'could' have pursued. *Or* we make understandable why, in consequence of his choice of means, a motive with which we are acquainted had a *different* result than that subjectively expected by the actor.

Weber does not regard this as a particularly profound contribution to knowledge. However, he suggests that it does tell us three simple but important things: (i) that we are not here concerned with the psychological analysis of 'personality'; (ii) that we are not moving into areas which exhaust or contradict the resources of our nomological knowledge; and (iii) that the interpretation of the phenomenon of action is equivalent to the claim that human beings can act 'purposefully' – i.e. act upon the basis of deliberations about the possibilities of future events given certain beliefs about the world. This last observation is of major significance, however, for the construction of conceptual schemes of great heuristic value. It allows, us, says Weber, to construct an ideal-typical explanation of the actions of an individual or, alternatively, these conceptual schemes can be ideal-typical constructions of a general character, such as economic theory.[44] In this latter case theoretical deductions concerning the outcome of certain economic conditions are made possible by presupposing strictly rational (i.e. instrumentally ideal) action.

It is clear that there is nothing arbitrary about the internal relations of the ideal-typical scheme of instrumental action. In fact it is this logical guarantee of the structure of rational action which leads Weber, in later work, to present the task of the sociologist as one in which the requirements of the ideal-typical scheme are taken as the ground of scientific policy formation. The fecundity of the insights which spring from realising the implications of 'agency', in this sense, is the key to the possibility of freeing social science, in Oakes's words, from its 'protracted adolescence'.[45]

3

The Limits of Verstehen

In Chapter 2 I have tried to illustrate Weber's views on the inadequacy of nomological explanation in the sphere of the socio-cultural, and present an exposition of the argument for the general alternative of a *verstehende* sociology. I want to go on from here to build on these fundamental points. My concern is with social science and not with Max Weber, but I think that it will be helpful to say something about the rudiments of value-freedom and the ideal-type, and something about the easily misunderstood notion of value-relevance. From here I want to go on to deal with what I consider to be the real problem of not just Weber's methodology, but all attempts to present a framework of interpretive social science. The basic idea of the ideal-type, and the concept of value-relevance, however, are not the stumbling-blocks, and I want to mount a brief defence of these general notions before going on to show that it is the assumption of ethical non-cognitivism, and a resultant formalism, which produces the fatal contradiction in the Weberian concept of *Verstehen*.

Weber's three later papers for the *Archiv fur Sozialwissenschaft*, 'The Meaning of Ethical Neutrality', 'Objectivity in Social Science' and 'The Logic of the Cultural Sciences', were collected in his more widely read work, *The Methodology of the Social Sciences*.[1] On re-reading these essays, the value of our examination of the Roscher-Knies monograph becomes plain. First, there is little in the 'Methodology' that is not contained in this earlier work. This is certainly true with regard to the logical analysis of the interpretive enterprise. Secondly, the reader who tackles these later essays 'raw' might be forgiven for forming the impression that they are flatly contradictory. The questions which immediately present themselves in respect of these essays are: (1) is the ideal-type a prescription for action, a description of typical behaviour, or 'ideal' in the sense of 'desirable'; and (2) how does Weber's claim that there exists a value-relevance to all sociological investigation square with his thesis of the possibility of objectivity in social science?

THE IDEAL TYPE

First, we may note that ideal-typical concepts are legitimately and edifyingly distinguished from nomological concepts in that they actually do bring us closer to what is 'essential' or 'concrete' in history. That is, they are concepts which allow us to understand cultural phenomena as being *fundamentally constituted by forms of practical reason*. At this point we may emphasise the important point that Weber's notion of an ideal-type is 'ideal' purely in a logical sense and not in any ethical sense. For Weber, the ideal-type is simply a logically convenient model for abstractly circumscribing the purely instrumental aspects of an example of social action. The need to draw upon both nomological *and* 'concrete' or interpretive concepts in the attempt to explain social phenomena is clear: nomological laws and concepts are presupposed by any conception of an objectively possible situation in which the practical-instrumental categories of means and ends embodied in social action may be applied. The notion of the ideal-type does require much more detailed examination. In fact I will suggest that the ideal-type involves us either in moral-judgment or arbitrariness. However, these preliminary remarks are enough, for the moment, to dispel the notion that Weber's whole project of value-free sociology crumbles as soon as the word 'ideal' is uttered in relation to his models of historical phenomena.

VALUE-RELEVANCE

When Weber speaks of the 'axiology' of action, he is referring to the specific interest in the value dimension of action. The cultural sciences must display this axiological interest because, quite simply, culture is that complex of phenomena upon which we confer value or significance, i.e. perceive to be important for us and to us.[2] In the cultural sciences, perception of the 'meaningfulness' (its value orientation) of an object is a presupposition of its becoming an object of investigation. Thus values, not necessarily our own, are the *sine qua non* of the very conception of culture. From this it seems to follow that all scientific analysis of culture ultimately rests upon value-judgments. It is axiomatic in Weber's work that value-judgments do not admit of a scientific demonstration of their validity – a point which we will pursue presently. However, Weber does claim that a true science of culture is possible. His point is that an ethically neutral or 'value-free' sociology is possible only through this realisation that our objects of investigation are constituted by our own judgments of value in the first place. Weber's claim, quite clearly, is that the selection of objects of investigation in the cultural sciences is, in all cases, culture bound, but the results of the analysis may be, in principle, universally valid.

VALUE-RELEVANCE AND VALUE-FREEDOM

It is at this point that we encounter difficulty in preserving the consistency of Weber's methodological theses. The widespread practice of referring to Weber and his contemporaries in the Heidelberg circle as 'Neo-Kantian', regardless of the usefulness of this label, is at least intelligible in regard to a particular epistemological point. That is, the insistence by Weber that the 'facts' of culture do not speak for themselves can also be generalised to all and any aspect of the apprehension of empirical reality, and presented as the thesis that all empirical observation is grounded in certain presuppositions which constitute a conceptual scheme. It is clear that Weber's discussion of the 'analytical ordering of empirical reality' as being conditioned by our theoretical interest in both the natural and cultural sciences is evidence for the attribution of this position to him. If all empirical knowledge rests upon certain presuppositions, the validity of these presuppositions is obviously vital to the validity of substantive empirical propositions which are inferred from them. If, as Weber holds to be the case, empirical propositions of the socio-cultural sciences are ultimately conditioned by presuppositions of value, and that such presuppositions are incapable of scientific demonstration, then this precludes the possibility of objectivity. Clearly, as an attempt to present the outline of a value-free sociology, this cannot be Weber's intention.

In attempting to reconstruct the most rational interpretation of Weber's views on this matter, Deryck Beyleveld has focused upon the distinction between 'cognitive interests' and 'theoretical presuppositions'.[3] We can clarify this by reference to our earlier discussions of Weber's views on the structure and adequacy of nomological concept formation. We recall that Weber speaks of the ordering of empirical reality in relation to 'natural phenomena'. Here we are content to formulate general equations which subsume certain relations between objects in the world under concepts which have a hypothetically infinite scope of validity, e.g. Newtonian laws of motion. In Weber's discussion of the splintering boulder in the previous chapter, we noted that our cognitive interest is satisfied at a certain point simply by the appearance of conformity of phenomena to our nomological scheme. This is so even though we are aware that the minutiae of the event are not susceptible of explanation in terms of causal regress. We simply satisfy ourselves with the a priori assumption that any aspect of a phenomenon does, in principle, conform to a scheme of causal determinism. However, in the sphere of cultural phenomena, our cognitive interest is not, and cannot be, so satisfied. We are aware that concrete events can be 'understood' – our cognitive interest, therefore, thirsts for a qualitative rather than a quantitative comprehension of the causal determinants of the phenomenon. In both cases, however, our cognitive interest is founded upon certain 'theoretical presuppositions'. Furthermore, in both cases, our cognitive interest is structured by similar theoretical presuppositions, namely, the presupposition of determinism *in some sense*. It can be seen, therefore, that there is a clear distinction to be drawn between the concept of cognitive interest and the concept of a theoretical presupposition: the latter being the more cognitively fundamental. 'Theoretical presupposition', as Beyleveld notes[4] is sensibly equated with the Kantian concept of 'category' as in 'category of the understanding'. Our problem, then, is to clarify whether or not 'cognitive interests' constitute a value-laden conceptual scheme which would invalidate any empirical research based upon it.

It is plain that Weber draws a distinction between facts and values. It is necessary, however, to clarify just how far this distinction goes in Weber's scheme. It is certainly not meant to be the distinction which the Logical Positivist uncompromisingly draws between, on the one hand, empirically verifiable propositions and tautologies, and, on the other, propositions which lie outside this class – such as metatheoretical claims, categorical imperatives or aesthetic judgments. The fundamental rationale of Weber's methodology is, at least in respect of metatheory, opposed to such an empiricism. This opposition is evident throughout his work, but the following remark makes the issue clear on this particular point.[5]

> We are, furthermore, completely free of the prejudice which asserts that reflections on culture which go beyond the analysis of empirical data in order to interpret the world metaphysically can, because of their metaphysical character fulfil no useful cognitive task.

Much will be said about the whys and wherefores of this particular view of theoretical reflection in later chapters, but the point here is to determine whether or not these views are consistent with the possibility of valuc-freedom and objectivity in social science in so far as our cognitive interests condition our theoretical (explanatory) framework. This is a little bit tricky, but Weber's discussion of the splintered boulder phenomenon may help.

Because our cognitive interest is satisfied with a partial view of the results of the event, this does not mean that we cannot, in principle, ascertain valid information, i.e. identify facts about the minutiae of the splintering. To direct our cognitive interest into this intricate aspect of the phenomenon is merely a difference in degree of a certain type of cognitive interest – a cognitive interest which can still be satisfied by nomological explanation. Therefore, we can assume that Weber uses the term 'cognitive interest' to denote a mode of explanation which satisfies our requirements of comprehension regardless of the intrinsic properties of a particular object or set of objects and their relations. Validity, therefore, is possible within a mode of comprehension conditioned by cognitive interests, regardless of the particular nature of those interests. This is, of course, self-evident: I may wish to know many things for may different reasons; *why* I want to know does not alter the nature of the things which interest me. I think this is the thrust of his notion of value-relevance.

We must recognise that Weber introduces the discussion of cognitive interests primarily to show the inadequacy of nomological explanation in our attempts to acquire knowledge of history and culture – and not to suggest that all knowledge is value-laden because of cognitive interests. Our cognitive interests in the sphere of history and culture go beyond the capacities of nomological explanation simply because the phenomena we wish to understand are conceived as being qualitatively different from natural phenomena. If we conceive the behaviour of an object as being conditioned or 'determined' by the motivation of values, then this conception functions as a theoretical presupposition which will facilitate a particular type of explanation. If we conceive an object as being inanimate, consciousless and devoid of purposivity then, from this presupposition, we are assured of the futility of attempting to explain its behaviour in such terms.

Following this, it is clear that cognitive interests are not to be confused with theoretical presuppositions which make possible the construction of ideal-typical concepts. Cognitive interests determine whether or not, for instance, we wish to acquire knowledge of empirical regularities in the history of a people or an economic process, or, alternatively, whether we wish to understand the meaning of history or economic activity. If we decide that the generic features of history are the 'essential' features, i.e. essential to our understanding of the concrete processes of history and culture, we do not make a value-judgment. Rather, we make a methodological error in that amassing knowledge of empirically valid regularities does not allow us to 'deduce concrete reality from laws'.[6] The nature of law-like generalisations, regardless of their empirical validity, still suspends our knowledge in the vacuum of abstraction.

In this situation we become aware of the incompatibility of certain types of concept formation and our cognitive interests. The logic of concept formation is related, therefore, to our cognitive interests, but the validity of heuristic (ideal-typical or analytical) concepts through which we are able to order empirical reality is in no way invalidated by the value-judgments which are manifest in our particular modes of cognitive interest. These are indeed relative to a particular historical and cultural constellation of values. We may say that the concepts which enable us to order empirical reality are formed from theoretical presuppositions which must be value-neutral if objective validity is to be possible; but that our values determine which aspects of the world are investigated. Conveniently, Beyleveld's analysis of the epistemological ramifications of this aspect of Weber's methodological theses provides us with some reassurance on this problem. He sums up his discussion thus:[7]

> We can attribute to Weber a two-tier conception of the constitution of our knowledge of empirical reality. At the first and more abstract level, there are theoretical presuppositions or categories which constitute our empirical knowledge in the Kantian sense. Within non-relativistic and universal frameworks so constituted there are points of view which are constituted by cognitive interests which are relative. The non-relativistic categories underlie a fixed reality which the relative ones give us different perspectives on, Weber's points of view, after all, are points of view about a fixed reality. If relativistic points of view are primarily rather than secondarily constituting of our knowledge of the world then this seems to be an impossible view. Of course, one might wish to dispute the adequacy of such a two tier conception, but I contend that such a view is the most plausible interpretation of Weber's position, the one which provides his position with more consistency than other alternatives.

In summary so far, we have a fairly clear picture of the methodological approach which Weber advocates. In particular we have noted the inadequacy of nomological explanation in its application to the phenomenon of social action. We have discussed the concept of social action as being the focus of sociological investigation and also seen how ideal-typical concepts of action might give us a heuristic device with which to identify and explain the rational and irrational aspects of social phenomena. In addition, we have seen that such constructs are grounded through reflection upon the categories of means and ends and how ideal-typical concepts of action, in conjunction with our nomological knowledge of possible, objective situations, may facilitate a causal (though not nomological) analysis of socio-historical processes and events. In order to deepen our understanding of this approach to concept formation we may now look at the crucial role and possible limits of incorporating the concept of rational action into a workable methodology.

FORMAL AND SUBSTANTIVE RATIONALITY

Rogers Brubaker's book *The Limits of Rationality*,[8] is an exceptionally lucid account of the unstable relationship between Weber's reliance on the notion of rationality as the basis of his conception of method, and his mistrust of its application to moral issues. Brubaker's clear presentation of the issues allows us rapid access into the Weberian problematic.[9] It points up the problems of reconciling *formal* notions of rational action, that is, the apparent internal consistency of employing means to any *given* end, with *substantive* rationality, that is, the ability to judge the rationality of *ends in themselves*. I think it is this dimension of Weber's methodology which will prove to be the most productive area of analysis.

Weber's concept of social action can be briefly explained as a conception of an explanatory framework in which aspects of cultural phenomena can be viewed as 'determined' (explainable), thereby rendering such phenomena susceptible to scientific analysis. His fourfold typology of action is well known:[10]

> Traditional action is determined by long-standing habits; affectual action, by strong feelings; *wertrational* action, by a conscious belief in the intrinsic value of acting in a certain way, regardless of the consequences of so acting; and *zweckrational* action, by a consciously calculating attempt to achieve desired ends with appropriate means.

Brubaker wants to emphasise the nature of the idealisations involved here. He notes that Weber was under no illusion as to the direct application of these types as descriptions of the actual conscious states of particular biographical actors. The degree to which an actual individual 'acts' rationally in one sense of the word as stipulated above is irrelevant. 'Traditional ways of acting may be more or less upheld; emotional impulses may be sublimated to varying degrees and consciously channelled in a certain direction.'[11] Furthermore, says Brubaker, although Weber characterised modernity as becoming increasingly rational in contrast to the static conventionalism of traditional societies, this is not intended to indicate a corresponding increase in rationality at the individual subjective level. He quotes Weber thus:[12]

> The subjective rationality of individual action does not typically progress *pari passu* with the objectified, supra-individual rationality of the social structure. Even in a highly rationalised social order, most action takes place 'in a state of inarticulate half-consciousness or actual unconsciousness of its subjective meaning ... [and] is governed by impulse or habit'.

Thus Weber is concerned with characterising the possibilities of consciously guided action from a methodologically idealised standpoint. It is not the subjectivity of an actual actor which we are discussing – it is an idealised conception of possible types of subjectivity itself.

Much has been made of the distinction between *Wertrationalität* and *Zweckrationalität*. The former is supposedly action guided by values regardless of consequences, and the latter is supposedly action which is shaped solely by an estimation of the consequences. Suffice it to say that I suspect that this is a quantitative rather than a qualitative difference.[13] However, we need only note here that it is the nature of the subjective orientation to action, rather than the action itself, which is the focus of analysis. What is really important to us, as I noted above, is the distinction between *formal* and *substantive* rationality.

For Weber, all action can be regarded as rational in that, ideal-typically at least, it is consciously guided. But he makes distinctions within this broad notion of action between '*subjectively* rational', taken to mean logically consistent within a framework of subjective belief, and '*objectively* rational', taken to mean practically efficacious *regardless* of the subjective belief of an actor or actors. The notion of *objective* rationality is, therefore, limited. Brubaker says that for Weber:[14]

> ... The notion of objective rationality does not apply to *wertrational* action – to action conceived as intrinsically rather than as instrumentally valuable, as an end in itself rather than as a means to some further end. This is because the value postulates to which *wertrational* action is orientated, unlike the expectation (about consequences) to which *zweckrational* action is orientated, cannot be objectively assessed.

This, of course, follows from Weber's basic epistemological assumptions concerning the scope of scientific knowledge: value-judgments are held to be scientifically indeterminable. This is methodologically expressed by the more fundamental dichotomy of *formal* and *substantive* rationality. Simply put, this is the notion that rationality may be predicated of all consciously guided action in that there may be *subjectively* coherent linkages within constellations of means and ends, *given* a particular end, and *given* the point of view of one who values the achievement of this end. Form a particular point of view, therefore, coherent means–ends activity can be regarded as *formally* rational whether it be the action of the *shaman* or of the technologist. *Formal* rationality exists in varying degrees in various cultures and epochs as a matter of fact:[15]

> Formal rationality is a matter of fact, substantive rationality a matter of value. Formal rationality refers primarily to the *calculability of means and procedures*, substantive rationality primarily to the value (from some explicitly defined standpoint) of *ends or results*. From the point of view of the purely formal objective of maximising the calculability of action – purely formal because maximally calculable action can be oriented to any of an infinite variety of possible substantive ends – capitalism, science, technology, and the modern legal and administrative system are highly rational.

Substantive rationality, on the other hand, is an evaluation from the point of view of a particular value-position. Brubaker clearly makes the point.[16]

> In emphasising the rationality of the modern social order, Weber is not justifying or defending this social order from a particular value standpoint, but is simply calling attention to social structural and social psychological 'mechanisms' that enhance the calculability of action. Such purely formal rationality is an objective property of the social structure of modern society. However one *evaluates* the

> increasingly important role of explicit calculation in social life, the *fact* of the growing importance of calculation must be acknowledged. The formal rationality of the modern social order is a matter of fact; whether or not this social order is substantively rational, in contrast, depends on one's point of view – i.e. on the ends, values or beliefs one takes as a standard of rationality.

The alleged empirical, non-evaluative nature of *formal* rationality structures, which appear as 'facts' for the 'value-neutral' investigations of the social scientist, is the focus of much criticism. The distinction between formal and substantive rationality is immensely important to us in that it points up the central problem of social science as being a search for an objective ethical theory or an adequate substitute. The following criticism of Weber's approach seems to make this clear: William Outhwaite notes that[17] 'Weber effectively divides the notion of rationality into one component which is narrowly descriptive and another which is a function of arbitrary values.' So, if the question is put as to whether capitalism is a rational economic system, Weber's reply would be that it is a *formally* rational system 'to the extent that calculation can and does take place within it and that whether it is 'substanti[vely] rational' or not depends on one's individual values – for example whether one considers the malnutrition of one third of a population to be a reasonable price to pay for the luxury enjoyed by another third'.[18]

Outhwaite says that this may be contrasted with a Marxist position which locates the presence of rational/irrational tendencies within capitalist systems not simply in terms of success or failure to 'deliver the goods' but in a more fundamental contradiction between social production and private appropriation.[19]

> The Marxist critique of this contradiction cannot be split up into a technical criticism of capitalist inefficiency and a moral criticism of capitalist injustice; it involves the rejection of this implied antithesis between fact and value.

This could be more simply put by suggesting that a successful sociological critique required the rejection of the antithesis between formal and substantive rationality. It is, of course, quite clear just what this would entail in terms of a science of human *ends*. Outhwaite goes on to note what he considers to be a more serious criticism from Marcuse, although it seems that the point is identical:[20]

> A more serious criticism of Weber's distinction is more clearly made by Herbert Marcuse who argues, in essence, that Weber collapses the notion of reason into formal rationality. The latter has substantive implications: it is really 'capitalist rationality'. 'Whatever capitalism may do to man, it must, according to Weber, first and before all evaluation be understood as necessary reason'.

We may ask, 'What, exactly, *does* capitalism do to man?' From the Buddhist point of view it robs him of the chance of a life of contemplation, which is a prerequisite of the ultimate value of enlightenment through Nirvana. From a Calvinist point of view it institutionalises the life of labour beyond the requirements of simple subsistence – an institution which is a constant act of worship to the glory of the Protestant God. The point here is obvious: to answer the question one must make judgments about the rationality of ends in themselves. Further, Weber does not collapse the notion of reason into formal rationality. He starts from the assumption that we cannot, with scientific propriety, make moral judgments, but we can evaluate the technical coherence between means and given ends. Thus formal rationality is the only possible object of an interpretative social science from a non-cognitivist viewpoint. He then characterises types of formal rationality in terms of criteria which may be operationalised to facilitate an empirical ordering of cultural phenomena.

We may say that Marcuse criticises Weber for being formally rational in this regard – for it is certainly an instance of necessary reason not to formulate value-laden methodological concepts when one has explicitly denied their scientific applicability. Outhwaite says of Marcuse's observations:[21]

> ... this criticism must not be overstated; Weber is fully aware of the potential conflict between formal and substantive rationality. Yet the latter concept, in being relativised to arbitrary value systems, loses any critical purchase on economic reality.

But again, we must note the assumption that there can be a critical purchase on 'economic reality'. This phrase reminds us of Weber's lengthy criticisms of the arguments of Roscher, who sought to grasp the 'concrete' and 'meaningful' reality of economic life. We saw that the attempt to ground the project evaporated into a poetic mist. Can we draw the conclusion from Outhwaite's remark that economic reality can be appropriated substantively only from a non-relative, non-arbitrary value standpoint. If we can, I fully concur – but as a criticism of Weber this point must be aimed at his fundamental assumption – which is perfectly explicit – of ethical non-cognitivism (/relativism).[22] To introduce criticism at the level of his complex attempts to systematise historically appropriate characterisations of culture *misses this fundamental assumption* and leads us into confusing and irrelevant debate.

To illustrate this tendency we need only consider the task of mounting a criticism of Weber from an ideological standpoint by noting the suggestion that his methodology is a product of his own cultural and ideological location. Löwith's influential work is representative of this approach, although there is a large body of literature with a similar orientation.[23] Outhwaite tells us that Löwith identifies the central theme of both Marx and Weber as the attempt to explicate the condition of Man in bourgeois society. Marx grasps this reality in terms of alienation; Weber in terms of rationalisation. It is the connection between Weber's methodology and his overall 'theory' of Western society which Outhwaite considers worthy of attention in Löwith's work.[24]

> As Löwith points out, Weber believes that science, like the rest of life, has become fragmented, specialized and 'disenchanted' with respect to ultimate values. 'Weber includes his own scientific cognitive orientation in the historical specificity and problematic of the whole of our modern life'.

Outhwaite goes on to say that Löwith detects this attitude in Weber's criticisms of Roscher and Knies in that he deprecates the non-secular tone of their analyses. Löwith considers that the notion of the ideal-type is based upon an 'illusion-free' human being,[25] ... thrown back on his own resources by a world which has become objectively meaningless and sober and to this extent emphatically 'realistic'. Outhwaite agrees that this criticism applies especially to Weber's conceptions of the State and nation so often 'mystified' through 'illusion'. He says:[26]

> Weber's minimalist concept of the state arises out of his critique of such illusions; it is not merely a matter of methodology but, despite this protestations to the contrary, has a substantial and evaluative significance which is broadly that of Western liberal individualism.

This allegedly unacknowledged value-orientation which, Outhwaite claims has been 'abundantly demonstrated' is taken to be evidence of an ideological stance within Weber's scheme of concept formation. However, Outhwaite believes that this encroachment of ideology is unavoidable as a starting point for social theory, and that it might be fruitful to attempt to assimilate Weber's work to that of Marx in this regard. In other words, this ideological orientation can be made epistemologically admissible if we view it from the 'more ambitious' perspective of Marx's philosophy of praxis. Outhwaite says:[27]

> For Marx, human knowledge of reality is partly sustained by that reality itself, he tries to show this with the example of the concept of abstract labour. Connections of this kind sustain a dialectical conception of knowledge involving not just a movement of thought from the whole to the part and back again, but also a practical dimension, which concerns the way in which the advance of knowledge is conditioned by changes in the object of knowledge. It may be questioned whether Marx can sustain his position as it stands without an unacknowledged reliance on a speculative conception of history which serves as the starting point of this whole process of knowledge. But it is clear that Weber could not even flirt with this approach.

This could not be more accurately expressed. He goes on to say:[28]

> Criticisms of this aspect of Weber's sociology can be divided into two: those which emphasize the lack of any overall theory of 'Western' capitalism of the kind offered by Marx (hence the arbitrary decisionism of Weber's account of concept formation) – and those which argue that he does have some such theory but merely fails, through methodological embarrassment, to make it explicit.

Thus, Outhwaite concludes that[29] 'Weber's account of concept formation is caught between the unattractive alternatives of "decisionism" (the view that we simply choose our concepts and the causal sequences to be investigated) and empiricism.'

There are three important points I wish to make concerning the foregoing discussion. The first is that any criticism of Weber's concept formation based on the suggestion that Weber's methodology is an ethico-political ideology in disguise is committed to substantiating the validity of the value-judgments which are presupposed by such a view. To accuse someone of peddling an ideology in any interesting sense of the word is to imply that what they say is false, and that the falsehood is being propounded in pursuit of sectional interests at the expense of the *real* interests of others. Fair enough – this is what critique should aim to do. But is it not obvious that this can be done only from a position of objective methodological and ethical knowledge? Such an accusation can play no constructive or coherent part in a debate about how we are to *acquire* such knowledge.

Secondly, dissatisfaction with Weber's lack of an 'overall theory of "Western" capitalism of the kind offered by Marx', and the proposal to furnish one which can provide a *substantive* theoretical account of cultural phenomena, again presupposes that the component concepts of such a theory have an objective validity. This complex of metatheoretical concepts must, therefore, contain objectively valid ethical concepts in the sense that the ultimate *ends* of forms of practical reason embodied in social action can be assessed as to their conformity to a standard of rationality which transcends all contingent formalism. In this way, and in this way only, we can speak of grasping a social or economic 'reality' in opposition to what is seen as being on offer in Weber's scheme: its hollow, formal content uncritically presented as 'fact' in the midst of scientifically inaccessible 'value'. In short, if we were to employ the notion of alienation as our overarching perspective on social action, we should have to be in a position to make judgments about practical activity not just in terms of the internal consistency of means and ends but from an external vantage point which had the benefit of criteria by which we could judge the conformity of *ends in themselves* to the ultimate interests of humanity. Marxism does claim to be able to do this, but it claims to be able to do it without making moral judgments. This position is indefensible – which might explain why we end up in debates as convoluted as this one.

Thirdly, when Outhwaite suggests that Weber's work languishes between the undesirable alternatives of a conceptual decisionism and empiricism, we must note that this criticism is misdirected. The decisionism in Weber's methodology operates at the level of *substantive* rationality. This decisionism is plainly entailed by Weber's ethical non-cognitivism – it is no great discovery to identify this state of affairs. That Weber is resigned to the limitations of the scope of social science by espousing this position as axiomatic is something which he at no stage attempts to conceal. Whether or not this admission on his part afforded him any inner spiritual peace is something quite distinct, and a topic which we may fruitfully discuss presently. However, the fact that writers of other persuasions do not accept these limitations is another matter – as is the fact that Weber's methodology of concept formation does not provide them with a basis for the revolutionary critique of capitalism. These two facts conjoined as premises, however, do not licence the conclusion that Weber's methodology of concept formation is flawed in any way, let alone that we have been given an argument which demonstrates that it should be rejected. Let us be clear as to the issue.

Weber's ethical non-cognitivism is the basis of his claim that *substantive* rationality does not admit of objective, scientific evaluation. That he holds that *formal* rationality structures *are* accessible in this way is not a view based simply on the fact that such phenomena are empirically observable (noting Outhwaites's reference to the empiricist alternative) – clearly formal rationality structures are not so observable prior to their operationalisation in terms of quantifiable criteria, i.e. calculation, control etc. The Neo-Kantian emphasis on the impossibility of theory-neutral observation is clearly in evidence here. Therefore, on this basis, Weber *must* hold that *formal* rationality structures are the only possible focus of sociological investigation. Thus Weber's observations in this regard have nothing whatsoever to do with his alleged, typically German, bourgeois-liberal-individualist psycho-political profile – unless such a political viewpoint has an essential monopoly on ethical non-cognitivism/relativism. Weber's methodological views are exclusively conditioned by his espousal of the belief in the irreducible indeterminacy of values, and this view subsumes a host of political persuasions (including Marxism) and cannot be reduced to a narrow conception of liberalism.

Now, no other candidate for a methodology of concept formation can overcome this gulf between, on the one hand a value-neutral scheme of rationality corresponding to empirically testable hypothetical imperatives (empirical norms), and, on the other, a normative-moral scheme of rationality corresponding to categorical imperatives which are validatable only through an objective ethical theory – a theory of *substantive rationality*. Weber's methodology of concept formation *is* coloured, therefore, by an ideology – the ideology of ethical or moral non-cognitivism. But to claim that such a standpoint is an ideology, in the Marxist sense of the term, or the generally pejorative sense of the term, is to do so from a standpoint which presupposes an ethical objectivism. The criticism of Weber should, therefore, be formulated in the most straightforward and unequivocal terms. That is, it is not because Weber is a bourgeois-liberal individualist or any other breed of political partisan that he presents *formal* rationality structures as the essential focus of sociological investigation, but that he is an ethical non-cognitivist in a universal and epistemological sense. Similarly, as the *substantive* evaluation of cultural phenomena strictly implies the possibility of a science of ultimate ends, those who refuse to accept the limitations of conceptual decisionism on the level of substantive rationality are, or should be, proponents of an ethical objectivism.

We may conclude, therefore, that our investigations should be directed along the following lines: (a) the axiomatic assumption of ethical relativism leads to the conclusion that social science must confine itself to the explication of *formal* rationality structures which can be *substantively* evaluated only from a plurality of arbitrary ethical standpoints, and (b) knowledge of culture in *substantively* rational terms is, therefore, impossible. What, then, are our options? There are two, only one of which is scientifically rational:

1. Accept the limitations and proceed in accordance with the strictures of Weber's observations on the need for a value-free sociology as presented in his essay 'Objectivity and Social Policy'.[30]
2. Question the unsubstantiated axiom of ethical non-cognitivism and explore its methodological implications.

WEBER AND MORAL PHILOSOPHY

Weber is not remembered or revered as a moral philosopher, yet his assiduous avoidance of judgments of value in his sociological and historical work is, as Brubaker and Löwith note, 'informed by a fundamentally moral impulse'. This attitude, as we have previously observed, attends the central theme of Weber's writings in that his work is concerned with 'the fate of man' in a world which has become 'disenchanted'. This fundamental moral impulse, therefore, should *not* be seen as a substantive attempt morally to evaluate this condition – a task which Weber holds to be impossible. Rather, it is to be gleaned from Weber's sense of tragedy in facing this situation as a social scientist. Brubaker's lucid reconstruction of Weber's ethic of responsibility and philosophical anthropology of personality shows how closely integrated these ethical reflections are with his conception of social action at the methodological level.

We have noted that Weber's idealisations do not purport to describe the actuality of individual agency. This is equally true of Weber's elucidation of the concepts of freedom and meaning as related to action:[31]

> We associate the highest measure of an empirical 'feeling of freedom' with those actions which we are conscious of performing rationally – i.e. in the absence of physical and psychic 'coercion', emotional 'affects' and 'accidental' disturbances of the clarity of judgment, in which we pursue a clearly perceived end by 'means' which are the most adequate in accordance with the extent of our knowledge.

Brubaker says:[32]

> Rational action, then, is at the same time free and meaningful action. Together, these qualities distinguish human actions from other events in nature. *Truly human action is rational, free and meaningful; natural events are non-rational, unfree and devoid of meaning.*

The concepts of rationality, meaning and freedom therefore, feature as components in Weber's construction of the methodological model of social action. *Wertrational* and *zweckrational* action are paradigm cases of social action and the categories of traditional and affectual action function as the parameters of action that can be considered as consciously guided, thereby demarcating behaviour which is properly classified as belonging to the realm of natural events. References to rationality, freedom and meaning on this level of idealisation are to be regarded as morally neutral; but, as Brubaker explains, these concepts become morally charged when we move from the employment of these terms as methodological constructions, which characterise and idealise individual action as an element of social action, to their employment in describing a consciously guided life as a whole. Brubaker explains:[33]

> A meaningful action can just as well be morally indifferent or even blameworthy as morally praiseworthy. A meaningful life, in contrast, is one endowed with *dignity* and thereby, in Weber's view, with moral worth. Meaning and moral dignity derive from the systematic integration of individual actions into a unified life pattern based on certain fundamental values. A life that lacks this systematic unity is not a meaningful life, even if it is composed of a string of meaningful actions.

This normative shift in the intentional scope of concepts also occurs in the cases of 'rationality' and 'freedom':[34]

> The rationality of an individual action, in short, may be no more than a matter of efficiency; the rationality of a complete life, on the other hand, is always a matter of *integrity*.

Similarly,[35]

> Freedom, finally, has a deeper and richer meaning when applied to life as a whole than it does when applied to an individual action. For a single action to be free, it is sufficient that it be uncoerced by physical or psychic factors beyond the agents conscious control. Life as a whole, in contrast, has the potential to be free not in the merely negative sense of being uncoerced, but in the positive sense of being *autonomous*, i.e. guided by norms of the individual's own making.

Meaning, rationality and freedom – for Weber, indispensable features of social action – can be seen, therefore, to converge in a conception of personality. This conception comprises the elements of dignity, integrity and autonomy. That this is consistent with Weber's methodological reflections and is to be understood as the logical extension of his most fundamental analyses of the nature of social science is quite clear. Weber says:[36]

> The freer the action ... i.e. the less it has the character of a natural event, the more the concept of personality comes into play. The essence of personality lies in the constancy of its inner relation to certain ultimate values and like meanings, which, in the course of action, turn into purposes and are thus translated into teleologically rational action.

Brubaker says of this observation:[37]

> Here Weber presents personality as a methodological ideal type. Only in so far as individuals have personalities can science genuinely understand individuals and their actions. Natural events, however regular, can never be 'understood', in Weber's special sense of this term, for they have no intrinsic meaning. They can be explained by being subsumed under general laws, but they cannot be understood in terms of their meaning.

Thus we can see that Weber's interests in these metatheoretical reflections remain on the level of methodology. In a purely formal sense, a person is an object of social scientific investigation by virtue of the property of personality.

Weber's moral philosophy, therefore, exhibits this formal emphasis. There is no substantive evaluation of particular values, just the insistence that a complex of values must be consciously and consistently integrated. This ethic of consistency for the individual imposes rigorous demands. Essentially, Weber suggests that the moral goal of human beings is to become fully human, by which he means the overcoming of the unfree elements of our existence as natural beings by the autonomy of being governed by the coherent values and meanings of a consciously formed personality. The 'heroic' nature of this task suggests comparison with the philosophy of Nietzsche's *Ubermensch*. Brubaker quotes a fragment of a letter from Weber which illustrates this theme:[38]

> All systems of ethics, no matter what their substantive content can be divided into two main groups. There is the 'heroic' ethic, which imposes on men demands of principle to which they are generally *not* able to do justice, except at the high points of their lives, but which serve as signposts pointing the way for man's endless *striving*. Or there is the 'ethic of the mean', which is content to accept man's everyday 'nature' as setting a maximum for the demands which can be made.

The moral message is clear. To be human is to rise above the chain of natural causality and to strive towards a meaningful autonomy. It is to choose one's own values and then to attend to the implications of coherently holding to them. For only if they are coherently followed do values function as components of the personality. And only as a personality, that is a thing with dignity, integrity and autonomy, is one human.

An uncomfortable paradox – or more accurately an explicit contradiction – is plainly evident in Weber's attempt to integrate his methodology of social science with a coherent ethic of personality. Brubaker states it clearly:[39]

> The truly human life is one that is guided by reason. To live a life informed by reason, an individual must become a personality. To become a personality, he must commit himself to certain fundamental values. But this commitment, though it is the foundation of every personality, and thus of every rational life, cannot itself be guided by a reason, for in Weber's view there is no rational way of deciding among the plurality of conflicting possible value commitments. Every rational life, in short, is founded on a non-rational choice.

The Nietzschean comparison has been drawn. The Sartrean connection is obvious – we must choose our own fate. There is a Kantian connection, too, with the emphasis on autonomy conceived as the state of being subject only to self-imposed obligation as opposed to the heteronomy of external obligation. But[40]

> For Kant, autonomy resides in the rule-making of the 'rational will' – a will that can adopt as its own ruling principles only maxims that can be universalized. Universality is a necessary and sufficient condition of the rationality – and thus the rightness – of a moral principle; autonomous moral legislation is thus purely rational, having nothing to do with arbitrariness ....

There is thus a clear departure here from the ethical rationalism characteristic of the tradition of the Enlightenment as represented by the Kantian conception of moral autonomy. This can be contrasted with the formal ethical rationalism of Weber's ethic of responsibility which I want to characterise as a form of emotivism. It should be clear that any attempt to present Weber's thought as a continuation of Enlightenment themes must do so in the face of this profound divergence of view and thus the fruitfulness of such a comparison is called into question. The Nietzschean and Sartrean themes are, however, egregiously relevant.

Weber's substantive ethical theory is elaborated in full cognizance of the tension between the exhortation, on the one hand, to guide one's life through reason, and, on the other, his acknowledgement of the ultimate absence of rational criteria on which to base such a life. His views on the value of ethical theory are typically modern in the this sense. In a 'disenchanted' world moral philosophy cannot address itself to the problems of validating value-judgments. Instead its role is changed by the severity of its scientific limitations. The task of moral education is to be geared towards the clarification of choices and the inculcation of an attitude of 'responsibility'; for clarification and responsibility are preconditions of the type of autonomy which Weber takes to be the mark of the fully human personality. The remit of the educator in this regard, therefore, is to be understood as the task of bringing individuals to the realisation '... that he must choose ...', even though he 'cannot help the individual to determine *how* he must choose'.

We must note from these reflections that the ethical prescriptions which follow from this characterisation of the scope of moral inquiry are purely formal. Not only that but they are constrained at the level of the individual. In other words, the formal structure of the moral universe is bounded by the individual personality – this latter concept again having only formal significance. Analysis at the societal level, for example, the description of formal rationality structures of particular institutions, derive from this individualistic conception of the universe of meaningful action. Whilst Weber's pronouncement that society must be 'treated as solely the resultants and modes of organisation of the particular acts of individual persons'[41] is not to be construed as the claim that society is identical with the individual, or a collection of individuals, it is to be understood as a statement of the propriety of a methodological individualism. That is to say, the nature of a social institution is to be presented as a formal rationality structure in terms of means conditioned by ends. The institutional model is a construct extrapolated from the root of the idealised model of the individual actor. So, in respect of institutions, Weber's sociology has not the slightest pretence to critical evaluation. Nothing can be said of an institution which cannot be said of an individual. And all that can be said of an individual is that he or she must be consistent. For Weber, beyond this formalism, the content of ethical prescription evaporates into non-rational mists of pure will.

The concept of duty which emerges from Weber's ethic of

responsibility is, fundamentally, a duty to self. More specifically, it is a duty of the emotivist self to be a formally rational self. The possibility of my acceptance of duty to others must depend upon my espousal of some basic value – which cannot be rationally grounded – which entails a regard for others. If I do not choose to adopt other-regarding values as the basis of my life plan, then no amount of discussion and argumentation can bring me to acknowledge such a duty. Conversely, it would not be rational for me to attempt to convert others to my values through argument, given that I accepted Weber's account of the scope of ethics, for the simple reason that I have already accepted the non-rational basis of my choice of basic values. This is an important point. The consequence of Weber's (and others') ethical formalism is a complete relativism at the level of content; and despite the 'civilised' overtones of the high intellectualism involved in the construction of this formal theory, there are no guarantees of egalitarianism, altruism or pluralist tolerationism intrinsic to it. I must choose – and follow the path consistent with this choice. When asked by another, 'What should I do?', I can only answer, 'You must choose.' Consequently, I cannot rationally make any *substantive* moral prescriptions – prescription must remain at the formal level. Thus if I do make any substantive moral prescriptions such as, 'One ought not to deprive one's fellows of basic resources to increase one's own wealth', all that I can coherently claim to be saying is, 'I have chosen to adopt the guiding value of an economic egalitarianism which, in a purely formal scheme of rationality, obliges me to hold to the view that one ought not to ... etc .

In short, one cannot hold to the formalist account of the scope of ethical rationality (an account which is entailed by Weber's ethical non-cognitivism) at the level of sociological method, which is extended into his philosophic-anthropological concept of personality, and thence emerges as the ethic of responsibility – *and* rationally hope to make substantive moral prescriptions which can be grounded in impersonal, non-arbitrary criteria. This follows because, on Weber's insistence, there can *be* no impersonal, non-arbitrary criteria for substantive, as opposed to formal, value-choices. This last observation is the touchstone of all modern ethical theory which can be subsumed under the general label of emotivism.[42]

THE CONSEQUENCES OF FORMALISM

I want to move towards a conclusion of this chapter by introducing what I think are serious problems for a social theory which wants to combine the interpretive approach with value-neutrality. There are two fundamental issues:

1. We must note that Weber's work has been discussed in three stages:

(a) a metatheory of the methodology of concept formation;
(b) a philosophical anthropology;
(c) an ethical theory.

These three stages are a fully integrated theoretical system. The fundamental insight upon which the whole system is built is that of the exposition of the nature of the dichotomy of natural and social phenomena. The essential purposivity of the social world leads to Weber's concept of social action in general, and his more specific characterisations in the fourfold typology of action. The core concept of 'meaningful', that is, consciously guided, goal directed activity, functions as the conceptual ground of the anthropology of personality and its substructure of component concepts – dignity, integrity and autonomy. These reflections lead to the concept of freedom in Weber's ethical theory – that is, freedom from the nomological chain of causation – and this concept is shown to close the system by its profound resonance and coherence with the initial dichotomy of the natural and the social: the free is that which cannot be subsumed under the nomological umbrella of causal laws – it can and must be 'understood'; whereas the unfree is that which lacks the properties of structured, consciously guided, means–ends rationality, i.e. nature. The latter category of objects is to be empirically ordered nomologically. It is the systemic nature of these reflections which focuses our attention. For, if it is the case, as it clearly seems to be, that a contradiction is generated within the system, then we are entitled to regard this as a *reductio ad absurdum* of the assumptions which lead to this contradiction. The tension between Weber's conception of the ethic of responsibility and the irrational moment of choice on which this must be founded has been plainly identified. Is it, as I suggested earlier, an explicit contradiction? That it is can be demonstrated by reference to the interconnections of Weber's system of thought which define the methodological functions of its component concepts.

Simply, 'choices' can be caused; in which case they are not choices. This is to say that the appearance of autonomous choice from the subjective, phenomenological perspective of the individual can, in some cases, be explained behaviouristically as an event consistent with the nomological conception of determinism. This cannot be denied from an emotivist perspective in general – the conception of moral discourse as rhetorical manipulation is simply a conception of the way in which the trickery of language operates on the appetites to induce (materially cause) a psychological state. Neither can it be denied from the specific Weberian position: the concepts of, for instance, *charisma*, or the outer parameters of 'traditional' or 'affective' action, are an analogue of the emotivist formulation. That such actions can be hypothetically distinguished from natural events in the chain of material causation by the conceptual apparatus of Weber's typology of social action implies that we have at our disposal an understanding of what it is that demarcates the spheres of the natural and the social – the unfree and the free, the nomological and the meaningfully interpretable, *Natur and Geist.* This pivotal criterion is supposedly embodied in the concept of the ethically responsible choice. But if there is no rational basis on which a choice can be made then how are we to characterise this moment of action? Further, why should we characterise it as a free, as opposed to a naturally determined, event?

We must recall that we are not concerned with actual subjective behaviour, but with idealisations of such behaviour. In fact, Weber's ethical theory is prescriptive only in so far as it exhorts the genuine self to act in accordance with the methodological idealisation of formal rationality. Thus given the value-orientation of an individual or a 'culture', it is a purely deductive, non-empirical enterprise to reconstruct the formal rationality structures which are implied by it. It could be suggested, then, that a truly ethical life is simply a matter of formal logic which stems from a foundational premise – a choice – and that the genesis of the particular choice of the basic premise is scientifically irrelevant. Indeed, whether we intuitively feel that the initial choice of value-orientation is important or not, we must ask ourselves whether it can be explicable from the point of view of a *verstehende* sociology. For it is non-rational, criterionless choice and, hence, cannot be 'understood'. If we disregard the moment of choice, all seems to cohere happily. But this tension between Weber's conception of meaningful action and the ethical integrity of a meaningful life, on the one hand, and the non-rational choice of value-orientation, on the other, leads us to a sobering conclusion concerning the explanatory worth of an interpretive sociology.

That is, it becomes plain that the idealised reconstructions of formal rationality structures appear as empty models of artificially rationalised social action built up by a plodding chain of deductions which, although offering a consistent 'explanation', seem quite plainly impoverished when juxtaposed with what now appears to be the really important question, namely, the reason for the initial choices of value-orientation. This question cannot be fended off by recourse to the insistence of the scientific inaccessibility of the validation of value-judgments. We are not asking whether the value-judgment which expresses the initial choice is valid or otherwise, indeed we may accept that this question is inadmissible scientifically. We wish to know why this choice was made. The type of explanation which must ensue must be a nomological explanation for the simple reason that the initial choice of values cannot be rationally made – it cannot even be idealised as a 'free' (i.e. non-natural) event on Weber's own criteria of concept formation.

This objection stands even in the face of Weber's strenuous objections to the 'dilettante's' search for an ultimate causal factor as the point of departure for historical investigation and explanation.[43] For we can still acknowledge the value-judgment involved in our interest in selecting a causal series, and admit the infinite regress of a chain of causation prior to a selected event. But it remains a fact that we have not discovered a mode of explanation which is satisfying, other than nomological explanation, if the non-rational conception of the moment of choice fails adequately to distinguish the realms of nature and culture. Thus it is reasonable to suggest that Mill's nomological scheme of explanation as envisaged in his concept of Ethology[44] seems appropriate to the phenomena which, in the light of this discussion, seem to constitute the real focus of sociological investigation. That is, why do actors choose *particular* value-orientations?

The point is this: an anti-nomological methodology conjoined with an ethical non-cognitivism/relativism must rely on an interpretive, or *Verstehende*, conception of social action. Thus *formal* means–ends rationality must do the explanatory work. But the emotivist conception of the actor, which leads to the characterisation of *substantive* rationality as beyond the scope of science, strips the reconstruction of formal rationality structures of its central role in sociological explanation. We might say that Weber's ethical non-cognitivism/relativism leads to a conception of social action which cannot adequately 'rescue' cultural phenomena from the realm of nomological causation. In Chapter 5 I want to examine this in detail in our discussion of Hollis, who seems to lead us to us this very point.

2. We have repeatedly stressed the idealising nature of the conception of action in Weber's methodology. Thus the conception of a particular rationality structure is a formalised account of a means–ends constellation of practical action. There is no logical objection to the notion, or the construction, of a formalised account of rationality given the purpose-guiding values which characterise it, as we have noted. There is no pretence in Weber's work to the suggestion that the construction of ideal-types of action correspond to the actual self-understanding of this activity by the empirical actors involved in it.[45] Thus, at the institutional level, we conceptualise, say, capitalism or law as a particular rationality structure employing particular means to a particular end. How do we glean the ends of these institutional activities in order that we may then build an ideal-typical reconstruction of its formal structure? How do we even separate the various goal-directed activities which are entangled within any form of institution? How do we judge among these interwoven aspects of action as to which are defining features of the institution and which are not. There is much in Weber's own writings to suggest that these discriminating procedures are largely hit-and-miss affairs. This point is echoed in a substantial body of literature which attends to the

actual business of applying his methodology. Attention to these texts show how differing conceptions of a particular institution may emerge as candidates for a datum line of empirical research.

It appears, therefore, that a conceptual decisionism surfaces on a different level. Not only are we to lament the fact that a non-cognitivist or ethical formalist conception of substantive rationality does not empower social science to condone or condemn institutions as 'truly human' or otherwise, but it appears that we face serious problems on a merely *descriptive* level.[46] Briefly, the question as to what constitutes the ideal-type of a particular institution boils down to a question about points of view – that is, points of view as to the essentially rational ends of these activities – not their contingent subplots or ulterior motives. If the question is put as to whose point of view is to be taken as being the correct point of view for social science to adopt, then we are again embroiled in issues of substantive rationality. An emotivist conception of substantive rationality, therefore, appears to raise further doubts as to the coherence of a *verstehende* approach premised upon it.

THE NEED FOR A SUBSTANTIVE VIEWPOINT

If ideal-typical heuristics are to be endowed with universal and non-arbitrary applicability, and are to claim significantly to explain the social world, then we must seriously reconsider our conceptualisation of substantive rationality. This claim is not based simply on a deep sense of injustice which flatly refuses to accept that substantive value-positions cannot be rationally defended or attacked. It may be the case that they cannot, and all the passion in the world will not alter this fact. However, if this is the case, we may also have to face the possibility that social science is likewise impossible. For it seems that a position of ethical non-cognitivism within a system such as Weber's generates a profound instability. That this position is fiercely upheld by modern theorists is a point which should acutely concentrate the mind. For, if these foregoing objections have any validity, this issue now appears as the central problem of sociological method.

4

Evaluation and Description

Chapters 2 and 3 have led us to the point where we must acknowledge the need for an interpretive or *verstehende* approach to sociological method. Yet, without a commitment to developing a conception of substantive rationality, it appears that we may face serious problems not only on the level of explanation but in simply attempting to describe the social world. In this chapter and the next, through the arguments of Finnis and Hollis, I want to show that this is indeed the case, and go on in the remainder of the book to sketch an objectivist outline of a solution to the problem.

I mentioned in my introduction that the dispute between Natural Lawyers and Legal Positivists is of general sociological significance. Perhaps I should express this claim more vigorously: the dispute between Natural Lawyers and Legal Positivists is of *ultimate* sociological significance. It can be characterised as a disagreement over a single proposition. The respective parties either affirm or deny that there is a *necessary* connection between law and morality. In fundamental terms the dispute can be presented as a disagreement over the positivist claim that it is possible to formulate a valid (non-arbitrary) conception of law without recourse to moral judgment. John Finnis has made a valuable contribution to this debate, and to the philosophy of social science in general, by presenting two interrelated theses. The first shows that all social phenomena, and, hence, legal phenomena, must be conceptualised as manifestations of practical reason – means employed to specific ends – and that ideal-typical descriptions of these phenomena require us to make judgments as to the practical reasonableness of the ends of these social enterprises. If this cannot be achieved in a non-arbitrary fashion, we must resign ourselves to the indeterminacy of an infinite plurality of interpretations of the social world; all of them 'consistent' with a particular 'point of view'. This much, I will suggest, Finnis demonstrates with the force of logical necessity.

In the second stage of Finnis's argument, he attempts to show that the practically reasonable point of view is, in fact, the moral point of view inasmuch as the practically reasonable point of view logically presupposes deontic criteria.[1] In other words, Finnis tries to demonstrate the validity, and ground the truth, of the following sequent of reasoning: general deceptions of social phenomena must be ideal-typically modelled from the perspective of practical reason. Practical reason presupposes moral reason and, hence, our descriptions of social phenomena (and, hence, legal phenomena) must necessarily involve moral judgment. Thus there is a necessary connection between law (and all other conceptions of social phenomena) and morality.

Finnis incorporates the sociological insights of Weber and the Aristotelian principles of basic concept formation in his argument for a theory of Natural Law.[2] In examining these elements of his methodology it will be possible to show that his first thesis is the correct point of departure for the contemporary debate concerning not only the concept of law, but concept formation in the social sciences. I want to argue that if disputes about conceptualisations of social phenomena are to be resolved, they must be resolved by following, *formally*, Finnis's methodological programme and refining the a priori techniques involved in the second thesis. Once this is accepted, we can begin to direct our efforts towards developing the common ground between theorists who attempt to validate the principles of deontic judgment through an analysis of the reflexive commitments of practical reason. It is for this reason that I think it worthwhile to examine closely the logical detail of Finnis's position.

PROGRESS VIA 'PSEUDO-POSITIVISM'

The key to the resolution of the dispute over the concept of law, which, I will suggest, vindicates the Natural Lawyer, is to be found in the adoption of a methodological approach which, ironically, is an implication of the type of analysis firmly advocated by those who are regarded as scientifically antithetical to the Natural Law thesis. I refer to the advocacy of some version of 'the internal point of view' or 'attention to practical point' propounded by Legal Positivists such as Hart in response to the inadequacies of earlier empiricist-orientated jurisprudence. But positivism in general, and Legal Positivism in particular, are contentious labels. 'Positivism', like 'law', may be called into question as the focus of conceptual analysis. I think, however, that for our purposes, and given what has gone before, the matter can be briefly and satisfactorily dealt with.

What unites the positivist tradition is the desire to replace 'metaphysical speculation' with 'science'. J. S. Mill and A. J. Ayer, the latter as a populariser of the programme of the Logical Empiricism of the Vienna Circle, are, though separated by many years of philosophical and sociological development, archetypes of the tradition. Hume is the illustrious forebear; Russell and Wittgenstein part of a recent generation; Popper a rebellious relative. The network of family ties which ramifies through the positivist and empiricist tradition in the natural and social sciences connects a multiplicity of persons and proposals. Notwithstanding this apparent heterogeneity, there is a central theme of the reliance on our physical senses as the primary source of all *informative* (i.e. non-tautological) knowledge. Popper, of course, argues strongly that our theories about the world condition our observations of it. But in the last resort his falsificationism relies on an *empirical observation* to settle theoretical problems. Nowhere is this confidence in our physical senses more in evidence than in the writings of John Stuart Mill. And it is his conception of scientific method which will serve as the necessary and sufficient condition of inclusion under the positivist nomenclature as I employ it – at least as far as social science is concerned. We have seen in our discussions in Chapters 2 and 3 that this is the nomological thesis of the 'unity of scientific method'. The position as far as Legal Positivism is concerned is a little different; in fact recent Legal Positivism is methodologically closer to what, in general sociological terms, is regarded as the anti-positivist position, and especially close to Wittgenstein's views on the explanation of rule-following and language use.[3] We may discuss this as an aside, but the debate is rather idiosyncratic, and we should not allow ourselves to be diverted from the arguments which we have developed so far.

We saw in chapter 2 that the consequence of nomological explanation is the thesis which holds that there is but one method of scientific inquiry, regardless of subject-matter, and one mode of scientific explanation. This unitary method comprises two main elements: (1) the primacy of empirical observation directed towards the identification of phenomenal regularity; and (2) the attempt to refer these particular observations to, and classify them in terms of, general causal laws which facilitate 'explanation'. This is the only methodological tenet we need to specify for admission to the positivist ranks – for its implications restrict and preclude a host of other methodological possibilities which may purport to differentiate a positivist from a nonpositivist. From this point on, therefore, self-ascribed nomenclature is of little relevance.[4]

In opposition to positivism we have discussed the repudiation of what I have called the 'Unitarian' thesis. The generally Neo-Kantian and specifically Weberian position advocates a serious reconsideration of the relationship between method and subject-matter. Social phenomena, being fundamentally constituted as a manifestation of the purposive consciousness of humanity, cannot be explained as if they were subject to the inexorable chain of natural causes and effects. Accordingly, we have made the case for a form of *Verstehen* as the appropriate alternative to the all-encompassing scheme of scientific explanation embraced by positivism. Ethical non-cognitivism, or value-neutrality, in the form of the thesis which holds to the impossibility of the scientific determination of judgments of aesthetic or moral value, may feature as a component of both positivist and anti-positivist methodologies. This is certainly the case in Weber's scheme of explanation. Thus, prima facie, this form of scepticism does not serve to distinguish the factions in question. Whether or not this position is *consistent* with both schools of methodological thought is, however, another matter.

To return, therefore, to my previous point concerning methodological nomenclature: if a theorist holds him or herself to be a positivist on the basis of asserting that a valid conception of law can be formulated without recourse to moral judgment, and yet denies the Unitarian thesis, we may be sure that 'positivism' here is being taken as synonymous with a version of value-neutrality. Weber himself would have had no option but to declare himself a Legal Positivist on this criterion. This fact, however, does not suggest any significant common ground between Weber's views, on the one hand, and those of Bentham, Mill or Austin, on the other. On the contrary, the distance between Weber and these three is, in philosophical terms, immense. These labels are, therefore, of little use. The real questions we must ask are as follows:

1. Is it possible to appropriate conceptually and order empirically social (e.g. legal) phenomena via the methodological framework of a Unitarian positivism?
2. Is it possible to reject the Unitarian thesis, adopt an interpretive or *verstehende* approach to investigating legal phenomena and still hold to the thesis that it is possible to formulate a valid concept of law without recourse to moral judgment.

If we accept the claims of Weber's rejection of Unitarian positivism, we acknowledge the necessity of orientating ourselves to social phenomena by first realising that purpose-guiding values give a structure to social action. By acquainting ourselves with (that is, *given*) the particular values of an individual or group, we are able to map the course of actions through time in a coherent way. In other words, we reconstruct an ideal-typical model of what an instrumentally rational being would do given the particular ends or values which constituted his, her or their purposes. Thus explanation is facilitated by reference to purpose-guiding values and not by the subsumption of the particular under the general in the manner of nomological explanation. Weber is emphatic, however, that the assumption of a nomological determinism operating in the world is an assumption which must be made by all agents if they are to engage in the employment of means to the achievement of ends.[5]

Yet it is the case that Weber acknowledge that this approach to the understanding of social processes is, if not hit and miss, a creative affair in many cases, and that ideal-typical constructs of major historical institutions have no claim to instantiation in reality. That is, they are an attempt to orientate the researcher to a logically convenient epochal or cultural value-system in the hope that the ideal-typical 'shot in the dark' may be refined by further investigation. This is most important as we shall shortly come to realise.[6] We must note that Weber insists that this approach to social science does not, and must not, involve value-judgments. We noted in our consideration of Brubaker's analysis and exposition that Weber insists that it is not possible to choose rationally between competing values and that the ideal-type rests upon a conception of rationality which is purely *formal*.[7]

In examining Finnis's discussion of the value of this type of approach to the phenomenon of law, we encounter the suggestion that there exists an evaluative dimension to this procedure beyond the primary conferral of significance upon social phenomena which Weber admits in his elucidation of the concept of 'value-relevance'. In establishing the connection between this interpretive methodology and Aristotle's teleological approach to functional analysis, Finnis suggests, however, that value-judgments are unavoidable at a second level of the enterprise, namely in the attempt accurately to *describe* the goals of various aspects of social action. His contention is that ethical non-cognitivism, or a value-free approach as espoused by Weber, imparts a methodological relativism to ideal-typical model building. Such a relativism cannot fix a non-arbitrary perspective through which hermeneutically to appropriate, and thus generally describe, aspects of significant social phenomena. In what follows I will try to show that Finnis is right in saying that the anti-positivist methodology is the only valid – that is non-arbitrary – approach to concept formation in social science, that this is indeed an evaluative procedure, and that a 'Legal Positivist' who flirts with this interpretive methodology (e.g. Hart) cannot uphold a morally neutral, non-arbitrary conception of law – or of any other social phenomenon. In other words, Unitarian Positivists (e.g. Mill) cannot appropriate the phenomena in question, non-Unitarian 'Legal Positivists' (e.g. Austin, Hart) are not positivist, and that, in virtue of their pseudo-positivism, cannot consistently deny the claims of the Natural Lawyer. Furthermore, I want to argue that Finnis, though ultimately unsuccessful in his attempt to provide a conceptually *necessary* demonstration of the solution to the problem, does in fact present the central problematic and the formal requirements of its resolution in a profoundly perspicacious form.

FINNIS: EVALUATION AND DESCRIPTION

Finnis's opening chapter in *Natural Law and Natural Rights* is entitled 'Evaluation and the Description of Law'. Consonant with the central tenets of Weberian method hitherto presented, he says:[8]

> A social science, such as analytical or sociological jurisprudence, seeks to describe, analyse and explain some object or subject-matter. This object is constituted by human actions, practices, habits, dispositions and by human discourse. The actions, practices, etc., are certainly influenced by the 'natural' causes properly investigated by the methods of the natural sciences, including a part of the science of psychology. But the actions, practices, etc., can be fully understood only by understanding their point, that is to say, their objective, their value, their significance or importance, as conceived by the people who performed them, engaged in them, etc. And these conceptions of point, value, significance, and importance will be reflected in the discourse of those same people, in the conceptual distinctions they draw and fail or refuse to draw. Moreover, these actions, practices, etc., and correspondingly these concepts, vary greatly from person to person, from one society to another, from one time and place to other times and places. *How then is there to be a general descriptive theory of these varying particulars?*

The diversity of conceptions of various social practices and institutions is a point which Weber readily acknowledges in his discussion of the various uses and modes of ideal-typical constructs. He is under no illusion that the ideal type of, say, Christianity or democracy, or in the case which occupies our attention here, law, accurately describes the multiplicity of interpretations which a host of individuals may place upon these particular conceptions. As Finnis says:[9] '... the practical concerns and the self-interpretations of the people whose conduct and dispositions go to make up the theorist's subject-matter – are not uniform.' Finnis sees the problem for the social scientist who wishes to describe these institutions as being self-evident: do the social sciences aspire to be something more than 'a conjunction of lexicography with local history, or even juxtaposition of all lexicographies conjoined with all local histories'.[10]

Finnis suggests that the improvements in methodological technique and explanatory power in the work of self-professed positivists such as Kelsen and, to a greater extent, Hart and Raz, are due to a decisive break with the naive empiricism of Bentham and Austin. This involves the methodological incorporation of three principal features: attention to *practical point*; selection of *central cases* and *focal meaning;* and *selection of viewpoint.*[11] As we develop the discussion we shall see that these three features converge into the foundational principle of concept formation in social science irrespective of the particular concerns of various disciplines within it.

My previous remarks concerning the pseudo-positivism of Hart and others may appear clearer in the light of Finnis's observation that Hart is concerned to develop a more accurate description of the specific character of law as a 'social technique' by devoting scrupulous attention to the practical structure of the enterprise of law. Hart wishes to make a distinction between pre-legal regimes which consist of simple rules backed by sanctions, and more mature systems which incorporate a secondary set of rules which pertain to the application, modification and scope of the primary rules. For Hart:[12]

> A legal system is a system in which 'secondary' rules have emerged *in order to* remedy the *defects* of a pre-legal regime comprising only 'primary rules'. Law must have a minimum content of primary rules and sanctions *in order to* ensure the survival of the society or its members and to give them *practical reason for* compliance with it.

Clearly, this view is an attempt to explain the enterprise of law by reference to is ultimate end; that is, the concept of law is a conception of a social practice geared towards a particular goal.

Finnis goes on to say that with Raz, the specificity of means and ends is refined even further. The goal is to institute a technique of authoritative dispute resolution by means of norms which apply not only to social conduct of those who are liable to be judged by the institutions, but these same norms provide guidance to the 'primary institutions' which settle the disputes by 'binding applicative determinations'. The law claims authority to regulate all normative institutions to which its subject members belong, and also contains norms 'the purpose of which is to give binding force within the system to norms which do not belong to it'.[13] For the moment the validity of these analyses is not our central concern. What is at issue is the descriptive approach. Simply, Hart, Raz etc. are trying to describe and differentiate a form of institutional activity by isolating specific characteristics. These characteristics, however, are not given or obvious, they are variously selected on the grounds of being considered the *most important* features of the enterprise. Finnis's point is that all these accounts of law are intended to be descriptive, and simply to describe is, ostensibly, to refrain from passing judgment on a particular situation. However, these descriptions of complex practical phenomena can approach generality only through the selection of particular features which, in the respective opinions of the observers, appear to be essential. What is essential to an enterprise is dependent upon the goal of the enterprise. In the light of this we must now ask whose opinion is likely to approximate to the correct understanding of the ends and thus the essential means of this enterprise.

The problem is that a value-free approach to the phenomena precludes any discussion of essence or importance. It has recourse only to isolating the lowest common denominator or highest common factor to ensure that descriptive or explanatory terms extend straightforwardly to all states of affairs which might, in non-theoretical discourse, be called 'law'. But we have seen that Weber regards this preoccupation with the 'typical', 'regular' or 'generic' features of historical or socio-cultural phenomena as the fundamental error of positivist (nomological) approaches to social science. Weber insists that this approach to 'explanation' clearly precludes the possibility of any significant understanding of the nature of social processes – rather it limits itself to empirically valid, but theoretically useless, claims about contingent historical circumstances.[14] We may add that on the level of linguistic analyses a conventionalist perspective seeks to report the typicality of ostensive definitions of the term 'law'. As far as providing a guide to the semantic content of the *concept* of law we must, again, regard these attempts as empirically valid but theoretically useless reports of the idiosyncrasies of language use This is important because there is much influential discussion of a conventionalist nature concerning the appropriation of legal pheno-mena.[15]

The suggestion that, for theoretical purposes, law must be regarded as a 'cluster concept' is attractive because of the empirical heterogeneity of the denotations of the *word*. That is, it is plain that the linguistically mediated manifestations of the legal enterprise encompass a multitude of practices which *more or less* involve themselves with rules, sanctions, etc. But this is only to say that we *more or less* understand what people mean by the word 'law'. The attempt to make theoretical capital out of word usage and ambiguous denotations *appears*, however, to carry more weight: Finnis agrees with Raz in saying that[16]

> The general traits which marks a system as a legal one are several and each of them admits, in principle, of various degrees. In typical instances of legal systems all these traits are manifest to a very high degree. But it is possible to find systems in which all or some are present only to a lesser degree or in which one or two are absent altogether ... When faced with borderline cases it is best to admit their problematic credentials, to enumerate their similarities and dissimilarities to the typical cases, and leave it at that.

This means very little unless we have a clear (and non-arbitrary) understanding of what constitutes 'the typical case'. Finnis is aware of the problem and adds a cautionary note of refinement:[17] 'Because the word "typical" may suggest that the relevant criterion is statistical frequency ... I prefer to call the states of affairs referred to by a theoretical concept in its focal meaning the *central case(s)*.'

ARISTOTLE: FOCAL MEANING AND CENTRAL CASES

It is at this point that we may discuss the relationship between Weber's views on the inadequacy of nomological explanation in social science and the Aristotelian notion of *focal meaning*. Methodologically, it is an interesting relationship, but one which is misrepresented by confusing word usage with the analysis of practical rationality. Confusion is engendered by the attempt to reject nomological explanation in social science without seeing through the implications of this radical shift in the approach to concept formation. I hope we can go some way towards clarifying the debate.

In Chapter 1 under the sub-heading 'Social Science as Moral Critique', I spoke of the impossibility of finding our ideal-typical descriptions of institutional phenomena instantiated in our empirical experience. This point is quite obvious once we reflect upon the diversity and intricacy of social life. In actuality any one institution, loosely conceived, is permeated by and permeates an enormous range of other institutions. It is understandable, then, that we encounter the plea for the 'multi-significance' of terms which purport to describe large-scale or even extremely small-scale institutions. But this is putting the cart before the horse. What we have done is embark upon our investigations with a loose understanding of the functions of the institution with which we are concerned, and encountered others with even looser understandings. In the absence of any conception of an essential function of an institution there is simply no good reason to differentiate what appear to be similar or analogous cases. Taking in these waifs and strays and accommodating them under the conception with which we first started may appear to be charitable, but theoretically it is pure obfuscation. We must remember that 'our' or someone else's initial loose understanding of the functions of an institution are arbitrarily conceived and may even be antithetical to each other. To present 'multisignificance' as being an advance on theoretical precision, therefore, is quite perverse. It amounts to saying that we are in a better position theoretically for admitting even more loose and arbitrary conceptions to parade under the banner of what was already loose and arbitrary. Weber's formation of ideal-types of institutional phenomena does not escape this problem. For when he speaks of practical ends which are unambiguously *given*, and from which we may reconstruct instrumentally rational models of these particular enterprises, we must ask, on whose understanding of the ends are we basing our ideal-typical analysis?[18]

Is it possible, then, to grasp the methodological core of focal analysis and endow it with the systematic rigour required by a social science? Finnis's reference to Aristotelian analysis in this focal sense proves to be illuminating, even though we shall see below that Finnis is hasty in invoking the authority of Aristotle to illustrate his conception of central and focal cases. These conceptions must not be conflated, and Aristotle's analysis of the multisignificance of terms takes us only as far as an 'agreed referent' for a problematic concept. In fact, Finnis is mistaken in thinking that Aristotle applies focal analysis in the example he cites (i.e. the concept of 'friendship').[19] However, the distinction we will draw between Aristotle's attempts to mitigate ordinary usage, on the one hand, and the actual possibility of employing focal analysis, on the other, is highly relevant to Finnis's critique of those who are apt to take pre-theoretical usage on trust, and his (Finnis's) subsequent attempt to formulate the concept of law as a specifically directed aspect of practical reason ultimately conditioned by the nature of its social goals.

Aristotle's employment of the concept of focal meaning is discussed in his analysis of friendship and citizenship. W. W. Fortenbaugh, in his paper 'Aristotle's Analysis of Friendship: Function and Analogy, Resemblance and Focal Meaning', examines Aristotle's attempt to clarify the ambiguities which arise from the employment of a single linguistic label in referring to a multiplicity of objects which differ in kind. Not surprisingly, this is a complex affair. However, I think that some detailed attention to Aristotle's approach to this problem will prove to be rewarding. Fortenbaugh reminds us of Aristotle's commitment to the principle of function as a determinant of the nature of being of any object:[20]

> It is an Aristotelian principle that the being of any functional thing consists in its capacity to perform its function. For any purposeful thing, whether a natural object or an organism, whether a man-devised tool or activity or association, its essential nature is determined by its function and is expressed by the *logos* which states its purpose.

Fortenbaugh suggests that friendship may be similarly conceived; and, we may add, so can law or any other practical phenomenon, and we should not be distracted by the substitution of this example in making the point. He notes that Aristotle regarded forms of practical action such as friendship as being[21]

> ... goal directed and so defined by their goal or purpose. Indeed it is because friendships are goal orientated that Aristotle begins his discussion of friendship by discussing the objects of friendship (*phileta*): the good, pleasant and useful. Friendships have a goal (*telos*) or purpose which determines their essential nature. Since there are three kinds of goals there are three kinds of friendship: those directed toward goodness, those directed toward pleasure and those directed toward utility.

Fortenbaugh is anxious to point out that the notion of focal analysis is not as clear-cut as many commentators on Aristotle's work have assumed. In fact, he wishes to show that the employment of focal analysis in the examination of friendship is not applicable. His arguments are instructive in that we may glean the subtleties of such an analysis by distinguishing the focal (case) from the analogous or the 'similar' – i.e. that which is related through 'resemblance' ('function' being a more fundamental aspect adequately described above).

Fortenbaugh shows that Aristotle *mitigates the ordinary usage* of the label 'friendship' by suggesting that different types of friendship can be related by analogy: 'When things are one by analogy, it is just as it they enjoy a single nature.'[22] This claim appears extravagant; however, intuitively, we may sanction ordinary usage in this way by recognising that analogies (attempt to) reduce differences to a common form or principle. Fortenbaugh says:[23]

> The possibility of an analogical relationship is clear when Aristotle says that the pleasant is a good to friends of pleasure. Filling out the analogy, we get: As the good is related to friends of goodness, so the pleasant is related to friends of pleasure ... Just as the good is related to friends of goodness and the pleasant is related to friends of pleasure, so also the useful is related to friends of utility. All three kinds of friendship may be related by analogy and therefore called friendships without simple, unmitigated equivocation.

We must bear in mind that this rather uninspiring point is made simply to *mitigate ordinary language use.*

Fortenbaugh tells us that Aristotle recognises common features which are logically necessary for the occurrence of friendship. These features are: reciprocal affection, wishing well and awareness [of regard]. Fortenbaugh, in noting Aristotle's concern with everyday notions of friendship, says:[24]

> Men say that it is necessary (*phasi dein*) to wish a friend well and for this reason a man's love of wine is not called friendship. Aristotle recognizes that wishing well, reciprocal affection and awareness are all necessary features of friendship as conceived of by ordinary men, and therefore is prepared to ask rhetorically how anyone could speak of friends who are unaware of each other's regard.

Again, we are on the level of language use and the logical necessity here should be understood as relating to the outer limits of the multisignificance of a linguistic label. This will presently prove to be of some importance to us. However, concerning the identification of necessary features, Fortenbaugh adds an interesting caveat which is highly relevant to Finnis's views on the relationship between description and evaluation. It concerns.[25]

> ... Aristotle's usage of the Greek verb *dei*. Certain uses which, might be thought to imply logical necessity need not be so construed. For example, when Aristotle says that the perfect friendship of morally good men includes within itself everything which ought (*dei*) to belong to friends, he is not saying that the features of perfect friendship are logically necessary for friendship. Such an interpreta-

> tion is ruled out by the fact that many friendships are lacking in one or more of these features. Instead, the verb *dei* may be construed as an evaluation: friendship ought (it's good) to have these features. And friendships which do are rated best. Alternatively, it may be a matter of hypothetical necessity: if friendship is to be lasting then it must have these features. ... Whatever the proper interpretation of *dei*, it is certainly true that Aristotle looks upon the friendship of morally good men as a kind of standard or central case which has everything expected of friendship.

Fortenbaugh suggests that Aristotle's reason for making the friendship of morally good men feature as a standard to which all friendships should aspire is clear. It is because such a friendship or association is complete in that it involves not only virtue but pleasure and advantage. Accordingly, such a friendship can *mediate* a relationship between friendships based on pleasure and friendships based on utility. Fortenbaugh says that in regard to pleasure and utility friendships based upon either need not *resemble* one another. He says:[26]

> The utility friendships of old men are most often lacking in pleasure and the pleasure friendships of younger people may be quite harmful. But both resemble the friendship of morally good men and so are related indirectly to one another.

Thus resemblances can be mediated by a central case – though not all resemblances need to be so mediated.

We have noted the common features (resemblances) of wishing well, reciprocal affection and awareness of regard. Here, and through these features, friendships of pleasure and utility resemble each other directly. In the important areas (i.e. the goal orientation) of a particular friendship, however, namely, pleasure and utility, direct resemblance fails. The central case of perfect friendship, therefore, functions as a focus of resemblance, even between friendships which are characterised by different goals. Perfect friendship, says Fortenbaugh, has 'the priority of mediator'. But this kind of priority, says Fortenbaugh, is not the priority of focal analysis. He says that other commentators, such as Aspasius, have introduced the concept of focal analysis as being founded upon the relation of resemblance discussed above; that is, the relationship of resemblance to the central case of the association of morally good men. But this kind of priority, says Fortenbaugh, is not the priority of focal analysis. He says:[27]

> As a mediator of resemblance perfect friendship may be described as a focus of resemblance. But resemblance is not an adequate basis for focal analysis as explained in the seventh book of the *Eudemian Ethics*. And if Aspasius and other commentators after him have thought that it is an adequate basis, they are mistaken. This point

> has already been argued by Professor Owen, who points out Aristotle's consistent refusal to apply focal analysis to artistic imitation. A painted eye resembles a living eye and is called an eye because it resembles a living eye. Nevertheless for Aristotle, this case of ambiguity is not to be mitigated by focal analysis. Aristotle's reason for not applying focal analysis is, according to Owen, clear and unvarying. A living eye 'is defined by what it does and a painted eye cannot see. It in no way shares the function of a living eye and can only be equivocally called an eye ...' The general case is clear. Aristotle does not apply focal analysis to things related by some resemblance, especially when function or purpose is involved.

It is important to note, therefore, that the business of analysis intended to mitigate language use is not to be confused with the much more profound search for identity through an analysis of the *logos* which expresses the purpose – *telos* – of the activity. Fortenbaugh's point is that a genuine focal analysis is directed towards an independent goal in each instance of its application. Initially, in the case of friendship a focal analysis is provisionally applicable in that it is directed to the object or goal of friendship (*phileton*). According to Fortenbaugh, in Aristotle's work the object of friendship (*phileton*) provides us with *two* focal series (*phileta*), each being an independent goal, these being the morally good and the pleasant. Each of these goals is a focus 'upon which conceptually depend several paronyms'.[28] In other words, from the focus of the good depend types of associations which are conceptually related to the pursuit of the good and, similarly, from the focus of the pleasant is generated a series of associations which are conceptually linked to the pursuit of the pleasant. It follows, then, that if friendship is to admit of focal analysis the two independent focal series must themselves be focally related to each other. In other words, there must be some relation of conceptual necessity implied by the definition of the good and of the pleasant. It is Fortenbaugh's aim in his paper to deny this possibility. His remarks below, although solely motivated by a desire to contribute to the excellence of Aristotelian scholarship, are, fortuitously, of immense relevance to our present concerns. In summing up his analysis of the pseudofocality of the concept of perfect friendship, he says:[29]

> If friendship directed toward pleasure is focally dependent upon friendship directed toward moral goodness, the focal relationship must proceed through the objects. This means that the definition of pleasure must mention or include the definition of moral goodness.

Fortenbaugh concludes with this most important observation:[30]

> Neither the *Eudemian Ethics* nor the *Nicomachean Ethics* gives us such a definition. And this is not surprising, for the problem is not peculiar to the discussion of friendship. It is the old problem of

> establishing some relationship between the various goals of human activity ...

It is important that we do not misunderstand the point. I am not holding up Aristotle's introduction of the notion of moral goodness as a focus for the definition of friendship as an argument to suggest that all definitions require this moral basis. The point is that *any* practical enterprise can be made to appear analogous to any other *if the actors involved can be said to subjectively regard their (disparate) goals as providing them with some utility*. Clearly, this leaves us with no possibility of differentiating any action from any other. We need a conception of utility which transcends mere subjective preference. Fortenbaugh's last sentence clearly states the problem which Finnis sees as being the essential task of the methodology of social science. As all social phenomena are to be conceived of as forms of practical activity, Finnis regards this task as being the identification of the central case of practical reason. But some confusion must be cleared up concerning the nature of focal analysis before we can move on to an analysis of Finnis's attempt to expose the core presuppositions of practical reason.

It is clear from Fortenbaugh's analysis that focal analysis in the Aristotelian sense is directed towards identifying a discrete goal in the various aspects of practical activity. A central case may mediate various associations directed to achieving various goals, but the focal case is conditioned by the essential purpose of a particular enterprise. Here we must note that Finnis handles the concept of focality somewhat loosely. That is, he conflates the focal case with the central case. This can be seen by noting that Finnis suggests that we may[31] '... call the states of affairs referred to by a theoretical concept in its focal meaning the *central case(s)*'.

We must remind ourselves of the important distinction between central and focal cases. In the Aristotelian scheme a central case may be either (a) an evaluative prescription which, as far as an argument for Natural Law in particular, and our efforts in general, are concerned, is question begging; or (b) merely an attempt to systematise ordinary usage – a conventionalist methodology which Finnis has clearly suggested we should avoid. This being the case, we should be cautious in our reception of Finnis's invocation of Aristotle's authority when he suggests that just as there are central and peripheral cases of friendship, so there are central and peripheral cases of constitutional government etc. Finnis suggests that our study of these 'related' phenomena is illuminated by thinking of corrupt versions of these cases (in this case he suggests Hitler, Stalin, Amin) as '... watered-down versions of the central cases, or sometimes as exploitations of human attitudes shaped by reference to the central case'.[32] Finnis' conflation of central and focal cases is more evident in the following passage:[33]

> ... one's descriptive explanation of the central cases should be as conceptually rich and complex as is required to answer all appropriate questions about those central cases. And then one's account of the other instances can trace the network of similarities and differences, the analogies and disanalogies, for example of form, function, or content, between them and the central cases. In this way, one uncovers the 'principle or rationale' on which the general term ('constitution', 'friend', 'law' ...) is extended from the central to the more or less borderline cases, from its focal to its secondary meanings.

This process may untangle a lot of confused or equivocal usage. The principle or rationale which Finnis suggests we would discover would, however, merely be the principle upon which equivocal usage of a term could be mitigated. Furthermore, and as we have noted, there can be no *focal* meaning of 'friend', as this concept generates a multiplicity of focal series. It remains to be seen whether or not 'law' admits of a focal analysis.

Fortunately, Finnis's conflation of central and focal cases is not too damaging to his attempt to untangle the methodological problem. In the section entitled 'Selection of Viewpoint', he poses the following question"[34]

> But by what criteria is one meaning to be accounted focal and another secondary, one state of affairs central and another borderline" ... From what viewpoint, and relative to what concerns, are *importance* and *significance* to be assessed?

This is where we came in. We may free ourselves from the hindrance of confused terminology by reformulating the question in line with the Aristotelian programme and, secure in the knowledge that we are not likely to confuse the *mitigation of ordinary language use* with *theoretical concept formation*, ask, 'What is the focal meaning of the concept of law?' Or, in other words, 'What is the essential goal of the enterprise of constructing a legal order?' the answer to this is, prima facie, simple: it depends upon one's point of view. There are, of course, as a matter of contingent historical fact, many points of view. The *focal* meaning of law, however, in the Aristotelian sense, is the viewpoint we must necessarily accept on the basis of a successful analysis of the *telos* of the enterprise.

How far, then, have we come with Finnis? Finnis has clearly shown the need for an ideal-typical construction of the phenomenon of law in line with the methodological prescriptions outlined in our analysis of Weber's interpretive sociology. Moreover, he has shown that although our theoretical intentions are primarily descriptive, we unavoidably encounter an evaluative dimension to the enterprise. This occurs because we are required hierarchically to differentiate functional aspects of the phenomenon in terms of value-laden criteria which attempt to characterise certain aspects as peripheral and others as essential. This, of course, rests upon our value-orientation to the goal of the activity in the first place. His invocation of Aristotelian method has pointed to the desirability, therefore, of exploring the essential aspects of multi-significance of a term *in opposition to searching for a common denominator or common factor in a pre-theoretically conceived conception of law.* But Aristotle's wisdom has not advanced our investigations beyond pointing to the possibility of systematising usage. This point, however, is not trivial. For what Finnis has shown so far is that before a systematic investigation of the phenomenon of law can begin, we need some justification for usage of a label which can sufficiently delimit the scope of the subject-matter. Rather than run the risk of confusion and conflation by using the terminology of secondary, central and focal cases, this stage of the investigation should be regarded as the attempt to isolate the 'agreed referent'. Beyleveld and Brownsword approach the problem in the following way. The first step is to '... specify the concept which is necessary for knowledge ... of a connotation agreed between disputants to be possible.'[35]

If prejudging the nature of the entity (law) is to be avoided, this referent must be acceptable to all who wish to *attempt* to elucidate its meaning in a focal or essential sense. It follows that such an agreed referent has scientific value only in a very general way, that of differentiating one object, in a qualitatively relevant sense, from another. The candidate for an agreed referent advanced by Beyleveld and Brownsword, following Lon Fuller, is that[36]

> Law ... refers to 'the enterprise of subjecting human conduct to the governance of rules', ... the choice of this referent is a stipulation and we can only have a genuine debate with those who are prepared to accept this starting point. Disagreement over the concept of law is to be viewed in terms of different ways of conceptualizing this referent.

Central case analysis, therefore, in Aristotelian terms is an attempt to introduce some systematisation and logical validity into the stipulation of an agreed referent. This stipulation does not reduce us to an endless relativity of usage, however. For, when Aristotle asks rhetorically, 'How can we speak of friends who are unaware of each other's regard?', he is not unaware of the physical possibility of so doing. Rather, it is a demonstration of where the buck stops in disputes over usage and the conceptual appropriation of prima facie subject-matter. Beyleveld and Brownsword refer to this as a starting point in their method of 'transcendental essentialism'. Simply, to disagree over the basic referent indefinitely and profoundly, *de facto*, is in no way inconceivable; but to do so is to demonstrate the impossibility of scientific discussion of the matter and, therefore, the impossibility of investigation of the matter. Where this level of basic intersubjective agreement is not possible, neither is dispute.

REFINING THE AGREED REFERENT

In the light of the above discussion we can take stock of our progress with Finnis. We have dealt with some general methodological issues satisfactorily; that of attention to the practical point of the phenomenon once this phenomenon has been conceptually isolated at the first stage by an agreed referent. The agreed referent must not prejudge the nature of the phenomenon in any focal sense or any sense which would, in a question-begging way, predetermine the results of a focal analysis. That is, the agreed referent must facilitate, as a potentially multisignificant concept, a plurality of contending conceptions of the focal case of the phenomenon whilst ruling out the set of all phenomena which cannot, with communicable coherence, be countenanced as a possible candidate for potential subject-matter.

The problem of *focal* analysis, however, remains. As this is the requirement of determining the essential, as opposed to the variously and disparately conceived goal of the enterprise of law, we appear to be set back to square one. However, this does show that Weber's conception of ideal-type construction in the social sciences suffers the same fate and that unless 'a point of view' can be isolated as the point of view from a scientific standpoint, then social science appears to be abandoned to the arbitrariness of a confusedly conceived subject-matter. Finnis realises that the problem of the selection of viewpoint appears as an evaluative one, and, like Finnis, I agree that there is a need to develop an argument which shows that this evaluation is not subjectively arbitrary. In attempting to do this Finnis notes that Hart and Raz are aware that the descriptive theorist must reproduce a practical point of view. By 'practical', 'practical reason' and 'practical philosophy', Finnis wishes us to understand that he does *not* mean[37]

> ... 'workable' as opposed to unworkable, efficient as opposed to inefficient; I mean with a view to decision and action'. Practical thought is thinking about what (one ought) to do. Practical reasonableness is reasonableness in deciding, in adopting commitments, in choosing and executing projects, and in general in acting. Practical philosophy is a disciplined and critical reflection on the goods that can be realized in human action and the requirements of practical reasonableness. So when we say that the descriptive theorist (whose purposes are not practical) must proceed, in his indispensable selection and formation of concepts, by adopting a practical point of view, we mean that he must assess importance or significance in similarities and differences within his subject-matter by asking what

> would be considered important or significant in that field by those whose concerns, decisions, and activities create or constitute the subject-matter.

Thus, Finnis notes that Hart wishes to give descriptive priority to the practical evaluations of actors with 'an internal point of view':[38]

> ... viz. those who do not 'merely record and predict behaviour conforming to rules', or attend to rules 'only from the external point of view as a sign of possible punishment', but rather '*use* the rules as standards for the appraisal of their own and others' behaviour'.

Finnis presents another possible point of view, this time from Raz, who suggests that the 'legal' point of view is that of people 'who believe in the validity of the norms and follow them'. Finnis adds that this is 'paradigmatically, the viewpoint of the judge *qua* judge'.[39]

But because these selections of a viewpoint reproduce the viewpoint of particular actors in particular historical situations we may simply ask, 'Why choose them?' Finnis makes a strong critical point here. In referring to Hart and Raz's attempts to reproduce *the* critical viewpoint he says:[40]

> But all this is unstable and unsatisfactory because it involves a refusal to attribute significance to differences that any actor in the field ... would count as practically significant. And, given the technique of analysis by central case and focal meaning, which elsewhere Hart and Raz use with such fruitful resolution, there seems to be no good reason for this refusal to differentiate the central from the peripheral cases *of the internal or legal point of view itself.*

Finnis makes this point in the light of the admissions from Hart and Raz that the 'internal' or 'legal' point of view is an amalgam of very different viewpoints. In Hart's case, allegiance to the system may be born of calculations of long-term interest, disinterested interest in others or simply an unreflective acceptance of tradition or inclination to follow the herd. Raz is even willing to accept that the hypothetical anarchist who becomes a judge in order to undermine the system from within is operating from the 'legal point of view'.

Clearly these respective distillations of a practical viewpoint from the plethora of actual or possible, genuine of dissembling, critical or unreflective viewpoints are at best hopeful heuristics and at worst purely arbitrary, and Finnis is right to make the point. Thus we require what Weber would regard as an impossible methodological synthesis: a *substantively* rational (as opposed to a *formally* rational) point of view as a precondition of any scientific *description* of social phenomena.

5

Evaluation and Explanation

We have seen that Finnis has shown that a methodology for social science requires, in its attempt simply to describe social phenomena, the viewpoint of the practically reasonable person. In other words, we are required to judge the rationality of *ends* of practical activity if we are to be able to offer a general theoretical description of the activity. Hollis, in *Models of Man*[1] claims that the attempt to construct models of social action which avoid the limitations of nomological explanation, arrives at a similar conclusion. His point is that if reasons and motives are to take the place of transitive causal explanations of events, then we are required to construct a concept of a rationally autonomous self which, on the one hand, provides an adequate conception of role distance and thereby frees us from the constraints of a structural determinism, and, on the other, effects an adequate closure in the explanation of action which is signally deficient in the conception of *formal* rationality hitherto presented. Briefly, he suggests that a good reason for action is its own explanation, but the teleological structure of this explanation can be characterised as non-causal only if the teleological 'pull' of the end state is itself rational. His arguments will help us clarify much of the confusion in the debate concerning causality, determinism, free will and the notion of personality in the structure of social-scientific explanation.

Hollis opens his work, *Models of Man*, by suggesting that the conventional wisdom of our age tells us that traditional political theory is dead. His point is that the quest for a theory of human nature which would license normative-moral inferences has been ruled out of court by philosophical developments which insist on a clear-cut fact/value distinction.[2] However, Hollis claims that metaphysical assumptions about human nature are buried alive among the roots of modern social theory. He suggests that as heirs of the Enlightenment we have inherited a problematic legacy. That is, we have inherited an anti-metaphysical attitude to scientific explanation which is wary of going beyond observable evidence, a belief that causal determinism provides us with the paradigm of scientific explanation, and a lingering hope, or at least a suspicion, that Man is capable of being improved, if not perfected, with the aid of science. There is, says Hollis, because of this, a basic tension in the view of man.[3] In speaking of the central assumptions of traditional political theory he notes the following:[4]

> Firstly, there are held to be, in Hume's phrase, 'constant and universal principles of human nature' (*Enquiries* VIII); secondly, social engineers are deemed to have a power of initiative and innovation, which somehow transcends these constant and universal principles; thirdly, human nature is taken to be fixed enough to have given needs or wants, yet mutable enough for those needs and wants to be satisfiable. These presumptions embody both the models of man, which are our point of departure.

These two models Hollis characterises as the passive and active, or Plastic and Autonomous, models of man which feature in approaches to social theory. The task now is to examine the methodologies appropriate to the respective conceptions, taking the passive/Plastic model first.

PLASTIC MAN

Hollis suggests that it is an Enlightenment orthodoxy to link the notion of constant and universal principles of human nature to the claim that we are natural creatures in a rational world of cause and effect. Hence, such passive conceptions of Man are *naturalistic* and *deterministic*. Both these terms require explanation.[5] Hollis says of the former:[6]

> Naturalism is ... the thesis [which holds that] ... Mind and Nature form a single system with those features of nature which make it a subject for science. ... Its sole implication is that there is only one general form of scientific explanation. There is no reason in nature to halt a chain of explanation at any point short of the system as a whole. In particular there is no boundary between inner states and environment or between self and society. ... Natural and social sciences attack the same one world with the same one method of validation.

Determinism is taken to be the thesis which points to the proper mode of explanation of this world. Hollis suggests that the formulation of this thesis which steers an acceptable middle ground between 'blandness and over-commitment' is the following:[7]

> ... *every fact which has an explanation is, together with some other fact, an instance of a natural law* ... Naturalism and determinism now go agreeably together, combining to assert that there is a unitary law-governed world and that knowledge of it depends on identifying its laws.

Hollis notes that the mark of a passive conception of Man is to suggest that human agency is susceptible to this mode of explanation.

In contrast, the active/Autonomous conception must rethink its philosophy of explanation. Hollis says:[8]

> Whereas Plastic Man, being formed by adaptive response to the interplay of nature and nurture, is only spuriously individual, his rival is to be self-caused. Where Plastic Man is an object in nature, his rival is the 'I' of the I and the Me. Where Plastic Man has his causes, Autonomous Man has his reasons.

Hollis's basic claim is that 'Autonomous Man' is the explanation for his own actions and that rationality holds the key to the possibility of explanation. He proposes that[9]

> ... a man's reasons for acting can explain his actions, without being the cause of them. Suitably worked out, this will imply that not all explanation is in the same mode, namely that of associating cause and effect with the aid of natural laws.

We are to develop a language of action, therefore, which asserts the existence of Autonomous Man in such a way that implies that human conduct cannot be fully explained by causal laws and conditions. Hollis's first step is to examine the notion of causality which underlies the naturalistic and deterministic conception of Man. He does this by first pointing out the epistemological constraints imposed on scientific investigation by an empiricist-based positivism.[10] The Humean insistence on the epistemic primacy of direct observation led to the evacuation of metaphysical notions from the concept of causality. Apart from the problem of induction, the concept of causality is rendered empirically applicable once stripped of ideas like production, force, purpose or necessity, and we are to proceed on the basis of correlating observations of events with a view to discerning their contiguity, order of temporal priority, regularity of occurrence and our habits of associating such events. Hollis points to the vast array of concepts which lie behind the application of the Humean principle and, in passing, refers to the complexities and epistemological problems of the relationship between ontology and validation. However, he is content to accept that the positivist criterion of empirical testability of hypotheses is at least intelligible. From this he suggests that the orthodox conception of a causal law is basically of the form, 'in conditions C, A is a sufficient condition for B'.[11]

Hollis then cites the application of this approach in Wallace's model of the hypothetico-deductive scheme of investigation[12] suitable to social phenomena (e.g. suicide), and similarly in Friedman's methodology of Positive Economics. Comparing the two, he draws the following conclusions concerning typicalities of positivist method:[13]

> A natural law is a regularity in nature holding in specifiable conditions; we know we have found one, when we have a well-enough

> confirmed theory; a theory is a set of logically-linked, high order generalizations; the only test of a theory is the success of its predictions; prediction and explanation are two sides of the same and only coin, in that explaining a phenomenon is finding a theory from which it could have been predicted. Also, taking a hint from what is left unsaid, we can add that the same method holds for all sciences and that normative statements have no place in science.

The question now posed is that of the validity of the conception that a causal law is a regularity holding in specifiable conditions. The riddle of induction first springs to mind and needs no elaboration. Secondly, there is the added confusion of noting the fact that there are many well-confirmed generalisations which are not regarded as causal laws.[14] We need to be able to distinguish a law-like generalisation from an accidental one. Again, we may note Mill's dictum: 'It is not the empirical laws which count but the causal laws which explain them.'[15] What, then, are the positivist replies to the problem of distinguishing between the (possibly) accidental correlations valid at the empirical level, and genuine causal laws? This question, however, as Hollis notes, is a little hasty:[16] '... asserting the distinction is a far cry from justifying it and we must ask what a Positivist can think it is a distinction between'. We are once again referred to the Millian principle (which he considered an adequate solution to the problem of induction) of suggesting that higher levels of generality approximate to the ultimate laws.[17] Hollis points to the epistemic inadequacy of this claim in that the validity of the higher generalisations are in as much doubt as the lower. Low-level hypotheses predict phenomena, or imply an observation statement. So, too, do high-level ones. But there are infinitely many possible theories which may achieve success at the empirical level. How do we know we have got the right one, i.e. the true one?[18]

The Popperian approach to this problem in the form of his falsifiability criterion is, inevitably, Hollis's next consideration.[19] The possibility of eliminating false hypotheses rests, says Hollis, on two crucial indeterminancies.[20] Bearing in mind that the logical form of the scheme of empirical testability according to Popper exhibits the structure of an argument *modus tollens* we get:

if T1, then 01; and not —01 so not T1.

However, as T1 is a conjunction of several hypotheses, 01 isolates no hypothesis in particular. Secondly, 'not —01' is itself a hypothesis in the sense that there are no theory-free facts and a theory cannot refute another theory. This last remark appears cursory, but it has been rehearsed at length in innumerable works in the philosophy of science and

I leave it at that in order to shorten the review of Hollis's argument.[21]

Hollis says at this point:[22]

> The temple of Positive science is giving us trouble partly because facts of observation are not as neutral as they need to be and partly because the distinction between matters of fact and the filing system [the theory] stops us finding any epistemic value in higher levels of explanation.

Here he notes W. V. O. Quine's contribution to the debate and quotes his famous 'web of belief' passage from 'Two Dogmas of Empiricism'.[23] Quine's suggestion is, of course, that causal laws are to be regarded as general statements which are so respectably and usefully ensconced in our framework of beliefs about the world to be above serious suspicion in that they may be trusted not to let us down as we go about our business. Hollis notes that the Pragmatist contention that all beliefs are revisable in the light of experience, and that experience is undiscriminated unless ordered by second-order beliefs which comprise a conceptual scheme, engenders a relativism which, at the very least, is not helpful in our quest for an intelligible concept of a natural law. After this review of positivist strategies and empiricist claims, Hollis concludes that[24]

> We need Mill's distinction between the 'empirical laws' and 'causal laws which explain them' but, epistemologically, cannot yet have it. Pragmatism, which lets us say what we want, does not stop us saying what we please. There is now a choice. We either enrich our ontology beyond what positivism allows or strengthen the claim of theoretical connections to do what Pragmatism asks. There needs to be more to a natural law than regularity, if we are to tell the law-like from the accidental, and the choice is whether to put the 'more' in the world or in the theory.

Briefly, Hollis suggests that we opt for locating the necessity required for explanation not in an unwarranted notion of the natural and universal regularities of the external world,[25] but in our theory, and to proceed by arguing, in Kantian vein, 'from what is theoretically true of experience to what must therefore be true in it'.[26] This means introducing *real definitions* into concept formation which assume a *necessity* which holds between *concepts of objects* in the world. We therefore cannot help but find this necessity in our investigations. But is this as futile as it sounds? Hollis says of methodology in this context:[27]

> ... it can only be virtuous to leave scope for enquiry and experiment. The scope would be analogous to the testing of conjectures in mathematics. In the end, no doubt, we shall be able to prove or disprove Fermat's last theorem but, until then, we seek negative instances, offer partial proofs and find ways of showing it more or less likely that the propositions at issue are indeed necessarily true.

> It is in principle no more a threat to empirical science than to mathematics that the aim would be to arrive at necessities.

Hollis suggests that the epistemological question then raised would be whether necessary truths can be shown to be importantly distinct from contingent truths without making them empirically vacuous. That is, whether the class of all synthetic propositions is not exhausted by contingencies (as Hume and the Logical Postitivists would suggest). This, says Hollis, raises complex questions in the philosophy of logic which he has little space to consider, but cites Arthur Pap as the guardian of this section of his argument.[28] Ontologically, says Hollis. 'We can rest content with wholly contingent connections among the referents of concepts, among which there are necessary connections.' Empirical notions of necessity, he reminds us, are forced into much bolder claims.[29]

In summing up this stage of his argument and its relevance to explanation in the social sciences, Hollis makes the following points: first, that the regularities of the moral world – the world of social action – must be treated as more than regularities. These regularities must be seen as the expression of some necessity 'making it a matter of theory to classify phenomena and to tell genuine laws from spurious concomitants'.[30] Secondly, there is common ground that causal explanation is explanation by citing causal laws; that the warrant for the assertion of subjunctive conditionals can only be derived from the validity of the causal law; and that the validation of this causal law entails the elimination of the merely accidental manifestation of regularity. Thirdly, causal connections are transitive. This is a key move in Hollis's argument. There is no reason to halt the chain of causation in explanation:[31]

> If *a* caused *b*, which caused *c*, which caused *d*, then whatever the exact interpretation of the arrow, $A \to B$, $B \to C$, $C \to D$ in the relevant conditions and so $A \to D$. The cause of the cause of *b* is the cause of *b* and the effect of the effect of *b* is its effect. If we do not accept this in everyday speech, the writing of history or courts of law, then either we should or there is something amiss with a passive conception of man. For combining naturalism with determinism, we cannot escape holding that the actions of Plastic Man have their antecedents far in the past and that responsibility, in so far as it exists, is transmitted undiminished from the past, through present action to whatever other agents do in response. As with freedom before, we can find analogues of everyday notions of responsibility and, once again, there are standard arguments to show that they can coexist with or even presuppose determinism. But they are analogues. Where there is no autonomy, the buck never stops.

Hollis holds that causal-cum-theoretical explanation holds for all sciences but will deny that it is the *only* notion required in the social sciences.[32] His aim is to find a frame of reference for Autonomous Man 'in the thin space between the inexplicable and the causally determined.'[33]

ONTOLOGY AND AUTONOMY

This being said, Hollis turns to the ontology of the social world with a view to exploring the nature of the social stage before attending to the condition of the actors. He suggests, employing a theatrical metaphor, that 'the individuals who interact are not prior to the stock of characters society provides; but neither are the characters identical with the actors'.[34] He promises to present us with a notion of the actor's identity which is 'a delicate blend of "private" self with social "self"' and, thence, offer a non-causal mode of explanation in the name of autonomy.[35]

In raising the thesis of a normative structuralism as a sociological ontology, whether of Durkheimian provenance or the more active conceptions of role negotiation (e.g. Goffman), he says, pursuing the dramaturgical metaphor:[36]

> The question pointed up by drama is whether roles create agents or agents roles. For Plastic Man social facts and individual programming (in whatever proportions) must account for everything in the human scene. The positions and roles attached, who is inducted into them and how, styles of performance and the impact of sanctions, general requirements and individual embodiments are all matters determining the agent's identity. By all means include subjective and intersubjective meanings, provided they are derived from somewhere like a central value system by processes like socialization and internalization. The crucial point is that the playing of roles is always *explanandum* and never *explanans.*

Conversely, for Autonomous Man, the notion of a role is the theoretical conception which gives us the possibility of an explanation. Autonomous man makes his roles essential to being who he is: he '... has a clear interest in a notion of role which is which both a source of reasons for action and a vehicle giving him control of his own life'.[37]

To take the agent, therefore, out of the chain of natural causality from social fact to autonomous action we require first an intelligble, and secondly an explanatory conception of role distance. For there is little scope to deny the fact that institutions are prior to the individual in the sense that we are born into a structured economic, ideological and linguistic environment as Durkheim so clearly emphasised. Hollis suggests that we may start with a scheme of explanation (requiring much amendment) as follows:[38]

1. The agent occupied a position with a role R requiring action A.
2. The agent knew that R required A.
3. The agent did A because of (1) and (2).

We shall see that this scheme is ambiguous as to the appropriate conception of reason and motive in autonomous explanation as we explore a concrete example. The example which Hollis employs is borrowed from Quentin Skinner's account (explanation) of Bolingbroke's hostility to Walpole in the 1730s.[39] Briefly, Bolingbroke's attacks on Walpole had two major themes: that of Walpole's retention of a major land force when Britain was no longer engaged in major hostilities; and that of Walpole's licentious use of patronage for his supporters. Skinner wants to know not simply why Bolingbroke attacked Walpole, but why he chose these particular lines of attack. Those who see Bolingbroke as a political adventurer reply that any means to hand will be employed by such a person to gain advantage.Others have suggested that Bolingbroke was a genuine patriot and was truly incensed by Walpole's unconstitutional activities. Skinner notes that the assumption here is 'that a man's professed principles enter into the explanation of his actions, only if he professes them sincerely'. So if Bolingbroke was an adventurer, says Hollis, his professed principles provide no explanation, while, if he was a patriot, they explain at face value.[40] Skinner holds that this overlooks the importance of the ideological framework in which men act and the atmosphere in which they can attempt to justify their actions. Skinner suggests that in the context of the time any form of opposition to the King's ministry would have appeared treasonable. Thus a strategy of appearing patriotic was required to facilitate any attack on the government. Using the constitutional premises of his Whig opponents, Bolingbroke was able to criticise the keeping of mercenaries and the centralisation of power from a patriotic standpoint. This being the only strategy available for criticising Walpole without facing accusations of treasonable conduct, the action is explained completely. Skinner's point is that Bolingbroke's actions would have been the same whether or not his patriotic principles were expressed sincerely. Hence, the explanation stands regardless of Bolingbroke's motives.

In terms of role-analysis, we may reflect upon the above argument as follows. Actors have positions and roles. The normative expectations of role are conditioned by an ideological context. The actor is aware of these expectations. When an actor fulfils the expectations we read this as the reason for the action. Hollis says:[41]

> At first sight the crux is whether the agent has internalized his roles and accepted their duties as his duties. In that case and no other his social positions would be the source of both reasons and motives for the action to be explained. But, on reflection, there is more to it.

In the basic scheme of explanation first presented, the final clause is ambiguous in that we can read 'because' in different ways:

1. The agent occupied a position with a role R requiring action A.

2. The agent knew that R required A.
3. The agent did A *because* of (1) and (2).

Hollis says:[42]

> We can read it as asserting that (1) and (2) caused him to do A in that he was so well socialized that he always acted on a normative syllogism with true premises. This makes (3) into a statement of motive, where motive is so defined as to suit a passive conception of man. But alternatively, we can treat (1) and (2) as reasons for doing A which apply to this particular agent and (3) as asserting that these reasons were his reasons. This reading leaves his motive enigmatic, the subject of a further and different enquiry.

Of course, agents are not confined to one course of action within a particular role. A passive conception of man allows for a multiplicity of possibilities within the scheme of explanation cited. Hollis admits that normative schemes of explanation of a passive man are more accurately rendered in the form of a 'role algebra' as follows:[43]

1. The agent occupied positions with roles R_1, ... R_j, requiring A.
2. The agent knew that R_1, ..., R_j, required A.
3. Conditions (1) and(2) were the agent's reason for doing A.

Given this, the indeterminancy of each role is made determinate in combination.[44] In specifying (1) and (2) as the agent's reasons we are not committed to claims about motives.[45]

> Where an agent does the only action his set of roles permits for the reason that it is the only action, then we have a complete and powerful normative explanation. The interesting question is whether a complete normative explanation is also a complete explanation.

After attending to some objections to the notions of position and role, and ideological context *per se*, Hollis suggests that we accept that agents do often have positions and roles which require a unique course of action, and, recognising these requirements, subsequently perform it.[46] But is this an explanation of the action? Well, it is if we make knowledge of the requirements into the actor's *motive* to action. Hollis says that if the actor is at one with the role, then explanation cannot refer to anything outside the role. (Here we must note that 'at one with' means 'constituted by the role'). The only direction open for further explanation would be the task of identifying the causes of role conformity (e.g. Durkheimian notions, or Marxian notions of system or a weak actionist conception of the social construction of the available stock of role interpretations). Consequently, we require a conception of role-distance for Autonomous Man which is provided by a different conception of 'motive'. We can be reasonably sure that this is what Hollis is driving at when we note that he says:[47]

> Granted that Bolingbroke could and did cite reasons for acting as he

> did, how can we know that these reasons were his reasons, in particular how can we know it without appeal to motives? [Obviously, 'motives' here refers to the as yet elusive alternative to the passive characterization of the term elucidated above.] The cap fits but was the actor wearing it? [That is, normative explanation is consistent, but is it true?] As a general problem about the scope of normative explanation, it depends on what we assert about human nature. We have already noted that *homo sociologicus* is certainly wearing the cap which fits. Quentin Skinner's assumption, however, is more refined. It is to the effect that, in recognizing good reasons for action which apply to him, the actor makes those reasons his own. The idea is to distance the actor from his context without thereby destroying the claims of context to explain action ... Similarly, the very concept of role-distance seems to imply that the actor's real reasons are not those supplied by his roles.

But to distance the actor from his context, and to suggest that his reasons for action are not those supplied by his roles, is to create a ghost in the machine. We now have a public stage populated by characters playing roles in accordance with a widely read script and we, the curious audience, are confined to studying the interconnections of the play. The private life of the actor is, however inaccessible to us. As Hollis notes:[48]

> ... we have a hidden world behind the scenes where the real actor lives his real life. In the privacy of this mental sanctum, he engages in real relations with phantoms of the actors in the public drama. He alone has access.

This dualism bodes ill for simultaneous possibilities of the reinstatement of Autonomous Man and a scheme of scientific explanation. What makes the reasons embodied in the role into the actor's own reasons is that the actor had a motive for doing his duty. But, as Hollis points out, the example of Bolingbroke shows only that reasons for choice of means may sometimes be distinct from motives for pursuing goals. If Bolingbroke was a patriot, then his legitimating reasons for action in context are conterminous with his motive. But we can never know whether he was a patriot or adventurer if there was (in the given context of action) no legitimate way of professing oneself to be an adventurer.[49] In this case we are stuck with a passive conception of man in that our explanation of action can refer only to role and legitimating reasons. Furthermore, the problem cannot be avoided by retorting that the concept of motive simply refers to another step beyond the initial selection of means with an attendant legitimating reason. This, of course, simply affirms that there is no actor – just character and role; or, equally obviously, postpones the problem if we are to maintain the concept of Autonomous role-distance. But Hollis remarks that this option does initially sound attractive:[50]

> By siting the actors on an indefinite means-end continuum, we can treat all their actions as *zweckrational* in their ideological context, without ever bumping up against an end which is not in turn a means. But there are two insuperable snags. One is that *Zweckrationalität* cannot stand on its own, since means are rational only if ends are rational, ... the other is that we cannot afford to make questions about motives unanswerable.

I think that Hollis's intention is to give us an explicable model of Autonomous Man by doing two things: first, he tries to give us an understanding of role-distance where this is to mean distance of autonomous self from role; second, he means to attend to a critique of *Zweckrationalität* in order to clarify the conception of motive and thereby give the self a reason for action in terms of rational autonomy as opposed to natural necessity. 'We need', he says 'to find motives in order to fit the cap to the actor's head, where our notions of role and legitimating reasons have so far only fitted his head to the cap.'[51] We shall look first at his reflections of the nature of a suitable self for science before attending to what kind of reasons this self can genuinely claim as its own.

STRICT IDENTITY OF SELF

Philosophical discussion of the concept of the self is extremely complicated. What is not complicated, however, is the realisation that without a theory of the self, there appears to be a strange lacuna in role-theory. Simply put, we wish to know who plays the roles. Hollis says of Goffman's famous descriptions of role-play:[52]

> Admirers of Erving Goffman, for instance, are well served with nuanced, cooly sardonic tales of how actors in the life-world play their parts with varying styles and skill, at varying degrees of distance and for varying ends. Interactions are far from mechanical and the actor can keep control of them by means of secondary adjustments, distancing rituals and elusive negotiations. If he succeeds, he has an identity not merely defined for him or thrust upon him; and this identity is crucial in understanding and explaining his conduct. Although 'identity' here is in part a set of attributes, it refers also to a subject or substance who manipulates his attributes and his *Umwelt*. Hence Goffman owes us a theory of self as subject, something more robust than a notional we-know-not-what, to sustain the active base for its social transactions.

Hollis notes that 'notoriously, the debt goes unpaid'.[53] His point is that putative explanations which speak of organic continuity (the 'code' which 'makes sense out of almost all the individual's activities and provides a basis for organizing them' or 'a repertoire of behaviour appropriate to a different set of contingencies'[54]) are not able to furnish us with a conception of self for Autonomous Man in that these suggestions are, in the end, simply statements of the view that the role, or totality of roles, constitutes the self. But, says Hollis, Goffman's actors can and often do construct and control. Hollis says, '... "personal identity" (especially in scare quotes) cannot be something imputed, if it is a crucial *explanans*. There must be more to it.'[55]

Must this something be the kind of self which philosophers wish to individuate? Hollis notes that there appears to be a divergence of approach between social scientists and philosophers here. His point is that philosophy has traditionally couched the problem of self in terms of a search for logical and epistemological criteria by which persons can be identified and reidentified.[56] Social science, he suggests, has conceived of the problem as one whereby a theory of personality can be fused with normative structuralism.[57] There is, however a common interest despite the employment of a different language of analysis. Hollis suggests that[58]

> ... philosophers cannot solve their philosophical puzzles without an excursion into social theory and, secondly, that strong actionism falls, unless the actor is so conceived as to satisfy what philosophers call strict or numerical criteria for personal identity.

The discussion of the possible identification of this criteria obliges us at least to acknowledge the massive corpus of literature which has accumulated throughout the history of modern philosophy. Hollis admits that his remarks in *Models of Man*, even on the basis of an attempt to pick out aspects of interdisciplinary interest as a 'gross pointer to problems which still beset the subtlest discussion', will appear 'superficial' and at best 'tentative'.[59] Rather than skimp on that which is admitted to be skimpy, I will omit any perfunctory reference to the history of the debate and present what Hollis considers to be a pointer to a solution.[60]

Briefly, Hollis suggests that William James may have pointed a way through the impasse of the seemingly impossible demands of the philosopher for strict, numerical (quantitative) identity and the sociologist's clearly inadequate, if convenient, qualitative notion of unity of role-set. James rejects the Humean 'bundle' theory on the grounds that the 'enduring substance' in which our perceptions inhere is merely a record of our discomfort in the admission that the 'bare existence' of phenomena is the 'total truth'. Similarly, the Kantian notion of the self as the synthetic unit of apperception is, for James, a transcendental restatement of the problem rather than a solution. We have already noted that the notion of the organic unity of role-set is qualitatively adequate as a definition of self in terms of role, but inadequate as an explanation of the phenomenon of role-play and its implied subjective origin. Further, this notion will not meet the philosopher's demand for strict, numerical identity of personal self for logical reasons, i.e. any set of roles may have more than one incumbent, etc.[61] Simply, the philosopher insists that '...there *cannot* be two persons who satisfy whatever makes me the particular person I am and the sociologist supplies a notion of who I am too lax to count as identity at all'.[62]

James's tack, however, does not appear to be qualitatively distinct from the Humean and Kantian notions he finds inadequate. Furthermore, his proposed conception of personal self appears to be disappointingly similar to the notion of a know-not-what which guarantees a unity of role-set. Hollis quotes him as saying:[63]

> 'Resemblance among the parts of a continuum of feelings ... constitutes the real and verifiable "personal identity" which we feel.' [My various selves need a unity and it consists in] ... 'the real, present onlooking, remembering, "judging thought"' ... 'a remembering and appropriating Thought incessantly renewed ...'. 'Personality implies the incessant presence of two elements, an objective person, known by a passing subjective Thought and recognized as continuing in time' ...

Hollis admits that this seems simply to affirm the adequacy of a qualitative definition of self. It also seems that this conception could, with a little ingenuity be construed as Humean in that it is a notion of the empirical impressions of remembering and associating experiences; Kantian in that a continuity of experiences *implies* a transcendental subject behind the phenomenon of experience; and, broadly speaking, sociological in that these formulations are several among the infinite number of ways of 'describing' whatever is meant by an organising 'core' at the hub of a plethora of 'I' roles and 'Me' roles. In one sense, therefore, we may have stumbled on an essential core of thought which seems to be common to apparently diverse perspectives on the problem. Strict identity is not achieved – that is certain – but is strict identity necessary? Hollis's approach is to present us with the possibility that we may have been asking for too much in this regard. However, to use Hollis's own phrase, we can suspect that he is merely 'loitering with rationalist intent'. He says:[64] 'There is an old Buddhist image of the self as a series of candles each lit from the stub of the last and, for James, it is enough. To ask more is a mistake...'. Hollis then quotes Ayer's refurbishment of James's analysis which would suggest that we really do make a mistake in demanding so much. I quote the following passage in full: first, because it is material to our present discussion; and second, because it shows how a pragmatic turn of thought is at its most seductive when we are faced with a problem that is *really* headache-inducing:[65]

> If one speaks of the construction of objects out of the flux of experience, it is indeed natural to ask who does the constructing; and then it would appear that whatever self is chosen for this role

> must stand outside the construction; it would be contradictory to suppose that it constructed itself. But the metaphor of construction is here misleading. What is in question is the derivation of concepts, not the fabrication of the things to which the concepts apply. To 'construct' either the material or the spiritual self is to do no more than pick out the relations within experiences which make it possible for the concept of a self of this kind to be satisfied, and these relations exist whether or not we direct our attention to them.

Hollis's point, in the light of all this, is that these conceptions of the self are acceptable in so far as they make intelligible the notion of a self in relation to social relations and thereby secure qualitative identity. Strict, numerical identity is not achieved.

I think we can interpret Hollis as saying that strict identity is an ideal which is a legitimate aspiration only if it acknowledges Autonomous Man and the attendant epistemological implications of the explanation of action. Qualitative identity suffices, conversely, only with the resignation to accept the limits of a passive conception of man. The point is that an actionist sociology/psychology which proffers a qualitative conception of personal identity presupposes Plastic Man – even if the attempt to reinstate Autonomous Man is the stated goal of the sociological or psychological enterprise in hand. I am prepared to suggest that Hollis's point is that one cannot have one's cake and eat it. For the philosopher who insists on the strict identity of persons, it becomes obligatory to acknowledge what John Searle has called 'the dreaded doctrine of *causa sui*'[66] as being applicable to agents, i.e. Autonomous Man. For the interactionist sociologist or the non-behaviourist psychologist, the adequacy of qualitative identity of persons becomes conditional upon the acceptance of passive (nomologically determined) or Plastic Man. I think Hollis's remarks below will support this reading.

Normative structuralism need not concern us here as the whole project – from Comtean and Durkheimian origins – is an overt attempt to conceive of the social world in a way which is compatible with the positivistic tenet of the unity of scientific method – a central component of which is the insistence that nomological explanation is the *only* form of scientific explanation. This conception of social science, unless stripped of all pretensions to the possibility of rational intervention in the world, is inconsistent with any notion of Man other than the purely Plastic, essenceless 'thing' transiently appearing as the effect of a determining role-repertoire. The interactionist who repudiates the emphasis (if not the existence) of a determining social structure is free of this basic contradiction but makes the construction of society from shared meanings an untenable thesis by its 'explanation' of action in terms of motives which themselves in turn must be derived from roles. However:[67]

> The characters in Goffman's world are played by actors who treat their roles as public means to private ends. The role yields a stock of reasons for action, which become good reasons in so far as the actor has good reasons for playing the character. So far so good – we are back again in Quentin Skinner's realm of social meaning, with the previous advantages [i.e. for a conception of Autonomous Man]. But we are also in the realm of pure individualism, where individuals enter social relations so well endowed with the essential attributes of human beings that roles are merely accidents. We grant that social relations secure the qualitative identity of characters but, having objected that the self has to be more than a 'repertoire' or a 'code', we still need strict identity for the actors.

Hollis's point is that the interactionist cannot conjure up some model of man in terms of a human nature which focuses upon universal needs or interests in the way that eighteenth-century liberal social theory was wont to do to square the circle of hope for mankind with naturalism and nomological determinism:[68]

> Goffman's actor is not in the altruistic business of investing effort and ingenuity for the benefit of later 'selves' just like him. He is working for himself, to preserve and foster what is strictly himself from one time and one role to another.

At this point I think it best to pull the argument together before it disappears in the complexity of its premises. At least we can demonstrate the soundness of Hollis's argument even if we remain incapable, through lack of space and time, to do justice to the profundity of the propositions upon which it rests. It seems that we can present the structure of Hollis's argument as follows, where the quasi-formal presentation at least identifies the pivotal premises:

1. If not-role-distance *then* not-autonomy.
2. If not-autonomy *then* structural determinism.
3. If not-structural determinism *then* role-distance.
4. If role-distance *then* autonomy.
5. If autonomy *then* personal identity.
6. If personal identity *then*(strict identity *or* qualitative identity).
7. If qualitative identity *then* (not-strict identity *and* not-role-distance *and* universal motivating model of Man).
8. If model of Man *then* (Autonomous Man *or* Plastic Man).
9. If Plastic Man *then* (not-Autonomous man *and* nomological explanation).
10. If nomological explanation *then* (not-role-distance *and* not-strict identity).
11. (If not-role-distance *then* not-autonomy) *then* structural determinism.
12. If not-sturctural determinism *then* Autonomous Man.

Therefore
13. If Autonomous Man *then* strict identity.
Which leads us to ask:
14. If strict identity *then* ... ?

THE DISCRIMINATING SELF

Hollis's point, initially, was concerned with the hidden premises of modern social theory. A tacit model of man was alleged to lurk beneath the anti-metaphysical protestations of the positivistic epistemologies of social action and, as we have seen, plugs the gaping hole in anti-positivistic, but avowedly ethically neutral, actionist hermeneutics. In the latter case, if the role furnishes the reasons for action it denies the agent '... any intrinsical quality which allows the requirements [of the role] to be good reasons. He is a free agent neither within his roles nor without.'[69] Thus the notion of qualitative identity implies a mode of explanation which must cite causal antecedents of action as being necessarily external to the actor – the actor here being, as Ayer suggests, an unexplainable implication of a theory which we are content to accept pragmatically. Ontology, it is suggested, is a metaphysical embarrassment. To press the point, Hollis says:[70]

> Pure individualism, taking men as the pre-social atoms of classical utilitarian and liberal theory, does offer to make action rational [i.e. cause of itself] by referring it to goals which are in turn rational because of what the agent is. Its classic snag, however, is that it cannot say what the actor is. It is no answer to Ayer to leave a mere Thing from Inner Space standing outside the construction. Yet an active conception of man must have a final category of creative self-expression, *not just in ethics but also in the epistemology of explanation* [My emphasis.] An active construction of the social world by rational initiative needs a purpose derived from a continuing, unmysterious self. Where relations within experience are the world of rational initiative needs a purpose derived from a continuing, unmysterious self. Where relations within experience are the work of rational initiative, it is not enough to hold that they 'exist whether or not we direct our attention to them'. Where Plastic Man is content with degrees of identity and individuality, Autonomous man still needs a strict principle of personal unity.

We move to the crux of the argument. 'What is it, then, that can continue numerically the same from one role and social scene to another?'[71]

Hollis suggests that the clue to the solution appeared in the discovery that historical explanation is possible only if the reasons for action which the agent has as the occupant of a problem-solving role are also his own reasons. For an active conception of man we noted that it was not sufficient simply to supply a conveniently consistent cap for the actor to wear – we need to know which cap the actor actually wore. If it is impossible to enter the actor's world – either (a) because there is not an actor; or (b) because the actor is conceived of as scientifically inexplicable by our conception of the scope of scientific explanation – we have, as Hollis says, only one move open to us:[72] 'It must sometimes be true that what the character has good reason to do the actor *eo ipso* also has good reason to do. Necessarily the autonomous actor must be himself in some of his characters.' We must remember that up to this point all we have done is (a) demonstrate the indispensability of a conception of self with strict identity if we are to hope to make Autonomous Man a subject for science, and (b) show that 'good reasons' are a candidate for the *explanans* of action. That is, good reasons are to be regarded as cause of themselves and thereby allow us a form of explanation which frees the actor from the chain of nomological causation. Hollis sums up this stage of the argument:[73]

> Prompted by the thought that bodies are just bodies unless relations between them are endowed with shared meanings we pass to a 'Who's What?' game. Here the shared meanings are externalized and given system in positions and roles. But occupancy of the same positions at different times is neither necessary nor sufficient for being the same person. Yet the 'Who's Who?' game, played with extra-social individual egos, yields only the qualitative criteria of memory. We need a more substantial 'I', one with both personal and social identity. Our final conjecture is that the strict identity is that of bodies, which in turn secures that of persons who perform individuating actions; their identity as persons is secured by their having rationally become occupants of social positions; where there are no suitable positions, their identity ceases to be strict and they become passive.

Hollis wants to say that I am who I am only if I can choose roles which are compatible with the rational acting out of what I have *rationally* chosen to become. A role may furnish reasons for action in terms of normative criteria intrinsic to the duties and interests of that particular role and which the actor as role-character may employ as a vehicle (means) towards ends which are legitimate for that role. But the interests of the character are supplied by the role. The actor must have real interests – his own ends – before the adoption of the role-vehicle as means. It is in the interests of a soldier to perform his duties because that is what the interests of a soldier are. The simple question must be: 'Why choose to be a soldier?' If a good reason can be supplied, then the actions of the soldier as character are not explained by the requirements of the soldier's role; they are explained by the actor's *good reasons for choosing the role.*[74] Thus the qualitative identity of Tommy Atkins is secured by his role-set as a soldier, but his essential identity becomes a function of his ability to justify his choice of roles.

It follows, therefore, that, even at this stage and in the absence of an explication of the criterion of a good reason, we have a formal description of what alienation can be. It is the situation in which an actor cannot find suitable roles in which to actualise his rational motivations. That it is impossible to sit out the play until a suitable role comes round means that we have the possibility of a subject-matter for social science which is at once Plastic – carried along by the vehicle of a behaviour-determining role – yet always potentially Autonomous in that compatability between role and rational motivation is always, at least in principle, possible. Hollis says:[75]

> Autonomy requires a choice of roles in which a man can rationally do his duty. If few men take this course, it is in part because few societies offer it. To create a Good Society where men can be themselves remains a task not for tinkers but for tailors.

CAUSA SUI: GOOD REASONS

At this point we have, as Hollis says, the stage and the actor, but no substantial conception of the self-motivating force which is to provide the alternative to nomological explanation. We need to put ontological flesh on the bones of our strictly identifiable actor who, as yet, subsists merely as a logical entailment of a conceptual scheme. To put it simply, the self we seek is to be identified by a distinguishing property, that of the capacity to generate good reasons for action and thereby become cause of itself – that is, a thing to which the concept of 'adequate' or rational causation can be accurately applied. This can explain the potential for freedom from nomological causality which is to be taken as a necessary, but not sufficient, condition of autonomy, and also the explanatory framework in which Autonomous Man becomes a subject for science as a potentially self-recognising actor. Rationality, therefore, becomes synonymous with the self-recognition of the adequate causation of one's own and others' actions. That this immediately raises the problem of Other Minds is not too disconcerting in that if a theory of rationality in this sense can be provided, so can a solution to the problem of Other Minds.

The inadequacy of Weber's reflections on the substitution of reasons, intentions and motives for nomological explanations is clear in the light of our recent discussions. Briefly, the whole baggage of such conceptions cannot lift us out of the chain of nomological causation unless we can isolate the self-causing reasons and motives from ones which are possibly functions of a natural determinism operating external to the actor, even if they permeate the self-conception of a character in his most intimate roles. Hollis says:[76]

> An actor can have a purpose and follow rules intentionally without acting autonomously. The rules are his stock; his intention marks his choice from the stock; rules and intentions between them settle the criteria of sameness and difference for types and tokens of action. But if there is no more to discern than a fabric of rules intentionally followed, the threat to the self remains, whether or not the resulting form of explanation is causal. We must therefore deny that explanation has yet been reached.

The candidate for a solution to this problem is to emerge from a critique of the concept of *Zweckrationalität*. A strong hint as to the inadequacy of this notion as presented by Weber was dropped in Chapter 3 *supra*. Our discussion in this section concerned Weber's conception of meaningful action, a notion which, when expanded into a philosophical anthropology, then became the basis of an ethical formalism. This scheme, as we noted, left the initial choice of values (ultimate ends to be pursued) floating in a limbo between the worlds of *Natur* and *Geist*. I suggested at this point in our discussion that Weber's conception of the origin of the personality, although described in a language reminiscent of the rationalist ethical tradition, did nothing more than leave the ultimate determinant of action firmly rooted in the sphere of natural causation. Our discussions in this chapter seems to provide us with a synthesis in that we can now clearly see the focus of the problem which might liberate a *verstehende* approach from its inconsistencies. Of the concept of *Zweckrationalität*, Hollis invites us to consider the following:[77]

> The most rational means to a goal are those which give the actor the highest chance of success at the lowest opportunity cost. Already there are signs of deep water but let us proceed in innocence, assuming the actor to have clear, consistently ordered goals, whose rationality is – for the moment – not in question. Let us assume also that, in calculating the best means to one goal, he avoids or discounts at suitable prices disturbance of all the others. In other words let us assume that there is an overall best means. The mere fact that the actor hits on it is not sufficient and perhaps not necessary for his action to be *zweckrational*. What are the missing conditions?

To which Hollis replies,[78] '... The only addition is that the actor must know that he has found the best means'.

THE RATIONALITY OF ENDS

The task which Hollis has before him is quite complex, but, for our requirements, the implications of it are perfectly simple. Hollis has shown that social science must, at some stage, treat the agent as *causa sui*. In other words, at some point, the *ends* of action must appear to be the complete explanation of the action. Hollis suggests that this is simply the doctrine that a good reason is its own explanation. A rational agent acts from good reasons, in the absence of good reasons, his or her behaviour must be said to be determined in some way. Thus the escape from the nomological chain is to be effected by way of a theory or rationality.

This is not just a simple matter of taking an agent's subjective view of what constitutes a good reason for action. As we noted with Weber's ethic of choice, this reduces to a formalism devoid of any explanatory value – other than to sink us firmly back into the nomological scheme. Further an unsophisticated interpretive or 'means–end' scheme of explanation is not, of itself, much help to us; neither is such explanation confined to the social sciences. Hollis furnishes us with several examples of such a scheme of explanation in biology, behavioural (rat) psychology and even mechanical engineering.[79] Thus plant behaviour may be explained in terms of a problem-solving strategy for maximising photosynthesis; animals hunt or attack to satisfy some need (goal) of appetite or survival'; or thermostats switch on and off to attain some goal-state of a mechanical system. This does not involve the explicit attribution of consciousness, or rationality or values to these phenomena. However, a rational end is postulated as inhering in a particular biological, chemical or electro-mechanical system *from the point of view of the observer*, thus facilitating an analogue of teleological explanation. Such explanation is, in fact, causal explanation seen as 'pull' instead of 'push', the goal or end state merely functioning as the final, rather than the efficient, cause.[80]

In the case of social action, the means-ends continuum upon which we site the actor does not, therefore, necessarily distinguish him or her from these natural systems. That the goal states of natural systems are posited as *explanans* and suffice as *explanans* is possible only because (or if) these explanations are ultimately reducible to causal laws. This, of course, cannot suffice for the anti-positivist sociologist. The upshot of this is that the agent who is to have strict identity, to be cause of its own action, must be regarded as a potentially *substantively rational* actor. We are brought back to square one. Social science requires a theory of substantive rationality, a science of ends, if it is to proceed with any logically defensible formation of its central and most basic concepts.

6

The Practically Reasonable Point of View

We are now in a position to state that social phenomena can neither be described nor explained in the absence of a theory of substantive rationality. In other words, unless we are able to make non-arbitrary judgments about the rationality of *ends in themselves* we will remain unable to claim a non-arbitrary status for the claims of interpretive sociology. Hollis is wary of entering into 'the mists of ethics' but pursues a project of conceptualising human skills.[1] Finnis, however, in presenting a criterion of reasonableness or 'the practically reasonable point of view', has suggested a solution. I must say at the outset that I do not consider this attempt to be successful. But this is not because I consider what Finnis has to say about the moral foundations of practical reason to be false, but rather because he does not show that his claims are *necessarily* true. However, we have benefited from Finnis's insights into the general problem, and it would be odd if we did not follow up his thinking towards a resolution of the matter. Moreover, Finnis's work provides the ideal occasion to examine some serious logical difficulties with the project of grounding a methodologically suitable conception of substantive rationality.

In Chapter 1 I suggested that the principles of moral reason may be adduced by reflection on our constitution as practical beings. The criterion of success for a phenomenologically reflexive method must be logical necessity. We cannot accept less and we cannot possibly hope for more. For only if a conceptually necessary result is achieved can such a reflexive critique provide rationally binding foundations. I want to look at Finnis's attempt to show that just as theoretical reason rests upon seemingly undemonstrable yet undeniable assumptions, so do the principles of practical reason, and that these principles entail moral commitments. For Finnis, these basic principles are 'presupposed' by all who engage in practical reason, but he holds that they are beyond any method of proof or demonstration – they are 'self-evident'. What I want to do in this chapter is examine these claims carefully in order to clear the road ahead for my analyses of Habermas and Gewirth. In particular, I want to show that the epistemological foundations of theoretical and practical reason are to be found by reflexively identifying the assumptions which make theory and practice possible, and that such principles are rationally defensible in that they can be shown to achieve *apodictic* status as transcendental or *dialectically necessary* presuppositions. In addition, we can look at the problem of moving from the *prudential* dimension of practical reason to the *moral* dimension. What we can consider here is the apparent impasse of universalising the *prudential* logic of the isolated subject's own well-being to an acknowledgement of other-regarding commitments.[2] Because Finnis asks all the right questions we can use his work as a platform for further progress by following, *formally*, his approach. I think that this chapter can at least prepare us to receive the arguments of Habermas and Gewirth as attempts to solve the same problem in broadly the same way. That is, they are all united in the attempt to ground the principles of moral rationality through an analysis of the presuppositions of purposivity.

BASIC VALUES

Finnis's aims are, as we have seen, on the one hand, general, in that he wishes to make a methodological point concerning the description of social phenomena, and, on the other, specific, in that he wishes to establish a non-arbitrary conception of the phenomenon of law. His general aim is to show that a non-arbitrary conception of any social phenomenon must be based upon the practically reasonable point of view, and that the practically reasonable point of view is, fundamentally, a moral point of view. Thus any social phenomenon will, at its ideal-typical core, be seen as instantiating basic values, or some permutation of basic values, which are constitutive of practical reason. It follows that legal phenomena, as a subset of social phenomena, will likewise instantiate basic values. Law will be shown to be, fundamentally, a moral enterprise and Legal Positivism[3] refuted. This approach is perfectly coherent and begs no question about the concept of law if it can be shown that the practically reasonable point of view has moral implications. Thus Finnis must provide a conceptual analysis which shows that the focal case of practical reason is logically dependent on moral principles. If not, it is no bar to reasonableness to engage in forms of practical reason which are not consistent with moral principles.

Finnis's suggestion is that the practically reasonable point of view can be shown to be a moral point of view, and that the moral point of view can be shown to be one which is constituted by the incorporation of basic principles which must be espoused by all who engage in practical pursuits. After examining claims which deny, in principle, the possibility of such a theory, and identifying them as ill-conceived, he turns to the Humean objection of the impossibility of deriving 'ought' from 'is'. Finnis suggests that the Humean 'is/ought' distinction and its employment in non-cognitivist or relativist objections to Natural Law theory or Moral Philosophy in general is invalid in that 'basic values' and 'basic practical principles' can be rationally adduced without inferential operations which proceed from factual premises. In opening part two of his work, he says:[4]

> The purpose of this chapter, in particular, is to illustrate (i) what I mean by 'basic value' and 'basic practical principle', (ii) how such values and principles enter into any consideration of good reasons for action and any full description of human conduct, and (iii) the sense in which such basic values are obvious ('self-evident') and even unquestionable. For this purpose, I discuss only one basic value, leaving to the next chapter the identification of the other forms of human good that, so far as I can see, are likewise irreducibly basic.

Thus the validity of these suggestions as to the nature of the basic values stand or fall with the arguments which Finnis is to put forward to demonstrate their 'self-evidence' or 'unquestionable' acceptability. Consequently, these values form a class, in that their validity rests upon a particular principle of cognition. Thus this principle demands attention.

Finnis begins with the assertion that knowledge is a basic value. By this he means theoretical or 'speculative' knowledge conceived as 'knowledge for its own sake', as opposed to knowledge which is required specifically to facilitate the pursuit of some end. Finnis suggests that we may as well speak of truth for its own sake, that is, inquiry motivated solely 'out of curiosity, the pure desire to know, to find out the truth about it simply out of an interest in or concern for truth and a desire to avoid ignorance or error.'[5] Knowledge is conceived as a good in the sense that it is simply 'good to know' something, i.e. that one desires to know something, on the one hand, but can also be conceived as 'a general form of good that can be participated in or realized in indefinitely many ways or indefinitely many occasions'.[6] This latter form of good is what Finnis intends by 'value' and, if knowledge is a value in this sense this is what we are to understand by a 'basic value'. A basic human good furnishes us with a basic practical principle in that it stands as the object of a particular desire to act which aims at participating in an intelligible and general form of good. That 'knowledge is good' is a practical principle which is hardly ever formulated as an actual premise for an action does not mean that it is not applicable (or instantiated) in all practical reasoning. Finnis says:[7]

> In this respect practical reasoning is like 'theoretical' reasoning which has its own basic, and usually tacit presuppositions and principles. We often say 'Too late!'; but how often do we formulate the presupposition on which our conclusion rests, the guiding presupposition that time cannot be reversed?

We must note here that Finnis's example of the basic presuppositions of our judgments quite clearly involves an inference.[8] This threatens to vitiate his claim that basic human goods can be established without violating Hume's Law, especially if the presuppositions of practical reasoning are seen to stand in the same relation to substantive practical reasoning as the inferential operation cited above. However, Finnis is right to say that such presuppositions, although not apparent to the actor, can be identified through reflection upon our own action and the actions of others. He suggests that[9] 'In trying to make sense of someone's commitments, projects and actions over a period, we may say that he acted "on the basis that" knowledge is a good worthy of a life-shaping devotion.' Commitment to knowledge is understood as a commitment to truth as a purpose-guiding value. This commitment is not innate:[10]

> On the contrary, the value of truth becomes obvious only to one who has experienced the urge to question, who has grasped the connection between question and answer, who understands that knowledge is constituted by correct answers to particular questions, ... A new-born child, for example, has presumably not had any such set of felt inclinations, memories, understandings, and (in short) experiences.

After further stating that the validity of the value of knowledge and truth cannot be inferred from the fact that it is universally desired, is commonly held by all human beings, or that the curious disposition of human beings is somehow ineradicably programmed, Finnis suggests that to claim[11]

> ... that knowledge *must* be a real value, because intelligent men, or great men, or mature men have regarded it as a value and as an aspect of their own flourishing, is not to make what could be called an inference. For one's assessment of a person as flourishing, mature, great, or, in the relevant respect, intelligent is made possible only by one's own underived understanding that what that person is and does is really good (in the relevant respects). The 'premiss' of the apparent inference thus rests on its 'conclusion'.

The last remark is certainly true. But this does not move us to regard Finnis's appeals to the self-evidence of this argument as any more justified than his mere assertion of its self-evidence. What we have above is simply a statement of the fact that people identify the great and the good in others according to their own values. This is particularly uninspiring in that their understanding of what is good is neither innate nor derived from any principles of reasoning. It is simply 'self-evident'. We are not surprised, then, to find Finnis ask immediately after this: 'But is there not something fishy about appeal to self-evidence?'[12]

Finnis attempts to support the plea for self-evidence by suggesting that the modern empirical disciplines also have recourse to principles which are undemonstrable yet unquestionable in the sense which he wishes us to understand it. He suggests that these principles are of a methodological nature and thus can be equated with the basic requirements of practical reasonableness. In examining the basic principles of the empirical sciences he says:[13]

> ... reflection on what it means to say that the principles or norms of sound empirical judgment are self-evident will help to eliminate some misunderstandings of what it means to say that the substantive principles of practical reasonableness are self-evident.

Finnis then proceeds to give eight examples of self-evident principles commonly employed by the empirical sciences, all of which are[14]

> ... not demonstrable, for they are presupposed or deployed in anything that we would count as a demonstration. They do not describe the world. But although they cannot be verified by opening one's eyes and taking a look, they are obvious – obviously valid – to anyone who has experience of inquiry into matters of fact or of theoretical (including historical and philosophical) judgment; they do not stand in need of demonstration. They are objective; their validity is not a matter of convention, nor is it relative to anybody's individual purposes. They can be meaningfully denied, for they are not principles of logic [,] conformity to which is essential if one is to *mean* anything. But to defy them is to disqualify oneself from the pursuit of knowledge, and to deny them is as straightforwardly unreasonable as anything can be.

In examining these following examples of allegedly self-evident principles of theoretical reasoning, I am not *primarily* setting out to present arguments which refute them, or to show why I disagree with the claims to actual validity of all the examples he cites. Rather, I am concerned to discover what Finnis means by 'self-evident', 'undemonstrable' and 'in need of no demonstration'. For, if these examples *cannot* be demonstrated – in some way which involves justified inference – I see nothing unreasonable in a person refusing to accept them. What we must succeed in doing is explicating the validity of such claims in a way which *does* demonstrate that they are rationally undeniable. In this way such claims become genuinely apodictic. Without at least showing, in principle, what such a form of justification is, and how, rationally, it is defensible, we cannot hope to succeed in transferring this type of analysis to practical issues. I will list the examples which Finnis cites and, if indeed this is possible, give good reasons as to why they should or should not be employed as sound principles of empirical judgment – reasons which do not appeal to a naked assertion of their self-evidence to any 'reasonable' person. My aim in this section is to attempt to expose and refine the a priori techniques involved in this stage of Finnis's methodological programme and make a case for a transcendental or dialectically necessary analysis.

1. *[T]he forms of deductive inference are to be used and adhered to in all one's thinking, even though no non-circular proof of their validity is possible.*[15]

This is true. However, that this is not a self-evidently valid prescription in the sense that it is universally regarded as being universally true can be noted from the fact that its straightforward denial is almost a commonplace in recent – and especially Post-Modern – philosophical literature. Regardless of their merit, there are a plethora of Relativist and Pragmatist theses propounded in opposition to this view which suggest that the circularity of logic which effects its own closure is merely a looping mode of thought specific to certain cultures.[16] Anthropological 'evidence' has suggested that the principle of non-contradiction is not employed by some cultures nor is the Law of Identity.[17] Similarly, Pragmatist writers have characterised logical systems as relative to interest orientations and denied the existence of any necessary principles.[18] The scholars who have followed up this suggestion are philosophers who are almost exclusively concerned with knowledge for its own sake in that they question the very grounds of epistemology itself. Neither are these scholars inexperienced in the business of scientific procedures of a highly sophisticated nature.[19] This is not to suggest that their inquiries, however sophisticated, do not imply the validity of the logic which they seek to deny and that, as Finnis suggests, they are unaware of their own tacit presuppositions. However, if this is the case, how are they to be brought to a reflective awareness of this situation on the basis of Finnis's contentions that these principles are not innate, must be arrived at through experience, yet are underived and undemonstrable? The fact is that the validity of deductive logic and the refutation of a cultural relativism or pragmatism which grants merely localised validity to such reasoning can be demonstrated *only* by argumentation which employs inferential processes.

First, and this is extremely important and largely ignored, we may note that circularity of proof has two modes which we may refer to as *vicious* circularity and *virtuous* circularity. Intelligent people do not take any notice of viciously circular or question-begging arguments. Why not? Is it because these arguments are not sound? Certainly not; viciously circular arguments do not necessarily exemplify forms of invalid inference. The reason we reject them is because it is always the premise of the argument which is in contention, and viciously circular arguments simply and arbitrarily assume the truth of their premises. The circularity is not the problem – this just means that the conclusion is inescapable given the premise, and, presumably, we object to accepting the conclusion because we object to accepting the premise. Pointing out the question-begging nature of the argument or the *petitio principii* does not show that there has been invalid inference or that the premise or premises are false, it merely shows that the simple assertion of the truth of the proposition in contention has been dressed up in the form of a supporting argument. The objection to question-begging argument is that there is always an absence of *material justification* for a premise, not that there has been invalid inference from that premise.

So, if the initial objection to the validity of logic is that proof of its legitimacy can be achieved only by 'circular' or question-begging argument, this objection, as Beyleveld and Brownsword point out,[20] is validly employed only against arguments which employ premises which are not necessarily true. But where a premise is phenomenologically, or dialectically necessary from the standpoint of the subject, as are the principles of deductive logic, the necessity of the inferences which flow from these premises cannot be dismissed as invalid due to circularity. Thus if I attempt to deny the principle of non-contradiction (or *modus ponens* or *tollens*)[21] I affirm it by suggesting that (if it is false) it (then) cannot be true, and thus, cannot be both true and false simultaneously. There is no way out. There is, of course, circularity, but this is rather different from the type of circularity which occurs characteristically in definitions dressed up as arguments: for example, in something as ridiculous as: 'gentlemen prefer blondes – because if they don't then they are not gentlemen', or (from Fowler) in simple assertions or denials of the point in contention dressed up as arguments: 'Fox hunting is not cruel because the fox enjoys it.' The principle is important, for upon it rests the intelligibility of any form of critique. I will say no more here, for we meet this objection at a crucial stage of the discussion later on, and there is little point in duplicating our efforts. But I explain in Chapter 9 why this view of logic itself as circular or 'question-begging' is wholly irrational and can serve no other purpose than to manufacture confusion.[22] It is important to deal with it fully to show that this kind of problem requires a *meta-logical* solution, and that such solutions are possible. The point to be made here is that logic can be argued for, not simply presented as 'self-evident' – for it clearly is not.

The next stage of the argument which secures the universal validity of logic proceeds from this demonstration of the misplaced objection to circularity. That is, given the validity of this argument, it may still be objected that this gives no guarantee that all cultures operate within these obligatory structures. Hollis, in his remarkable paper, 'The Limits of Irrationality', and in his book, *Models of Man*,[23] shows that this is a rationally impossible position to adopt. This is so notwithstanding the fact that many people have adopted it and persist in propounding it. Its demonstration would require that we could identify belief systems which operated outside of 'our' logical scheme. In order to find out what people believe we must translate what they say. If we did not assume a fundamental logical correspondence between our own language, perceptions and those of our target culture, translation would be impossible because a successful translation depends upon consistency. In other words, if we were to identify, say, an instance of the violation of the principle of non-contradiction, how would we be able to decide whether or not our translation was accurate or simply a mistake on our part? If only logic can guide us here then we have no way of deciding the issue. In short, if we have assumed enough about them to claim to be able to translate their language, we have assumed that they employ the principles of deductive logic – at least the principle of non-contradiction. This principle is the *sine qua non* of deduction and we can be sure that if another mind/culture operates with it then they must also employ all other logical principles of any interest to this debate.[24]

In *Models of Man*, Hollis spells out the implications of these preconditions of intersubjectivity for social science. He says:[25]

> To understand utterances in an unknown tongue, the Enquirer must relate them to one another and to the world. Since relating *x* to *y* does not let him translate *x* unless he can already translate *y*, he must in any case relate some to the world. To gain a bridgehead, by which I mean definitive interpretations of enough terms to restrict possible renderings of others, he needs a set of utterances whose empirical conditions of use he can specify. Hence, he must assume that the Other Mind perceives very much what he perceives and says about it very much what he would say.

It is upon this bridgehead that the further possibility of translation is made possible. In effect, the assumption that there is one world describable in two languages is the starting point of the project. In addition, the translator must assume that the Other Mind speaks truly in these first simple experiments and that his utterances express some sort of coherent belief. The bridgehead is a patchy guess at a few simple ostensive definitions, the signs for 'yes' and 'no' etc., and it is from here that one tries to explore the complexity and subtlety of the Other Mind's language. There is room for flexibility and revision of the bridgehead, therefore, to take account of sarcasm, or idiosyncrasies in naming etc., but there are limits to this flexibility. The basic principles of the bridgehead, the foundational assumptions, cannot be revised. This is because they are assumptions about the rationality of the Other Mind.

The translator must assume that the declarative utterances of the Other Mind express beliefs and that there is some set of relations which exist between these beliefs. But, it is alleged, these relations may be radically different from ours: where we make simple inferences of the form, 'Necessarily, if P then Q, and not–Q, then not–P', the Other Mind may have a rule of inference that, 'Necessarily, if P then Q, and not–Q, then P'. In other words, the Other Mind organises his or her beliefs by different laws of thought. Hollis drily observes that:[26]

> Luckily for social theory, the supposition cannot be intelligibly stated. It requires that the Enquirer, faced with the expression
>
> '$\Box(((P \rightarrow Q) \,\&\, {\sim}Q) \rightarrow \vdash P)$'
>
> already have firm grounds for reading '$\Box$' as 'Necessarily', '$\rightarrow$' as 'if ... then', '&' as 'and', '~' as 'not', P and Q as variables with constant sense, the brackets as indicators of scope and the whole as a valid formula. He is hesitating only over how to read '$\vdash$', which he has some grounds for taking as 'therefore'. At first sight he can, thus showing that whereas we use L_1, where this is an invalid formula, the Other Mind uses L_2, where it is valid. But, on reflection, to do so would destroy at least one of his previous identifications. Consider for example, his identification of '~' in L_2, with '~' in L_1, as an expression of the English word 'Not'. A condition for '~' expressing 'not' is that it is impossible to change the truth while preserving the sense of an expression by substituting 'not' for '~'. Whatever else '~' means in L_2 it is evidently not what the Enquirer means by 'not'; or, if it is, then at least one other term has been misidentified. The translation of each element singly is a hypothesis to be discarded when the incoherence results. But the test is incoherence and so what is true of each singly is not true of all at once. The global hypothesis at stake is not that the Other Mind has an alternative logic but that he has a logic at all. It is a hypothesis which any success in translation confirms all too completely, since that is precisely the very mark of success.

The other mind may have curious ways of relating beliefs to one another but we must assume that he has some way of relating his beliefs. The minimum amount of assumptions we must make are summed up by Hollis:[27]

> I have tried to show that the Enquirer must impute before he can discover, since in interpreting it is not enough just to pay attention. He must also judge. He says to himself, 'I assume the Other Mind to be a rational man. I take it that his beliefs are, on the whole, rationally connected and that, usually his utterances express his beliefs. I take it that he uses words as tokens governed by the rules for their type and that literal sense informs the stock from which the richest patterns are wrought. I take it that he seeks to make himself understood, recognizing that verbal arabesques are mere sound, if they destroy the sense of the stock. So, when I hit upon a translation which would show him not to be a rational man *uberhaupt*, I reject the translation.

Finally he says:[28]

> Language is not a mere vehicle or device, a set of external rules for

> generating well-formed strings of words. It is a way of uttering thought with the intention of being understood. To grasp the rules I must grasp the thoughts, to grasp the thoughts I must grasp the rules. I can break the circle only by imputing rationality.

Thus we can see that the thesis which posits the existence of fundamentally alternative cognitive systems is intelligible only as a *noumenal* possibility.[29] But this refutation of the thesis of cultural relativism is not applicable solely at the level of culture. This would presuppose that members of the same culture do not face the difficulty of overcoming the problem of translation in the fundamental sense of understanding what they took to be a familiar language. I must impute the basics of rationality to my next-door neighbour if I am to communicate via the medium of language and not directly via unmediated thought transference.

For present purposes the important point is this: there are reasons which can demonstrate the apodictic validity of the claims for the universal applicability of deductive reason put forward by Finnis. To be sure, these reasons are the product of transcendal arguments and not self-evidence, unless, that is, this latter phrase is a wholly inappropriate choice of putative synonym for 'dialectical-necessity'.[30]

2. *[An] adequate reason why anything is so rather than otherwise is to be expected, unless one has a reason not to expect such a reason ...*[31]

This is a tautology and consequently cannot be a regulating principle of anything. In passing we might mention that there is nothing self-evident about tautology. Moreover, the validity of a tautology as a substitution instance of the Law of Identity is a matter which has engendered much critical debate. The assumption that such a law is self-evident or 'primitive' is an error which characterises the logical empiricist theory of the alleged triviality of the a priori.[32] However, if the above is to be interpreted as the claim that every event has an explanation, or at least that it must be assumed that every event has an explanation, then we can say something about it. The first thing we can say is that it is not straightforward. For instance, do human volitions have explanations and, if so, are motives or purposes capable of being explanations or are there only material causes? We noted that Weber encountered more than a few contemporaries who were prepared to speak of the 'unpredictability' and 'inexplicability' of the human will. In social science we can square the epistemological requirements of both explicability and the need to admit autonomy. With Hollis we saw that 'adequate' or rational causation can be construed as the conception which reconciles determinism with free will in that rational, as opposed to irrational, actions are free from the material chain of causation and that rationality provides the sufficient explanation of its own efficacy. Again, arguments which support this latter claim are features of a transcendental epistemology. As with all transcendental arguments, the process of inference moves from the hypothetical question of the possibility of knowledge to the conditions of that knowledge. Simply presenting the claim will not do – even if the claim does turn out to be true in a dialectically-necessary sense, i.e. an unavoidable, rationally undeniable assumption.

3. *Self-defeating theses are to be abandoned ...*[33]

Bearing in mind that Finnis holds the theoretical principles here presented to be unchallengeable by any reasonable person, we must note that this claim has been rejected outright by the most eminent of mainstream analytical philosophers and logicians. This is, of course, logically irrelevant to the status of the claim; but I wish to make a more subtle point. Bertrand Russell did not accept the universal validity of this principle for what appeared to be perfectly logical reasons. In fact, he saw the above principle as the ruination of logic through the creation of intractable paradoxes. Self-reflexivity as a refutation, he alleged, was responsible for the creation of paradoxes which threatened to undermine the whole edifice of mathematics and logic.[34] His theory of types outlawed this rule on the grounds that the grammatical structure of the proposition, as opposed to the logical structure of the proposition, was too ambiguous to allow us to proceed with reasoning which was not limited by stringent extra-linguistic rules which were counter-intuitive to ordinary language users.

One of the arguments against Russell's objection to this maxim is that the set theory which he attempted to logicise, and preserve by abandoning the universality of self-reflexive critique, cannot be so reduced.[35] If a simple statement of this claim is regarded by some as sufficient, undemonstrable, underived from other claims and principles and non-inferential, it is easy to see why Russell was unimpressed. If Russell was wrong, we must know *why* he was wrong. I can only suggest that it is because there are arguments to show that the arbitrary outlawing of reflexive critique is a device which demonstrates the failure of Russell's initial analysis. And if there are arguments, then there are inferences – and these inferences must be defensible.

4. *[P]henomena are to be regarded as real unless there is some reason to distinguish between appearance and reality.*[36]

This is either *very* interesting or not interesting at all. It cannot, given the complexity of the current debate within the philosophy of science, be legitimately interpreted as the assertion that the thesis of realism is unchallengeable by any reasonable person. Neither can we assume that it means that any and every phenomenal experience, however strange, must be assumed to be veridical unless proved otherwise. The likeliest interpretation is that solipsism must be rejected by any reasonable person. Solipsism, in essence, refuses to recognise the distinction between appearance and reality; it denies the independent existence of a world of reality beyond one's own consciousness. The solipsist adopts this position on the basis of philosophical reflection which results in the rejection of the vulgar self-evidence of our experience of 'the world'. In other words, solipsism reverses Finnis's statement and holds that there are *no* good reasons to regard phenomena as being real. The solipsist has a lot going for him here.

Descartes tackled the problem by asking how we might ascertain the difference between real experience and dreams. He did not intend to invite suggestions for a list of features which would count as evidence for or against the reality of an experience. The point is rather to illustrate the fundamental intelligibility of asking the question. Descartes' answer to this question is, of course, that there is no empirical evidence for this claim.[37] This is why the thesis of solipsism is, prima facie, coherent. The solipsistic impasse can be avoided only by a transcendental reduction – an argument which transcends the debate about evidence and proof and attends to the conditions under which the employment of such concepts is possible. Thus we must acknowledge that if empirical knowledge is possible then there must be something external to our consciousness. The difference between real experience and fantasy turns upon the intelligibility of the assumption that sometimes our experience is caused by external objects and that sometimes it is not.

Given this, we then face the problem of distinguishing between phenomenal appearances *within* what is assumed to be real experience, and phenomena which are to be excluded from it. We need to distinguish three categories of phenomena: the phenomena of dreams and delusions; non-veridical appearances; and veridical appearances. Thus the concept of *phenomena* is to be explicated in a way which subsumes both appearance *and* 'reality' (i.e. veridical experience). The problem for empirical science is to establish empirical techniques which allow us to distinguish between what appears to be the case and what really is the case.[38] Given that it is true to say that the sun appears to revolve around the earth today, notwithstanding Copernicus, the hasty acceptance of Finnis's principle would actually prove to be antithetical to the scientific attitude. It exhorts us to accept appearance as reality (truth) as a kind of default position. This is not likely to encourage the kind of critical curiosity which has resulted in the most startling findings of the natural sciences. It is worth noting that the default position of accepting appearances as real is unlikely to be modified in the absence of an understanding of what constitutes 'a good reason'. In ideological terms, then, Finnis makes a highly contentious claim. Any critical social theory (e.g. Marxism) must challenge the interpretation of phenomenal reality – it must challenge the *given*. Marx suggested that we subject that which is seen to be natural and inevitable to the scrutiny of his dialectical methods of analysis. His justification of this position is far from being self-evident and is considered by many not to be a good reason at all. In the light of these observations it seems that far from being unchallengeable by any reasonable person, what constitutes a good reason to accept or reject appearances as real is the central question of the philosophy of natural and social science.

5. *[A] full description of data is to be preferred to partial descriptions ...*[39]

If this means that if we wish to know the whole truth then we shall be better pleased with more of it than less, then it is a tautology. More importantly, if it is to be taken to mean that comprehensiveness is to be regarded as an epistemological category, then it is demonstrably false. The divine conception of the solar system in all its poetic beauty and fullness is not to be preferred to a single proposition in Kepler. Neither was there ever any good scientific reason based on comprehensiveness to prefer it as being true.

6. *(ii) [A]n account or explanation of phenomena is not to be accepted if it requires or postulates something inconsistent with the data for which it is supposed to account.*[40]

Arguments for and against Popper's extensive analysis of scientific rationality will be of much help to us here and in example 7 *infra*. Detailed criticism of Popper's falsificationist criterion[41] has shown that accounts or explanations – theories – are always constituted as a complex of hypotheses, and lack of consistency with data does not license refutation of a complete theory. This is so because inconsistency rarely pinpoints one particular hypothesis. We came across this in our discussion of Hollis. Logically, the problem is that an empirical test, mapped onto the propositional calculus as a systemic argument, can result in a 'refutation' of a hypothesis where the move to *modus tollens* is effected by the incongruity of data – mapped as a propositional function – which serves as the denial of the consequent of the general hypothesis. But the complexity of implicit sub-hypotheses and their empirical 'implications' is such that this 'refutation' does not allow us to identify, and thereby falsify, the particular hypothesis which implies it.

An example which shows not only the non-self-evidence but the scientific imprudence of the cited principle is the experiment which Popper regards as 'bold conjecture' *par excellence* – Einstein's theory of relativity. As accounts of the less than spectacular empirical testing of this hypothesis show, confusion concerning the theoretical import of apparent anomalies, faulty equipment etc., could have resulted in the 'refutation' of this hypothesis owing to the said hypothesis's inconsistency with the data.[42] Assuming the theory to be true, which it could be, it appears that a true hypothesis can be inconsistent with the 'data' because the relations between theory and data are precariously complex at the level of empirical testability.

7. ... *[A] method of interpretation which is successful is to be relied upon in further similar cases until contrary reason appears.*[43]

If this is to suggest that an hypothesis is to be relied upon until it becomes inconsistent with the phenomena it seeks to explain, then it is a methodological error. For, as Popper has clearly shown,[44] a scheme of explanation can – in fact *must* – condition its own evidence. Furthermore, some hypotheses are unfalsifiable and, hence, appear as eternally adequate to the phenomena. Others are so limited in explanatory scope that they are 'safe'. In addition to these problems, Popper regards this maxim as scientifically erroneous in a prescriptive sense – i.e. a practical-technical sense. This is because it leads to the production and subsequent protection of hypotheses which timidly limit themselves to a paucity of explanation at the empirical level – he terms this 'confirmationism'. Thus far from being self-evidently reasonable, this practice is pernicious from the point of view of the practical application of theoretical reason. Popper suggests that hypotheses should be constantly attacked despite their repeated confirmation and that the constant struggle to refute hypotheses is the rational scientific approach which, incidentally, he claims to be historically supported by the greatest practitioners from Copernicus to Einstein.

8. *[T]heoretical accounts which are simple, predictively successful, and explanatorily powerful are to be accepted in preference to other accounts.*[45]

Far from being self-evident, this pronouncement actually runs counter to Finnis's position on the primacy of the pursuit of truth as the basis of all practical reason. The statement above is a classic formulation of the Pragmatist/technologist case for scientific method.[46] Both schools are either sceptical of, or positively deny, the possibility of objective knowledge in the sense of justified, true belief. The above formulation of method is then used to rescue the rationality of science in the face of the dependence of empirical 'evidence' upon the infinite plurality of conceptual schemes.

Furthermore, this injunction is plainly at odds with both the commitment to truth and the belief in the possibility of a non-instrumental rationality. First, it is highly unlikely that the world is simple – therefore it seems reasonable to assume that simple explanations of it are always false. Secondly, predictive success is technologically desirable from the point of view of the amount of instrumental control it may afford; but it is necessarily the case, if not self-evidently the case, that theories may work because they are true, but they are not true because they work. Only the instrumentally oriented would be satisfied by predictive success. It cannot satisfy one who regards 'knowledge-for-its-own-sake' as a basic value. Thirdly, 'explanatorily powerful' equivocates on the concept of explanation – 'explanations', if not true explanations, explain nothing. However, the technologist, concerned with the pragmatics of control, is untroubled by the distinction. Again this is inconsistent with Finnis's claim that knowledge and truth are basic human goods. If the example of sound empirical judgment cited above is true, it follows that the claims made for truth and knowledge as basic goods of practical reason are self-evidently false.

FIRST SUMMARY

The preceding pages are not intended to deny that knowledge and truth are basic human goods and form the basis or intrinsic ends of all practical reason. Neither am I primarily concerned to show that all or some of the above examples of empirical judgment are false, or not even necessarily true. If they are objectively true, as Finnis alleges, they are true regardless of the beliefs or opinions of the whole world. What I hope to have demonstrated is that these maxims are in no way self-evident in the sense that they cannot be substantiated by inferential reasoning. If they are true, they must be demonstrated to be so by inferential reasoning. It is also important to note that to challenge these maxims is neither unreasonable nor does it bar one from the pursuit of knowledge. In fact it is vital to the process of science that debates occur concerning these matters, and that they are examined from every conceivably coherent viewpoint. For it is in the process of argument that the undeniability of foundational truths is made plain.

That some of the above examples *are* false is damaging to Finnis's theory of the requirements of practical reason which he attempts to develop into a moral theory. This attempt is based on the claim that the other basic goods to which he refers (and which he wishes ultimately to establish as universal values) are dependent for their derivation as moral principles upon the same method as that which he employs in the case of the basic good of knowledge. This obliges us to infer that they are, as apodictic claims, similarly unsupportable. However, it would be much too slick to avoid his ethical arguments entirely, even on the basis of this sound logical point.

In respect of Finnis's arguments concerning the maxims of empirical science, I think it reasonable to suggest that, notwithstanding the contentious nature and demonstrable falsity of some of his substantive examples, it is possible, without unwarranted presumption, to reformulate his philosophical intentions on a *formal* level. By this I mean that Finnis is right to say theoretical reason and its practical or methodological orientation is based upon assumptions which have a special mode of validity. This validity, which Finnis wishes to characterise as 'self-evidence', is not to be construed as denoting that property of propositions which is immediately perceived by all and sundry to be the property of truth – Finnis is clear about this.[47] Rather, we can interpret his notion of self-evidence as being synonymous with a conception of apodictic validity – even though his substantive examples do not meet the criterion of such validity.

THE FORMAL STRUCTURE OF FINNIS'S CLAIMS

What, then, is the criterion of apodictic validity? A proposition is apodictically valid if, as a regulating principle of inquiry, it cannot rationally be denied. Thus the principle of non-contradiction is affirmed by denying it, i.e. the claim that 'A proposition and its denial cannot simultaneously be true of the same set of circumstances' implies the impossibility of this claim and its denial being simultaneously true. *Formally*, a proposition is apodictically valid if, from the point of view of one who attempts to reason, it instantiates an ineluctable law or, because of the confusion which this phrase may cause, a rationally unquestionable principle of reason *from the point of view of one who attempts to reason.* I give an example of how to synthesise a deductively apodictic or meta-logical principle in Chapter 9 *infra*.[48] We may extend this to theoretical reasoning by substituting theoretical principles akin to those suggested by Finnis. These apodictic principles of reasoning must, however, be the products of inferences, and these inferences must be transcendental or dialectically-necessary inferences which all take the form of a conditional proposition which, from the point of view of one who attempts to reason theoretically, is inescapably valid. That is, they take the form: 'If empirical knowledge is possible then "x" must be accepted as true', whereupon 'x' achieves apodictic status. Similarly, we may formally posit the existence of apodictic principles of practical reasoning. Thus we may accept Finnis's claims to the effect that there exist principles of practical reasoning which are categorically prescriptive and which do not violate Hume's Law – for they are not inferences from contingent facts – although we cannot hold to the claim that they are inferentially underived. Thus the Humean objection to the possibility of an ethical objectivism or an objective theory of Natural Law is not an insurmountable obstacle.[49] The formula will be: *a principle of deductive/theoretical/practical reasoning will be apodictically valid if and only if it is dialectically-necessary from the point of view of one who reasons deductively/theoretically/practically.*

It may be true, then, as Finnis thinks it is, that apodictic principles of practical reason can be identified and that they have moral implications. What is it that will turn practical-instrumental principles into moral principles? We have hitherto used the notion of substantive rationality as being interchangeable with the notion of moral reason in the sense that we know what it is that a value-free approach to science wishes to exclude from its corpus of legitimate explanation. In Weber we noted that reflection on practical reason allowed us to construct a model of instrumental rationality which, we stressed, did not go beyond the purely technical evaluation of empirical facts. This kind of rationality is a matter of making one's means consistent with one's ends. Substantive rationality, on the other hand, is a value-concept in that it seeks to make judgments about *ends in themselves*. This is to claim that some ends are categorically rational. Now this has been a definition of 'the good' which has featured in thousands of years of discussion in ethics. But does it suffice to furnish us with a full notion of what is entailed by a moral judgment? The point is that even if we can hone down practical reason to its bare logical structure, and show that there are some ends which *prudentially* must be regarded as categorical, we still face the problem of logically grounding principles which involve our relations with others. Following Gewirth, we can say that it is the *other-regardingness* of a principle which defines its moral nature.[50] Thus the quest is for principles which are rationally undeniable, action-guiding, overriding, categorical and other-regarding – *from the point of view of one who attempts to reason practically.* The task before us, then, is to show that from the fact that we have any purposes at all, it can be demonstrated that we logically must accept one or more principles which are conditioned by all the criteria noted above.

We may make an interesting point here: the reference to other-regarding criteria will prove to be the central problem for us. For the sake of argument we could imagine a plausible solution to the problem if we were allowed to omit other-regardingness from the equation: thus, if we are to pursue purposes, then we need to be alive, we must value life as an end in itself, thus life is a basic or intrinsic good and this basic good conditions at least one basic principle – one must categorically value one's life. It is possible to carp at this for several reasons – suicide is a problem, extreme hedonism, etc. The point I am making, however, is that there may be apodictic *prudential* criteria of a categorical and overriding nature, and demonstrating that there are may not be too difficult. In fact, prudential rationality is simply instrumental rationality applied to one's own problem of attaining the wherewithal to act for one's own (self-defined) interests. Simply, I need my life for the pursuit of my purposes, but I do not need yours. Prudentially, therefore, it seems that even if I have to value my life as an end in itself, I do not, logically, have to value yours. The moral dimension to practical reason, however, involves taking into account the interests of others as relevant action-guiding considerations, and this is the type of principle we are seeking to synthesise. We must bear this in mind as we consider Finnis's conception of practical reasonableness.

Finnis offers some suggestions as to what might constitute the implied set of basic goods and then a further set of principles which incorporate them into a rational life plan. I will mention briefly the arguments Finnis offers in respect of the basic values which he holds to constitute the moral foundations of practical reason. I do not think that they achieve apodictic status in the way in which Finnis presents them, but the following reflections are, however, interesting to us formally for three reasons. (a) They are presented as a system which attempts to unearth a complex set of interrelations between various basic ends to be pursued and thus illustrate the possibilities of constructing an ethical system by reference to some possibly apodictic principle (or principles) of practical reason. (b) They illustrate the possible depth and scope of practical reason which may underlie a simple (Weberian) conception of formal rationality. (c) They show us what an integrated theory of substantively rational social theory would look like, and exactly what details need to be established in such a theory.

Finnis suggests that we may work towards a conception of the subject-matter of the good by realising through reflection that we and others are orientated to diverse forms of practical activity by participation in general or basic forms of good. These are purpose-shaping values. He asks, 'What then, are the basic forms of good for us?'[51] I will simply list those basic goods which Finnis wishes to make central to the shaping of our practical reason.

Life

This is to be understood as 'bodily (including cerebral) health, and freedom from the pain that betokens organic malfunctioning or injury'. This basic human purpose 'or internally related group of purposes' is to be regarded as the substructure upon which many diverse expressions of purpose are founded from the 'prayer of a man overboard' through the complex network of the medical services to road safety laws, famine relief expeditions or taking care when crossing the road.[52]

Knowledge

That is, 'for-its-own-sake'.[53]

Play

For Finnis this is an 'irreducible element in human culture'. It is the basic good of seeing the 'point' in activity which has no point other than enjoyment of the performance of the activity.[54]

Aesthetic experience

This is 'the creation and/or active appreciation of some *work* of significant and satisfying form'.

Sociability (friendship)

This, in a minimal sense, is realised by the value of maintaining a 'minimum of peace and harmony amongst men',[55] yet also goes considerably beyond this:[56]

> Some of the collaboration between one person and another is no more than instrumental to the realization by each of his own individual purposes. But friendship involves acting for the sake of one's friend's purposes, one's friend's well-being. To be in a relationship of friendship with at least one other person is a fundamental form of good, is it not?

Practical reasonableness[57]

This would appear to be the generic concept under which all these aforementioned basic goods are subsumed. But Finnis here intends that special property of practical reason which is regarded as a basic good by all who act for purposes. This special property is that of the *integrity and authenticity* combined in practical reason which guarantees the essentially human character of purposive action. This idea is close to that of Weber's conception of personality. Finnis says:[58]

> Negatively, this involves that one has a measure of effective freedom; positively, it involves that one seeks to bring an intelligent and reasonable order into one's own actions and habits and practical attitudes.

This order has internal and external aspects. Respectively, these appear as striving to 'bring one's emotions and dispositions into the harmony of an inner peace of mind that is not merely the product of drugs or indoctrination nor merely passive in its orientation'. In addition, we strive for an external cohesion in the attempt genuinely to realise our own 'freely ordered evaluations, preferences, hopes, and self-determination'.[59]

Religion

By this Finnis intends to encompass sacred and secular conceptions of the term. Simply stated, a religious orientation is one which concerns itself with the universal order and one's location within it:[60]

> Misgivings may be aroused by the notion that one of the basic human values is the establishment and maintenance of proper relationships between oneself (and the orders one can create and maintain) and the divine. For there are, always, those who doubt or

> deny that the universality-of-things has any origin beyond the 'origins' known to the natural sciences, ... But is it reasonable to deny that it is, at any rate, peculiarly important to have thought reasonably and (where possible) correctly about these questions of the origins of cosmic order and of human freedom and reason – whatever the answer to those questions turns out to be, and even if the answers have to be agnostic or negative?

This list can be modified and reformulated in a host of different ways but no essential characterisation of the basic forms of good will result. In other words:[61] '... those seven purposes are all of the basic purposes of human action, and that any other purpose which you or I might recognize and pursue will turn out to represent, or be constituted of, some aspect(s) of some or all of them'. Furthermore, all are equally fund amental:[62]

> First, each is equally self-evidently a form of good. Secondly, none can be analytically reduced to being merely an aspect of any of the others, or to being merely instrumental in the pursuit of any of the others. Thirdly, each one, when we focus on it, can reasonably be regarded as the most important. Hence there is no objective hierarchy amongst them.

In summing up this outline of the basic values constitutive of practical reason, Finnis says:[63]

> So it is that the practical principles which enjoin one to participate in those basic forms of good, through the practically intelligent decisions and free actions that constitute one [as] the person one is and is to be, have been called in the Western philosophical tradition the first principles of natural law, because they lay down for us the outlines of everything one could reasonably want to do, to have and to be.

FINNIS: THE ETHICAL DIMENSION

In Chapter 5 of *Natural Law and Natural Rights* Finnis says the understanding and acknowledgement of the nature of basic goods 'creates, not answers the problem for intelligent decision'.[64] In other words, ethics, as a systematised discipline which attempts to answer the questions of 'What is to be done? What may be left undone? What is not to be done?' starts from a reflective acknowledgement of the self-evidence of the basic goods or, 'the principles that express the general ends of human life' and then aims to work out how they are 'brought to bear upon definite ranges of project, disposition or action, or upon particular projects[,] dispositions or actions'.[65] He says:[66] '"Ethics", as classically conceived, is simply a recollectively and/or prospectively reflective expression of this problem and of the general lines of solutions which have been thought reasonable'.

'How does one tell that a decision is practically reasonable?' Finnis states that:[67]

> In the two millennia since Plato and Aristotle initiated formal inquiry into the content of practical reasonableness, philosophical reflection has identified a considerable number of requirements of *method* in practical reasoning. Each of these requirements has, indeed, been treated by some philosopher with exaggerated respect, as if it were the exclusive controlling and shaping requirement. For, as with each of the basic forms of good, each of these requirements is fundamental, underived, irreducible and hence is capable when focused upon of seeming the most important.

The business of ethics, then, is that of identifying the basic goods and then working out a method of practical reasonableness which incorporates and applies them to the evaluation of particular courses of action. The second order principles of this method are clearly identified and explained by Finnis. We must assume that these second order principles of practical reason are held to be analogous to the eight methodological principles of theoretical reason which we discussed above in relation to the basic good of knowledge. Just as those methodological principles were alleged to constitute the unquestionable canons or laws of theoretical reason (or empirical science), the following principles are to be regarded as the laws of practical reason. Finnis says:[68]

> Speaking very summarily, we could say that the requirements to which we now turn express the 'natural law method' or working out the (moral) 'natural law' from the first (pre-moral) 'principles of natural law'. Using only the modern terminology (itself of uncertain import) of 'morality' we can say that the following sections of this chapter concern the sorts of reasons why (and thus the ways in which) there are things that morally ought (not) to be done.

I will examine only the first three of the nine principles in order to show the nature of the claims involved. This will suffice to make the general critical point.

A coherent plan of life[69]

Finnis invokes the wisdom of Rawls and the Christian teachings which counsel the prudence of taking a long-term perspective of the project of life. 'It is unreasonable to live merely from moment to moment, following immediate cravings or just drifting. It is also irrational to devote one's attention exclusively to specific projects which can be carried out completely by simply deploying defined means to defined objectives.'[70] Here there is resonance with Weber's notion of integrity – meaningful life does not consist of randomly cobbled together pieces of 'social action' which may be interpreted individually as 'rational, and goal-directed. The rational life-plan is one where 'Implicitly or explicitly one must have a harmonious set of purposes and orientations, not as the "plans" or "blueprints" of a pipe-dream, but as effective commitments.'[71] Thus we may say that a coherent plan of life participates in the pursuit of the basic goods in a fashion which is logically consistent and with a view to the uncertainties of the future in a way which conditions each decision in respect of others which have been or will be made in an attempt to create an overall harmony to a life seen as a whole.

No arbitrary preference among values[72]

A coherent life plan will fail if it seeks to base itself on[73]

> ... a devaluation of any of the basic forms of human excellence, or if it is on the basis of an over-valuation of such merely derivative and supporting or instrumental goods as wealth or 'opportunity' or of such merely secondary and conditionally valuable goods as reputation or (in a different sense of secondariness) pleasure.

This, of course, follows from Finnis's previous remarks on the equality of importance of the basic forms of good which cannot and must not be seen in terms of a hierarchy of significance.

No arbitrary preference among persons[74]

This is a statement of the irrationality of a failure to adopt an egalitarian outlook on the basis of the realisation that the basic goods are human goods '... and can in principle be pursued, realized and participated in by any human being'.[75] Although there is scope for self-preference, this third requirement is understood as a critique of[76]

> ... selfishness, special pleading, double standards, hypocrisy, indifference to the good of others whom one could easily help ... and all the other manifold forms of egoistic and group bias. ... In the modern philosophical discussion, the principle regularly is expressed as a requirement that one's moral judgments and preferences be universalizable.

The other basic requirements of practical reason are Detachment and Commitment, the (Limited) Relevance of Consequences: Efficiency, within Reason; Respect for Every Basic Value in Every Act; the Requirements of the Common Good; Following One's Conscience.[77] All of these principles are held to constitute morality:[78]

> Each, of these has a place in rational choice of commitments, projects and particular actions. Each, moreover, contributes to the sense, significance and force of terms such as 'moral', '[morally] ought', and 'right'; not every one of the nine requirements has a direct role in every moral judgment, but some moral judgments do sum up the bearing of each and all the nine on the questions in hand,

and every moral judgement sums up the bearing of one or more of the requirements.

FINNIS: A CRITICAL SUMMARY

It would be inappropriate to embark upon a hair-splitting critique in the manner of that which was directed at the alleged irrefutability of the principles of theoretical reason. The only point which needs to be made in this vein is that the foundational principles of the basic goods and the secondary principles of ethical method presented above stand or fall on the same claims to self-evidence and undemonstrability as those which we found to be wanting in our previous analyses. I suggest, therefore, that we take stock of some of the claims involved in Finnis's outline of the canons of practical reason and, without a great display of logic chopping, pose a simple question in respect of them.

We have seen that Finnis makes claims of apodictic validity for principles such as altruism, egalitarianism, the denial of hedonism, the irrationality of an ethical egoism, the failure to adopt a broadly religious view of self, etc. Most importantly, in his remarks which rule out arbitrary preference among persons, he suggests that practical precepts must be universalised. Now even if we accepted one or two or even all of Finnis's contentions concerning basic goods and basic values, without this universalisation step we cannot make progress. Before I introduced his outline of the basic goods I made this point concerning the jump from the prudential to the moral. It is quite clear in Finnis's remarks on universalisation and in his comments on 'Sociability' that an 'interest in the well-being of others' is assumed to be self-evident. Let us simply consider the basis of these claims.

These principles are located within a system of reasoning which is held to be common to all who adopt the pursuit of ends by the employment of means. In other words, for one who reasons practically, these principles are held to be presuppositions which can be shown to be dialectically entailed – even though it is in no way suggested that all who reason practically are consciously aware of these presuppositions. It is held to follow, therefore, that courses of action which violate these presuppositions can be objectively regarded as being violations of the principles of practical reason *per se* and thus violations of moral reason which is intrinsic to the structure of practical reasoning. The test of this violation of practical reason would be to imagine a situation where one who pursued a particular end could be shown to be, implicitly, denying or flouting a basic form of good or a principle of practical reasonableness which conditions the pursuit of these goods. A particular action or course of actions could be shown to contradict a principle which features as a basic presupposition of practical reasoning. Given the systematic breadth of the principles presented by Finnis, it does not prove difficult to construct examples. Thus an ascetic, a recluse, a lotus eater – even a Conceptual Pragmatist – would, in terms of Finnis's criteria of practical rationality, be characterised as irrational. They would be guilty of contradicting the basic laws of practical reason.

At this point the 'self-evidence', or, in our characterisation, the apodictic validity, of the basic canons of practical reason would come into question. If no grounds for their universal validity could be presented, then no argument between parties could take place. The most that could be said is that an individual who does not accept the seven basic goods and nine principles of application is an unreasonable individual. By Finnis's own emphatic tenets, no justification can be presented. An unreasonable individual in this case is one who does not accept the aforementioned principles of practical reasoning. We have seen that these principles can be doubted, denied and, in some cases, shown to be necessarily false. It is therefore *a fortiori* the case that the canons of practical reasoning propounded by Finnis can at least similarly be reasonably challenged or refuted. In other words, we cannot, with the force of *necessity* formulate an apodictically valid prescription for practical reasonableness of the form: 'If one is to act in accord with the principles of practical reason then one must do *x*', where *x* is one, all or any of the basic principles presented by Finnis. To be able to make such a prescription is surely the goal of the enterprise we are here undertaking. Thus of the two steps of Finnis's theory I offer the following conclusions.

1. His first contention, which holds that social phenomena must be conceptualised as aspects of practical reason and that the avoidance of arbitrariness requires that such conceptualisations (ideal-types) must appear as focal cases of the phenomena from the practically reasonable point of view, is necessarily correct. That is, it is a logico-philosophical analysis of the structure of social-scientific explanation which, on the basis of an epistemologically orientated examination of concept formation, exhibits logical necessity in its conclusions.

2. The second step, which involves the characterisation of the practically reasonable point of view as a moral point of view, is a perspective which, albeit eruditely, simply prescribes its moral nature on the basis of assumptions which are bluntly stipulated as unchallengeable. If these assumptions, which are themselves categorical imperatives, were logically necessary, they would indeed be unchallengeable by any reasonable person. This is implicitly to define the unreasonable person as one who refuses to accept the force of logical necessity. This is perfectly justified. But to define the unreasonable person as one who cannot, or will not, see the alleged universal validity of debatable moral imperatives *simply stated* is viciously circular.

The value of Finnis's work is to show the practically reasonable point of view to be the required viewpoint of social science. Finnis has also alerted us to the possibility that a successful logical analysis of practical reason may widen our practical perspective to reveal a vast complexity of interrelated assumptions and entailments which may, from their surface origins of simple instrumentality – their naive practicality, be shown to lead us into moral commitments. The most exciting aspect of Finnis' reflections is that the vast panoply of interrelations between seemingly unconnected ends rests on the possibility of establishing a logically necessary link between our own instrumental rationality and the deeper universal ends which Finnis suggests may underlie the whole of our constitution as practically rational beings. That Finnis is unsuccessful in establishing this link beyond question should not lead us to infer that it is an impossible task – Habermas, through the concept of communication, and Gewirth, through the concept of agency, pursue just this line of inquiry. Their work should be assessed in the light of the formal structure of Finnis's Natural Law project. Finnis takes us from a simple problem of description to a fundamental methodological shift in social science. For his reflections on the problem of constructing a non-arbitrary, non-conventional concept of law are valid for *every* instance of such concept formation pertaining to *any* aspect of social phenomena.

7

The Presuppositions of Communication

Enough has been said up to this point to suggest that if issues of substantive rationality can be objectively grounded, then the principles upon which this validity rests are likely to inhere in the presuppositions of practical reason. In general, we may say that the cognitive operations which are required to produce *theoretical* knowledge of practical activity trail in their wake, especially in the field of social theory, a complex of unavoidable assumptions which have immense significance for our understanding of the moral dimensions of the concept of practical rationality. The analysis of these cognitive operations constitutes the focus and subject-matter of metatheoretical or epistemological investigation. Such investigations need not start out, and, in many cases, have not started out, as substantive programmes of investigation in the field of moral theory. Indeed, in the case of Habermas and his contemporaries and predecessors in the field of Critical Theory, involvement with ethical issues, in the traditional sense of the search for the Good and the Right, has arisen out of the theoretical tensions produced by an emphatic attempt to avoid such problems. In true dialectical fashion, the thesis of Marxism, in interaction with the antithesis of Weberian analysis, has produced the synthesis of Critical Theory which appears as the complete *negation of the negation* of the Marxist theory of ideology.[1] It will be useful to sketch in some of the background to these theoretical developments and remind ourselves of the methodological theses which we have encountered in our discussions so far.

As we first noted in our analysis of Weber's methodology, we require a conceptual vantage point from which we are able first to formulate a distinction between natural and social phenomena, and then to discover that these aspects of phenomena, if they are to be systematically investigated, oblige us to formulate different explanatory concepts. The fundamental category of analysis employed is that of social action, i.e. action which is structured within a framework of means and ends. We noted, in addition, that the presuppositions of such action embraced the concepts of nomological explanation, in that the objective possibility of such action was dependent upon the assumption that a simple determinism obtained in the world and that objects were susceptible to our manipulation in a predictable way. In other words, practical action and its presuppositions form the base of a conceptually valid scheme of methodological assumptions.

In the work of Finnis we then noted that the construction of ideal-typical concepts of social phenomena demands that we find an Archimedean point from which we are able to evaluate the essential from the epiphenomenal. In Finnis's illustration of the problem of description and evaluation we find that it becomes impossible to avoid arbitrariness in description of social phenomena unless we commit ourselves to a definition of practical reasonableness which exhibits a universal validity. If we do not, then all social science is simply commentary 'from someone's point of view'.[2] Similarly, Hollis's reflections on social action show us that teleological explanation cannot content itself with a 'one step at a time' continuum of *Zweckrationalität*. We must judge the rationality of end states in order to satisfy the requirements of a concept of *adequate* causation, and thereby reinstate a coherent concept of the agent in social theory. Our investigations are, therefore, directed to the realm of ends.

THE RATIONALITY PROBLEMATIC

Where the social phenomenon in question is rationality itself, or at least that mode of rationality which is held to hold sway in a particular epoch, it becomes obvious that only a rational being could recognise when and if he was in the presence of reason. Sociology, therefore, cannot avoid what Habermas calls 'the rationality problematic'. He says[3] '*any* sociology that claims to be a theory of society has to face the problem of rationality simultaneously on the *metatheoretical*, *methodological*, and *empirical* levels'. In orthodox Marxist terms, bourgeois ideology is a phenomenon which can only be identified from the vantage point of a true proletarian consciousness. This latter proposition is the one which excites so much theoretical *Angst* in Marxian theory; but it is simply a restatement of the logical dilemma which all attempts to construct a science of society eventually meet head on. In Marxist and Neo-Marxist theory this collision has produced a version of a theory of Natural Law which has been variously described as 'universal pragmatics' or 'discursive will formation'.[4] The problem hinges on the attempt to develop a universal theory of rationality which allows 'critique' to be possible. Where this critique is focused upon social phenomena, i.e. that which is constituted by practical action, the project becomes no less than an attempt to construct a universally valid scheme of practical rationality. In other words, it attempts to answer the question, 'What ought I to do – if I am to be rational?' In social terms this raises the question of what constitutes rational institutional design and thus, which norms and, hence, what rules are to be rationally imposed and for what reasons. It is quite clear, therefore, that this project is nothing less than an attempt to integrate fully ethics/natural law/moral philosophy and social theory.

This simple statement of the problem belies the complexity of the interrelations between Weberian and traditional Marxist approaches to social theory and praxis. In this chapter I will discuss how it comes about that a search for a universal pragmatics is implied by Weberian and Marxist schemes of social theory, and how the alleged principles of such a universal pragmatic can be grounded only in a fully transcendental framework of analysis – despite claims to the contrary on behalf of its principal authors. The attempt to ground a universal pragmatic in this synthesis of Weberian and Marxist theory appeals to the possibility of identifying universally valid norms by way of rationally reconstructing the implicit principles of *Communicative Action*.[5]

EVOLUTION AS THEME

It is not unusual, these days, to find criticisms of Marxist theory which point to the pernicious influence of Enlightenment illusions concerning the concept of a continuum of progress which suggests a parallelism between technological and moral development. Comte, and later Durkheim, as inheritors of the critical shift in social and political thought, saw emancipation – or at least moral progress – as a possibility brought about by the scientific-technological age.[6] 'Industrial society', as a basic sociological category, was conceived by them to be a 'higher' stage in the evolutionary development of humanity in the moral and technical senses of the term. Durkheim, in particular, saw the emergence of a complex division of labour brought about by industrial development as being, by virtue of its structural features alone, the bearer of an emancipatory potential in that the archaic forms of normative regulation which denied the reality of the individual would, by virtue of their pathological 'lack of fit', disappear. Habermas draws upon this Durkheimian theme in an attempt to locate this insight within a Piagetian and Kohlbergian framework of cognitive development.[7]

Habermas interprets Durkheim as presenting the view that normative regulation moves from a tacit 'conventional' mode to a linguistified, 'post-conventional' mode in accordance with the development of system complexity from mechanical solidarity to interdependency states.[8] This is not to say that Durkheim saw the shift from mechanical to organic solidarity as being without its dangers. There is much in his work which advocates the necessity of constructing institutions which moderate the individualistic and alienating tendencies of modernity. Nevertheless, the belief in the evolutionary progress of human morality tied to the attendant developments in technical control are clearly evident in his work.[9]

For all the differences between Durkheim and Marx, it is undeniably the case that they shared first, an evolutionary model of society, and secondly, a belief in the emancipatory tendencies of the development of productive forces. In the case of Marx, the exact nature of this evolutionary theory – and its philosophical pedigree – will prove to be a crucial element in our analysis of the curious orientation of the Habermasian project. However, it is true in a general sense to say that they shared a theoretically grounded confidence in the coming of a more rational, more free, more human existence; and that the explosion of technical mastery over production was, far from being an impediment, a necessary condition of this progress. It is for this reason that modern theorists indict Marx as being rooted within the traditions of the Liberal Enlightenment with its worship of, and unshakeable faith in, the development of Reason – this, of course, is a criticism which identifies reason as being synonymous with the positivistic conception of rationality, i.e. 'scientific' rationality.

DISENCHANTMENT

This criticism of Marx reaches its height with the historical-empirical vindication of Weber's darkest fears concerning the 'disenchantment' of the modern industrialised world and its attendant mode of instrumental and bureaucratic rationality. The concept of moral progress is shown to be a superstition born of an uncritical acceptance of the validity and superiority of Western values which are assumed to have a universal application, when, in fact, they are simply one among a vast plurality of fundamentally unsupportable *Weltanschauungen*. As McCarthy explains:[10]

> The progress of societal rationalization was indeed well along by the end of the nineteenth century; but what this progress turned out to be, according to Weber, was the ascendancy of *purposive* rationality, of technique and calculation, of organization and administration. The triumph of reason brings with it not a reign of freedom but the dominion of impersonal economic forces and bureaucratically organized administrations – a 'vast and mighty cosmos' that 'determines with irresistable force the lifestyles of all the individuals who are born into (it)'.

Weber held out no hope of this situation being improved by the advent of Socialism. Rather he regarded this possibility as being the final and highest stage of bureaucratic domination.

For orthodox Marxism, the analysis presented by Weber, together with the historical developments of the twentieth century, has forced a theoretical and practical crisis of immense proportions. McCarthy notes that[11]

> Writing in the early 1940s, Max Horkheimer and Theodor Adorno surrendered, in effect, to the force of Weber's diagnosis. The rise of

> fascism in Europe, with the complicity of large segments of the working class; the degeneration of Socialism into Stalinism, with its bloody suppression of any dissent from party rule; and the apparently seamless integration of the American populace, including the working class, into what appeared to be a thoroughly commodified and totally administered society – left them, they felt, no realistic basis for hope.

This pessimism was compounded by the force of Weber's analysis of modernity as characterised by the domination of pure instrumentality embodied in calculation and control. Where Marx had welcomed the proliferation of any development of the forces of production of capitalist society and, simultaneously seen within it the positive dialectic of the increasing contradictions of the social relations of production, Horkheimer and Adorno saw only an overwhelming, ineradicable domination which pervaded all spheres of life. McCarthy quotes Horkheimer thus:[12]

> Subjects who, in Horkheimer's words, 'have to form themselves, body and soul, in relation to the technical apparatus' are no longer potential subjects of revolution ... 'All life today tends to be increasingly subjected to rationalization and planning ... [T]he individual's self-preservation presupposes his adjustment to the requirements for the preservation of the system.'

In other words, the task of revolutionary critique, which was supposed to be theoretically impossible in isolation from practice according to orthodox Marxism, is now seen to be *practically* impossible due to the massive hegemonic power of modernity with its crushing institutionalisation of an instrumental rationality in a 'disenchanted world'. The Enlightenment hope of rational emancipation first necessitated the eradication of traditional ethical world views, and the stripping away of ethical meaning superstitiously and anthropomorphically projected as constituting the structure of reality. Modern science and secular, empiricist logic in the field of a theory of meaning succeeded in doing this,[13] but created, in its naivety, a dehumanised vacuum. Meaning and unity in and of existence are dissolved by the power of this development of 'Reason'.[14]

> ... the disenchanted world is stripped of all ethical meaning; it is devalued and objectified as the material and setting for purposive-rational pursuit of interests. The gain in control is paid for with a loss of meaning. And the control that we gain is itself value-neutral – an instrumental potential that can be harnessed from any one of an unlimited number of value perspectives. This subjectivisation of 'ultimate' ends means that the unity of the world has fallen to pieces. In place of the one God or the unitary ground of being, we have an irreducible plurality of competing, often irreconcilable values, and

as Weber says, 'over these Gods and their struggles it is fate, and certainly not any "science" that holds sway'.

A NEGATIVE DIALECTIC?

In such a world then, the possibility of the emergence of a coherent and politically advanced proletariat capable of transcending the ideological distortions of bourgeois society is seen to be a dream induced by the ideology of Reason itself. Reason has, to be sure, a dialectical mode of development, but this turns out to be a negative dialectic, turning in on itself.

The uncomfortable problem here for revolutionary theory is a simple one to understand. The need to give an a priori justification for the prescriptions of Marxist praxis, before the developments of the twentieth century, had been countered by the materialist argument which posited labour as a fundamental category of historical development. The species-being of humanity was its capacity to labour creatively, to interact with and transform the world. Through the historical process of development, the proletariat would, as the most advanced class produced by this process, inherit the capacity to unmask the distorted features of their existence as creative beings. Following this, they would be capable of overthrowing the last stage of their oppression and would instigate a new order characterised by an awareness and responsibility based on the realisation of their own freedom to determine the course of history. Leaving aside for the moment the serious objections to this theory as exhibiting a 'scientific', i.e. value-neutral character, there is some plausibility in suggesting that explicating the nature and content of normative regulation before the historical realisation of this epoch is impossible, and that the proletariat will develop its own moral system from within the fundamentally rational mode of production which is alleged to be the *telos* of the development of history in the materialist theory.

This position was most systematically developed in response to the historical crisis of Marxism by Lukács in *History and Class Consciousness*. This work is the supreme example of the attempt to solve the moral-practical impasse created by the gap between theory and practice, through the complete ontologisation of Reason into the single process of history.[15] I will presently consider this project and its epistemological implications in the light of William Outhwaite's systematic analysis of the problems of appropriating the object domain in social theory.[16]

However, once the concept of the emergence of a proletarian consciousness in a mass revolutionary form has been abandoned, the obligation to produce a theoretically valid justification for practical-critical activity becomes desperately important. If such a justification is not forthcoming, then talk of 'praxis' geared towards emancipatory change is simply nonsensical in a historicist/materialist framework. It is this position in which Critical Theory finds itself in the post-war period.

AVOIDING THE DEAD END OF THE DIALECTIC

Habermas is anxious to avoid the 'dead end' of the negative dialectic as conceived in the work of Horkheimer and Adorno. However, he does not see the possibility of continuing the theory and practice of the heritage of Marxism without fundamental reorientation. He says:[17]

> The destruction of the historico-philosophical certainty that the industrial working-class and the European labour movement were targets for possible, theoretically induced processes of enlightenment and bearers of a politically pursued, revolutionary transformation is not, in my view, entirely a disadvantage. ... Theoretical attention is [now] directed not so much to the conflict-engendering mechanisms of the economic system as to the defence mechanisms following in the wake of crisis, to the ways in which the state deals with conflicts, and to cultural integration. In consequence of this displacement of conflicts, warded off at the institutional level, to the periphery, to the geographical, social and psychological margins, the groups in which conflict potentials accumulate need not be identical with the bearers of politically enlightened and organized action.

Simply, then, without recourse to the arguments of orthodox historical materialism (à la Lukács) Habermas wishes, and believes it to be possible, to furnish a critique of capitalist society and its power structures in a way that will provide rational support for organised action to effect a transformation of this society into a better one. The abandonment of faith in the proletariat is a serious obstacle to overcome from a purely theoretical point of view as we have noted. The normative validity of practical-critical activity must be established without appeals to the historically determined privileges of potential bearers of a new order.

But Habermas creates even greater difficulties for himself by mounting a comprehensive critique, and ultimately a rejection, of the Marxist category of labour as providing the normative grounding for the critical validity of the concept of alienation. Finally, Habermas compounds the difficulties of his task by suggesting that a theory of universal pragmatics can be normatively grounded in truth by exposing the presuppositions of communicative action geared towards producing intersubjective understanding, and yet simultaneously denies the possibility of a successful transcendentalist programme in providing foundational anchor points for theoretical or practical reason. Habermas's sociological and moral vision is a complex affair – it is an ambitious attempt to synthesise the contributions of several classical thinkers previously regarded as proponents of irreducibly antagonistic theories of man and society

It is difficult to disentangle Habermas's thought from developments within the more traditionally orientated Marxist framework. Moreover, Habermas insists that we should not try to do this. He has proclaimed that he wishes to carry on the task of constructing a critique which '... is guided by the intention of recovering a potential for reason encapsulated in the very forms of social reproduction'.[18] In this sense his work is to be regarded as a continuation, with much revision, of the Marxian heritage in 'different historical circumstances'.[19] Yet the task remains the same: it is the task of analysing[20]

> ... power constellations that suppress an intention intrinsic to the rationality of purposive action and linguistic understanding – the claim to reason announced in the teleological and intersubjective structures of social reproduction themselves – and that allow it to take effect only in a distorted manner.

This statement of intent is, of course, consistent with an orthodox approach in that it is characterised by a focus of analysis which seeks to explicate the relationship between power and false consciousness. There are several features of Habermas's approach, however, which distance it from orthodox Marxist theory. I will deal with these under two headings: one which examines the shift from the vision of the proletariat as bearers of the capacity to transcend the false consciousness of 'distorted communication', and a second which examines the shift from conceiving the source dynamic of rational emancipation as grounded in the 'externalisation theory' of social labour, to the revised Habermasian theory of Communicative Action.

FAREWELL TO THE WORKING CLASS?

I use this phrase from Andre Gorz in full awareness of its irony for theory which still links itself with the Marxian heritage. The context of the emergence of Critical Theory has already been discussed at some length. The historical realities of Fascism and Stalinism were cited as being decisive factors in reorientating theory away from the article of faith which suggested that 'the industrial working class and the European labour movement were targets for possible theoretically induced processes of enlightenment and bearers of a politically pursued, revolutionary transformation ... '. The scale of these historical tragedies is immense, yet it is not a pathologically optimistic dogmatism which refuses to accept these phenomena as historical-empirical refutations of Marx's theory of revolution. Indeed, the rise of Fascism can be explained consistently in Marxian orthodoxy as a gruesome stage of alienation induced by economic crisis and the triumph of reactionary ideologies.[21] Similarly, the enormities of Stalinism are actually entailments of the orthodoxy under perfectly uncontentious interpretations which suggest that the development of productive forces in Russia could not possibly sustain a successful socialist polity. It has often been said that a proletarian revolution requires a proletariat.

I have no wish and no obligation to embroil myself in this debate. I am simply making the point that it is not the dialectic of history which has necessarily engendered the revisions in theoretical consciousness manifest in the emergence of Critical Theory and its rejection of large chunks of the orthodox corpus of historical materialism. 'History', under certain consistent interpretations, can still be adequately handled by the orthodoxy. Rather, it is the a priori significance of the critique of instrumental rationality which, together with the tragic scale of dashed hope in the face of the cataclysms in Fascist Europe and Stalinist Russia, has made major revisions in the orthodoxy easier to countenance. But the historical genesis of these *intellectual* revisions is quite distinct from the validation of the revisions.

What must be explained and demonstrated, theoretically, is why the proletariat no longer feature as the bearers of the potential for emancipation. I think this will become clear in the second point to be discussed, i.e. the revision of the normative grounding of social critique in the displacement of Marx's category of labour by a theory of Communicative Action. For the grounding of a project of theorising a universal pragmatic in the Habermasian sense requires a jettisoning of the limitations placed on intersubjectivity in a conventional, historical materialist conceptualisation of the proletatiat, an appropriation of Weber's critique of modernity and, simultaneously, a refutation of Weber's emphatic insistence on the impossibility of a scientific validation of moral-practical principles which are, after all, the aim of the whole Habermasian project. But the irony of all this is that a theory which does not want to detach itself from the fundamental tenet of the primacy of history in the development of consciousness – i.e. Habermas's theory – must provide an a priori rejection of the role of the proletariat; for, as we have argued above, history has not provided one. What has happened is, as Habermas says,[22]

> ... *revolutionary self-confidence* and *theoretical self-certainty* are gone, and not only because in the meantime bureaucratic socialism has turned out to be a worse variant of what was to be fought against.

This is a very guarded statement as to why we should abandon the orthodoxy, and I hope to shed more light on the reasons behind Habermas's cautious approach to dismantling the orthodoxy in the course of this examination of his work. But for the moment we may summarise the Habermasian divergences from orthodoxy which come under our first heading before we delve into the subterrain of Marxist theory.

The suggestion is that for various reasons there has been an emotional breakdown of resolve. Because of this, Habermas suggests that the place of 'very general theoretical assertions' which have hitherto provided the basis for political praxis, must be replaced by less ambitious and more rigorous insights into our socio-historical situation. We require[23]

> ... an empirical analysis that is sensitive to contemporary history and is social scientifically well informed – an analysis that differentiates its object not only according to stages of development, mode of production, class structure and political order, but according to national traditions, regions, subculture and according to contingent historical relations.

The materialist base of the orthodoxy, therefore, is now supplemented by an analysis of superstructural variables. This is not heretical in itself, bearing in mind the conventional insistence upon a dialectic of interaction between base and superstructure in orthodox interpretation. However, the primacy of the materialist reduction and the role of the proletariat disappear with the next programmatic prescription – a reiteration for which I apologise:[24]

> Theoretical attention is [now] directed not so much to the conflict engendering mechanisms of the economic system as to the defence mechanisms following in the wake of crisis, to the ways in which the state deals with conflicts, and to cultural integration. In consequence of this displacement of conflicts, warded off at the institutional level, to the periphery, to the geographical, social and psychological margins, the groups in which conflict potentials accumulate need not be identical with the bearers of politically enlightened and organised action.

In addition to this, Habermas eschews the relevance of what for generations has been the watchword of Marxist struggle, that of the unity of theory and action in praxis. In reply to Agnes Heller's suggestion that the Habermasian project exhibits a disquieting tendency to fall into the academic trap of distancing theory from action, Habermas refers to important developments in systems theory which has ' ... sharpened our eye for the consequences of a[n] ... extremely heightened social complexity'.[25]

He goes on to say[26]

> One who uses the word 'revolutionary' in more than a metaphorical sense has to acknowledge that with the incalculability of interventions into deep-seated structures of highly complex societies, the risk of catastrophic alternatives ensuing also grows.

The theoretical distance from orthodox Marxism, therefore, is clear even at this point. A more fundamental revision of doctrine is, however, effected by a complete restructuring of the normative groundings of revolutionary critique in that Marx's basic tenet of Historical Materialism, the primacy of the category of labour, is to be replaced by the concept of Communicative Action.

COMMUNICATIVE ACTION VERSUS THE CATEGORY OF LABOUR

Habermas first mounted his critique of the Marxist conception of social labour as the normative ground of revolutionary critique in *Knowledge and Human Interests*. His thesis that all knowledge was the product of irreducible human interest orientations was an attempt to construct epistemology as social theory in a way that avoided the traditional impasses of philosophical reflection anchored in a monological concept of the knowing subject. In this work he suggested that the universality of the category of labour as embodying an emancipatory *telos* was flawed in that Marx's conception of human labour led us only to an understanding of theoretical knowledge in an instrumental-technical sense. Control of nature was the guiding cognitive interest which appeared in the form of scientific rationality in its modern, nomological, hypothetico-deductive scheme of explanation. The evacuation of moral-practical interest from this form of rationality results in the Weberian vision of the 'disenchanted' world. Emancipatory interests are banished from discussion as being beyond the grasp of reason, where reason is circumscribed by the limits of instrumental-technical operations authorised by the *methodology* of the natural sciences. Epistemology is replaced by a concept of theoretical validity which operates within pragmatically orientated parameters of predictive success or failure. Habermas suggested that Peirce's systematisation or rational reconstruction of these pragmatically orientated processes captured the essentially historical nature of the particular interest orientation characteristic of natural science.[27]

In presenting this conception of the nature of natural science Habermas linked the modern institutional practices of the scientific community with Marx's philosophical anthropology. In short, Habermas suggested that the *telos* of social labour had indeed come to fruition in the technological mastery of the modern world, but that the emancipatory potential of the teleology of labour envisioned by Marx had signally failed to materialise. Again, this is not to be regarded as an empirical matter. The Marxian notion of the teleology of labour is not to be dispensed with by the Popperian procedure of 'falsification'. Indeed, it is an entailment of Habermas's reconstructivist theory of science that such methodological operations are exposed (as ideological) by the theoretical validity of the Marxian category of labour. Rather, it is Habermas's contention that the category of labour has only limited validity in that it correctly captures the essence of a particular interest of humanity that has universal application, that of the historically universal interest of mankind to control nature. It is valid, therefore, only as a category of human action which heuristically appropriates the essential relationship between man and nature. In other words, as the basis of a theory of history with a critical intent, it fails to capture the multi-dimensionality of the practical activity of humanity. The category of labour as it operates in Marxian theory, therefore, shrinks the concept of species-being to that of an instrumental historical potential. The development of Reason, by consequence, is, and only can be, conceptualised in its instrumental orientation. The emancipatory interest postulated by Habermas must, therefore, be located in relations of practical activity other than those orientated to a mastery over nature.

Habermas's contention in *Knowledge and Human Interests* was that a new 'action-theoretic' category which captured the essential relationship between man and man over and above the relationship to nature must be developed, systematised and integrated into a social theory which could once again ground its own critique and future praxis. In brief, this emancipatory interest is identified and theoretically appropriated in the concept of *Communicative Action*, or action geared towards 'reaching understanding'.[28] Critics have been voluble in attacking this attempt to shift the grounding of Marxian theory away from the category of labour. Among them Heller and Giddens have suggested that to do so is to remove the possibility of establishing a concept of alienation which furnishes the basis of critique. I append a small discussion of this debate here and refer the reader to it.[29] (It is important to us in that here we can see that both camps seem to confirm the point I shall make later, which suggests that the notion of *human purposivity* subsumes both labour and communication. My point will be that the emancipatory *telos* which Marx sought and which Habermas seeks is contained in this irreducible 'category'.) However, Habermas is fully aware of the impressive history of the 'expressivist' or 'externalisation' theory of objective spirit which is proffered as the philosophical-anthropological backing for these theorists' reading of Marx's conception of labour. Habermas rejects this whole school of thought, culminating in Hegel, and says that we must construct social theory without ontological or transcendental backing.[30] In other words, he suggests that there is a middle way of epistemology which does not, in a non-immanent way, posit the Hegelian absolute or, in Kantian fashion, assume the universal validity of reason without recognising reason itself as historically located.

THE REINSTATEMENT OF RATIONALITY

It is Habermas's contention that theoretical developments in the human sciences and philosophy have had to orientate themselves to the project of constructing a theory of rationality. This much has been suggested by our review of Finnis, who, from the standpoint of the Natural Lawyer, recognises legal science as a sub-category of social science and, in addition, acknowledges that the empirical ordering of social phenomena requires a scheme of ideal-typical concepts which, if a pluralistic subjectivism is to be avoided, must be constructed from a point of view of practical reasonableness which claims a universal validity. That we have found his attempt to ground the normative-moral validity of such a standpoint deficient in no way invalidates the analysis which holds such a project to be obligatory. Habermas is similarly disposed to this requirement. Although his normative theory focuses upon the rational reconstruction of Communicative Action, his thoughts on the construction of a general social ontology are germane to our discussion in that they continue and develop the themes of integration in social science, Natural Law and moral theory; a theme which I am anxious to pursue as comprehensively as the vehicle of this work will allow.

Habermas suggests that philosophy has surrendered its 'relation to totality' by abandoning, or more accurately, being forced to abandon, that intention which Habermas holds to have been common to all philosophies, that is '... the intention of thinking being or the unity of the world by way of explicating reason's experience of itself'.[31] In the language of modern philosophy, as Habermas puts it:[32]

> Philosophy can no longer refer to the whole of the world, of nature, of history, of society, in the sense of a totalizing knowledge. Theoretical surrogates for worldviews have been devalued, not only by the factual advance of empirical science but even more by the reflective consciousness accompanying it. With this consciousness philosophical thought has withdrawn self-critically behind itself; in the question of what it can accomplish with its reflective competence *within the framework* of scientific conventions, it has become metaphilosophy. ... [I]nterest is directed to the formal conditions of rationality in knowing, in reaching understanding through language, and in acting, both in everyday contexts and at the level of methodically organized experience of systematically organized discourse.

In emphasising the central role which his theory of communication will play he says, in the light of these remarks:[33] 'The theory of argumentation thereby takes on a special significance, to it falls the task of reconstructing the formal-pragmatic presuppositions and conditions of an explicitly rational behavior.'

Habermas wants to explain the role that sociology can play, and what qualifications of competence it claims in addressing itself to this rationality problematic. He suggests that following the (alleged) refutation of all attempts to provide a first philosophy or a foundational structure for knowledge, a new constellation of relations between philosophy and the sciences has opened up.[34] The normative and universal claims of theories of modern empirical science can no longer rely upon a transcendental-philosophical guarantee of validity. Habermas refers us to the work of Kuhn and others[35] in the history and philosophy of science as authority for this remark. In a dense formulation he suggests the following relationship between science, history, and sociology:[36]

> This claim [i.e. the claim to the embodiment of a universally valid scheme of cognitive rationality at the core of modern scientific claims to the theoretical knowledge] can be tested only against the evidence of counterexamples, and it can hold up in the end only if reconstructive theory proves itself capable of distilling internal aspects of the history of science and systematically explaining, in conjunction with empirical analyses, the actual, narratively documented history of science in the context of social development. What is true of so complex a configuration of cognitive rationality as modern science holds also for other forms of objective spirit, that is, other embodiments of rationality, be they cognitive and instrumental or moral-practical, perhaps even aesthetic-practical.
>
> Empirically oriented sciences of this kind must, as regards their basic concepts, be laid out in such a way that they can link up with rational reconstructions of meaning constellations and problem solutions.

I think that this means that the universalistic claims of modern science do not transcendentally ground themselves and, therefore, are to be regarded as pragmatically rational in a provisional sense dependent upon their favourable comparison with other external candidates or counter schemes of problem-solving. In other words a conceptual pragmatism reigns, and, simultaneously, appears as the problem for theory. The ultimate task of evaluation of the rational authenticity of scientific schemes of cognition falls to an all-encompassing socio-historical methodology of the 'rational reconstruction of meaning constellations' in which 'problem solutions' can be analysed from a privileged perspective. That is (bearing in mind the fundamental theoretical tendencies of the Frankfurt School in general, and Habermas's approach as presented in *Knowledge and Human Interests* in particular)[37] from the perspective of critical reflection on the multi-faceted processes of historical development which does not take analytical categories as *given*, but as *constituted* by and in the dialectic of development. Thus a historical sociology is now to be the arbiter of rationality. But, we must ask, how can we do sociology without accepting the methodological prescriptions of that stage of reflective consciousness which, it is alleged, arrogated to itself a now-invalidated universalism. Perhaps, in the light of this last remark, the question should be: how *did* we do it?

By this I mean what *a priori* warrant do we have for making these assertions concerning the inadequacy of metatheoretical systems? For if Habermas is asking us to reject the ontological project from Fichte to Hegel to Marx, and to reject the transcendental/critical approach of Kant, he cannot argue that the ontological project implies the falsity of Kant's system, adduce reasons to show the falsity of the ontological system, and then conclude that both are false.[38] In other words, Habermas requires an Archimedean point from which to criticise epistemology. It is the epistemological debate to which we will now turn our attention.

APPROPRIATING THE OBJECT DOMAIN: CONSTITUTION THESES

We can formally present the epistemological problem to which Habermas turns by noting, as Outhwaite says, the absence of a systematic examination of the role of 'object constitution' in the philosophy of science.[39] Constitution problems are those which concern '... the establishing of an object of scientific inquiry'.[40] He suggests that there are two main approaches. The first, 'constitution (e)', he refers to as epistemic constitution and quotes Thelma Lavine thus:[41]

> ... the epistemological principle that mind does not apprehend an object which is given to it in completed form, but that through its activity of providing interpretation or conferring meaning or imposing structure, mind in some measure constitutes or 'creates' the object known.

The second approach, 'constitution (o)', exhibits an ontological emphasis and is exemplified by Marx's comments in the first and third Theses on Feurbach:[42]

> The chief defect of all hitherto existing materialism ... is that the thing, reality, sensuousness, is conceived only in the form of the *object* or of *contemplation*, but not as *human sensuous activity, practice*, not subjectively. Hence it happened that the *active side*, in contradistinction to materialism, was developed by idealism – but only abstractly ... The materialist doctrine of the changing of conditions and of education forgets that it is people who change circumstances and that the educator must himself be educated.

Outhwaite wants to show how these two distinct approaches are often assimilated to each other in unsatisfactory ways, and to illustrate the importance of the specificity of the constitution problematic in metascientific analysis. The assimilation of (o) and (e) can be presented, says Outhwaite, in the following way:[43]

> One can construct a crude sort of continuum between a strong and a weak thesis of constitution. Both ends of the continuum share an emphasis on the creative activity of the knowing subject, but whereas the strong version holds that the subject is entirely free
> whereas the strong version holds that the subject is entirely free to

> construct its own 'world', weak versions hold that this creative activity of the subject is guided, either by the nature of the object known or by the transcendental conditions of any (human) perception.

There is no continuum of constitution stretching through to empiricism. Rather, empiricism can be perceived as the antithesis to the whole project of constitution in that its basic tenet is to take the object as 'given'. Consequently, concept formation from the empiricist point of view becomes the central concern of analytic philosophy in the form of language analysis. (Notably Carnap etc. – 'thing language'.)[44] The strong extreme of constitution (e) is represented by the philosophical perspectivism of Nietzsche:[45]

> To the extent to which knowledge has any sense at all, the world is knowable: but it may be interpreted *differently*, it has not one sense behind it, but hundreds of senses – 'Perspectivity'. It is our needs that *interpret the world.*

This view, characterised as an epistemic or subject-centred view, is curious in that the connections with Marx's thinking is obvious: the emphasis on needs shaping knowledge, a theory of ideology in the sense of 'perspectives' given the interests of a ruling class. But Marxism lends itself to a constitution thesis nearer to the ontological end of the spectrum as in the work of Lukács:[46]

> In this tradition, the emphasis is on acts of practical constitution (o), which may include constitution (e) as a subordinate activity. Cognition, and theoretical activity in general, lose the privileged place which they enjoy in most philosophical systems. Instead they are understood as aspects of human practice as a whole, and may, further, *be judged* [my emphasis] by their contribution to this practice.

We may suggest, then, that the Habermasian programme, as with Marx, can be characterised, from an epistemological point of view, as an attempt to furnish a constitution thesis from a perspective of human needs or interests. For Habermas, however, the suggestion is that the orthodox Marxist approach to the problem of a fully developed theory of history and society constitutes its object domain in an impoverished way – i.e. from the perspective of technical control – and that this precludes the possibility of reaching an understanding of the conditions which can satisfy our ultimate need – emancipation.

However, Habermas is not suggesting that Marx's approach to epistemology is altogether flawed. Habermas recognises Marx's identification of labour as an interest perspective as perfectly valid in the domain of theoretical or technical discourse. Bearing in mind Habermas's conception of a consensus theory of truth for both theoretical-descriptive and normative-practical statements, the possibilities for redeemability in truth of criticisable validity claims in this former mode of discourse are, ultimately, to be referred to the ontological reference point of the natural world. This is the object domain appropriated by the hermeneutic intent conditioned by this technical perspective – the interest in material reproduction of the species expressed in the fact of labour. The possibility of knowledge of the natural world, therefore, rests upon universal consensus, or, as Peirce would have it, upon the universal conformity with experience of empirical hypotheses. The growth of this mode of technical rationality in the modern world, however, has assumed massively hegemonic proportions and now lays claim to settling normative-practical issues which lie beyond its scope. The 'need-perspective' of humanity which can provide universal consensus – and thus, for Habermas, truth in these matters – is the need-perspective of emancipation announced in the fact of language which, like labour, announces a universal intent of the human species-being. This intent is intersubjective understanding through communication in order to fulfil the need to reproduce genuinely integrating structures. These structures are 'genuine' in that they meet the essential requirements of all. At this point we may try to clarify the ideas which Habermas has on the way in which these two need-perspectives feature as epistemological categories in legitimate and illegitimate ways.

Briefly, the epistemological function of human interests rests upon the universality of these interests. We interpret the world in ways conditioned by our interests. Our essential interests, therefore, provide essential interpretations. Universal consensus, therefore, if achieved in a free and co-operative manner, becomes the sign of essentiality and thus lays bare the fundamentals of the human condition. But with the growth of an instrumental orientation to knowledge we lose sight of the essential nature of our species-being and its potentials. This last observation is important in that it introduces us to the dichotomous conception of System/Lifeworld. This will be examined presently, but for the moment we must note that it is a crucial distinction in Habermas's social theory which facilitates the identification of, on the one hand, strategic (power-backed – sectional interest), as opposed to genuinely Communicative Action, on the other. In short, the Lifeworld is the accumulated, hermeneutically produced stock of knowledge and practices of a communication community which serves as the independent reference point for the validation through rational debate of normative – practical claims to rightness. 'System' refers to that complex of institutions which exert steering effects upon society in this domain by rigidifying, narrowing and constraining the autonomous development of the Lifeworld through the legitimation of sectional interest.

This conception can be assimilated to Marx's notions of reification in general, and commodity fetishism in particular. That is, a complex of hegemonic institutions determined by the economic base and serving the sectional interest of the economic élite, serve to produce a legitimating background of 'common sense' which conditions the distorted hermeneutic activity of a community. Thus interpretations, explanations and claims to normative rightness are furnished by reference to a false 'Lifeworld' which is not the product of unfettered, co-operative attempts between actors to reach understanding, but is rather an ideological storehouse of legitimating disinformation produced by the perverse, and strategically orientated, categories of interpretation which are instrumentally efficacious in a limited, non-generalisable form. The cognitive categories of this system, however, masquerade as being universal in their application. Thus, from a Habermasian conception of epistemology as being grounded in need-perspectives, system knowledge, as opposed to Lifeworld knowledge, can never achieve ultimate validity in universal consensus – the criterion of truth – as the perspectivity of system knowledge does not derive from universal needs. If, however, we operate with this consensus criterion of truth, we need to know what it is that makes a consensus genuine as opposed to a system-steered integration effect.

We may approach Habermas's work, therefore, by asking how successful he is in coping with the constitution problem he sets himself, bearing in mind the requirements of universality of such a thesis if it is to serve as the normative grounding for critique and emancipatory praxis. The question will be directed therefore, at the transcendental validity (or 'quasi-transcendental' as Habermas claims) of the identification of the human interests which provide the 'perspective', that is, condition the object domain, appropriated by the constitution thesis suggested by Habermas.

OUTLINE OF THE SOCIAL THEORY

For Habermas, labour and language are presuppositions of the concept of society. Society reproduces itself through structures which facilitate material reproduction and socialisation. The interest perspective of material reproduction is instrumental-technical. The interest perspective of the socialisation process is normative-practical, and, Habermas contends, emancipatory as opposed to simply integrational. How, then, does Habermas attempt to demonstrate this emancipatory potential?

Briefly, the contention is that we can 'reconstruct' the stages of the moral development of society and relate it to the ontogenetic development of the individual personality to show that there exists a developmental logic to the capacity for handling normative-practical issues. In this way we can show that the *telos* of normative development aims at an integration of personality and society through the institutionalisation of debate free from coercion where rational consensus guarantees the generalisability of interests.[47]

The generalisability of interests is guaranteed in this way because it is secured by reason: disagreement over interests presupposes inter-subjective agreement over the conditions possible for such disagreement. These conditions are embedded in the 'deep structure' of communicative competence and may be revealed by analysis of the presuppositions of discourse. The dimensions of this theory are synchronic in that we are able 'quasi-transcendentally' to ground the universalisable aspects of Reason-now-constituted, and diachronic in that we can reconstruct the developmental stages of our present competence. This latter dimension distinguishes the theory from a Kantian conception of transcendental critique in that Reason is not abstracted from history and that the programme of universal pragmatics is made refractory to empirical analysis. I shall examine the synchronic dimension of the theory first, and then discuss the claims that its central contentions can be derived and supported by a (diachronic) reconstruction of its historical development.

COMMUNICATIVE ACTION

In his inaugural lecture of 1965, Habermas said:[48]

> What raises us out of nature is the only thing whose nature we can know: language. Through its structure, autonomy and responsibility are posited for us. Our first sentence expresses unequivocally the intention of universal and unconstrained consensus.

Although I will suggest that we need to know much more about ourselves if we are to know the nature of our language, this statement provides the focus of the Habermasian programme of universal pragmatics. Support on a synchronic level is adduced from a theory of argumentation conjoined with an analysis of speech acts. Starting from a theory of rationality, and with reference only to the dimension of descriptive knowledge, Habermas distinguishes the cognitive-instrumental model of knowledge characteristic of the self understanding of the modern era, from a wider conception of rationality connected with the ancient conception of *logos*.[49] Communicative rationality is characterised, therefore, as:[50]

> ... the unconstrained, unifying, consensus-bringing force of argumentative speech, in which different participants overcome their merely subjective views and, owing to the mutuality of rationally motivated conviction, assure themselves of both the unity of the objective world and the intersubjectivity of their lifeworld.

We shall first examine the argument which seeks to demonstrate the presupposition, through argumentative speech, of a mutually accepted conception of an objective, external world before examining the implications of the 'Lifeworld' or social world of intersubjectively understood normative expectations.

In the elucidation of this point we are asked to consider a piece of knowledge (*p*) shared, in the form of identical beliefs, by A and B. A, as a speaker in a group of communicators, asserts *p*. B, as an isolated actor, selects means, conditioned by his belief that *p* is the case, in order to achieve a desired end. Thus the knowledge *p* is utilised in two different ways. In the case of A, the utterance of *p* in relation to the facts is directed towards reaching understanding amongst a community of speakers and hearers. The utterance of *p* by A is rational in that it presents a criticisable validity claim – a claim that can be accepted or rejected for a good reason.[51] In the case of B, the relation of *p* to the facts and the possibility of grounding the belief make possible a successful intervention in the world. The rationality of the action is constituted by the fact that the actor's plan implies both a belief in the truth of *p*, and the expectation that such a plan can be brought to fruition under given conditions. The significance of the above considerations are summed up by Habermas:[52]

> An assertion can be called rational only if the speaker satisfies the conditions necessary to achieve the illocutionary goal [i.e. the genuinely social goal of successful (authentic) interaction which attends the solely cognitive, propositional component of the speech act] of reaching an understanding about something in the world with at least one other participant in communication. A goal-directed action can be rational only if the actor satisfies the conditions necessary for realizing his intention to intervene successfully in the world. Both attempts can fail; the consensus sought can fail to come to pass, the desired effect can fail to take place. But even the nature of these failures shows the rationality of the expressions – *failures can be explained.* [My emphasis]

An analysis of the conditions of rationality begin, therefore from the concepts of language as communicative medium, propositional knowledge and its intersubjectively presupposed referent – objective world. The ways in which knowledge is used in the above examples generates two perspectives from which we may judge the *telos* of rationality: instrumental mastery to allow successful intervention in the world (orientation to success); and communicative understanding (orientation to understanding). This, obviously, bifurcates our route of analysis. Habermas characterises these separate routes as (i) 'realistic', and (ii) 'phenomenological'; the former being the instrumentally orientated aspect of rationality and the latter communicative.[53]

The 'realistic' mode of rationality starts from the ontological presupposition of the world as the sum total of what is the case and characterises the rationality of action on this basis.[54] In this sense we are speaking about problem-solving in the sphere of instrumental orientations. We can derive an analogue of rationality, therefore, by imputation of a problem-solving capacity to a system. The system's change in state can be interpreted as a solution to a problem and understood as a *quasi-action* as though it were an expression of a subject's capacity for action.[55] We must note, however, bearing in mind our earlier discussion of the distinction between Lifeworld and System, that[56]

> ... this is to speak of rationality only in a figurative sense, for the susceptibility to criticism and grounding that we require of rational expressions means that the subject to whom they are attributed should, under suitable conditions, *himself* be able to provide reasons or grounds.

The 'phenomenological' mode of rationality does not initially assume the realist ontological position. It concerns itself with the problem of constitution of the object domain. 'The world gains objectivity only through *counting* as one and the same world for a community of speaking and acting subjects'.[57] The point here is that the concept of an object world is relativised to a community of communicators, but that such a conception is necessary if intersubjective understanding and co-ordinated action is to be possible within it:[58]

> Through this *communicative practice* they assure themselves at the same time of their common life-relations, of an intersubjectively shared *lifeworld*. This lifeworld is bounded by the totality of interpretations presupposed by the members as background knowledge. To elucidate the concept of rationality the phenomenologist must then examine the conditions for communicately achieved consensus; ...

The phenomenon of disagreement will prove to be of much interest to us as we progress. Let us note for the moment that it involves the following: where A disagrees with B – about *p*, A is reflexively committed (or, as we may put it, that it is dialectically-necessary) for A to acknowledge the fact that he understands B, that B's belief that *p* is at odds with his (A's) belief that *not-p*, that both beliefs cannot simultaneously be tenable (by virtue of the necessary 'one world' condition of the possibility of intersubjectivity) that the world is as it is independent of the subject's beliefs, and that resolution of the disagreement demands recourse to criteria which are external to both parties to the dispute. Habermas quotes Pollner with regard to the challenges which arise for communicators once these fundamental issues of overcoming disagreement are acknowledged:[59]

> ... a mundane solution may be generated by reviewing whether or not the other had a capacity for veridical experience. Thus, 'hallucination', 'paranoia', 'bias', 'blindness', 'deafness', 'false consciousness',

> etc. insofar as they are understood as indicating a faulted or inadequate method of observing the world serve as candidate explanations of disjuncture. The significant feature of these solutions – the feature that renders them intelligible to other mundane reasoners as possible correct solutions – is that they bring into question not the *world's intersubjectivity* but the adequacy of the methods through which the world is experienced and reported upon.

Thus the realist and phenomenological perspectives merge into a concept of rationality based on their recognition of the conditions of intersubjectivity. But we need to expand this argument to encompass characterisations of rationality in modes of communication other than those of descriptive truth or instrumental calculations. Habermas says:[60]

> ... we call someone rational not only if he is able to put forward an assertion and, when criticized, to provide grounds for it by pointing to appropriate evidence, but also if he is following as established norm and is able, when criticized, to justify his action by explicating the given situation in the light of legitimate expectations.

This is also true of situations where expressions of desires, moods and feelings are the subject of attempted communcation. We must, therefore, examine the way in which normatively regulated actions and expressive self-presentations relate to criticisable validity claims.

It is here that we must examine Habermas's incorporation of a theory of speech acts, notably from Austin and Searle. First, we must note the distinction between the locutionary/constative force of a speech act, and the illocutionary/performative force of such. Simply, the constative act can be seen as the use of language to affirm or deny a proposition. The intention is to make a claim containing an objective reference to something in the external world which may be assessed as to its truth or falsity. The illocutionary or performative dimension of speech acts, however, can be seen as an aspect of social action in that:[61]

> Truth is merely the most conspicuous – not the only – validity claim reflected in the formal structures of speech. The illocutionary force of a speech act, which produces a legitimate (or illegitimate) interpersonal relation between the participants, is borrowed from the binding force of recognized norms of action (or evaluation); to the extent that a speech act is an action, it actualizes an already established pattern of relations.

An example of the genuinely interactive content of the speech act can be easily presented. 'The snow is melting' contains the unstated element, assumed by speakers, 'I hereby assure you that ... '. In other words, we have a normative expectation attendant with the constative element which leads us to consider the interactive use of language and the[62]

> ... vast array [of] tacit warnings, guarantees, admonitions, cautions,

> recommendations, and promises, and the like, that are just as mu[ch] part of ordinary speech as the propositions proffered in the *cognitive use of language*.

There are, thus, at this stage, two intersubjectively presupposed worlds: the world of external objects and the world of recognised norms of social action that we may or may not accept, thus raising the issue of validity claims of normative rightness. Pusey notes that[63]

> In the cognitive use of language a speaker and hearer may not choose explicitly to bring normative validity claims into question. Conversely, of course, an interaction that focuses explicitly on the legitimacy of this or that norm may not involve any explicit reference to external facts. Yet both types of claim are *internally connected in the very constitution or ordinary language communication*. In this sense both are simultaneously joined in the typical speech-actions of (adult) speakers with a minimum of communicative competence.

A third world of reference is implied in speech acts, that of the inner world of authenticity or otherwise which is, at the very least, at issue in the interaction between speaker and hearer:[64]

> In the expressive use of language, every typical speech action carries the voiced or silent guarantee of the *sincerity* or truthfulness with which I, the speaker, am expressing my inner feelings, needs, and intentions to you, the hearer. It is in that dimension that speech orients you, the hearer, to 'my' inner world of feelings and motives, and so to an assessment of the *authenticity* (or inauthenticity) of what I say.

The concept of Communicative Action is important in allowing us to understand the essential difference between (and the possibility of integration of) 'system' and 'action' perspectives on the approach to modelling society. On the one hand, it reorientates debate concerning the universal applicability of moral prescriptions, and, on the other, it offers the opportunity of developing a new scheme of ideal-typical heuristics with both critical intent and possibly apodictic validity. In opposition to the typology of action formulated by Weber, which is structured in a means–ends framework of limited application, Habermas speaks of an additional category of action orientated to reaching understanding. The former typology Habermas characterises as instrumental and 'strategic', the latter as 'communicative'. Habermas makes four distinctions in the concept of action:[65]

Purposive

> In the model of purposive-rational action, the actor is orientated to the realization of an end; the success of his or her actions is measured by the extent to which he or she succeeds through

intervening in the world ... in bringing the intended states of affairs into existence.

Instrumental

Actions orientated to success are termed *instrumental* when they are understood as following technical rules and can be appraised from the standpoint of the efficiency of goal-orientated intervention in the physical world.

Strategic

Actions orientated to success are termed *strategic* only if they are understood as following rules of rational choice and can be appraised from the standpoint of the efficiency of influencing the decisions of rational opponents. Instrumental actions (as well as the corresponding tasks) can be *combined* with social actions as elements of roles; strategic actions are themselves a class of interactions.

Communicative

I speak of *communicative actions* when social interactions are co-ordinated not through the ego-centric calculations of success of every individual, but through co-operative achievements of understanding among participants. In communicative action participants are not orientated primarily to their own success but to the realization of an agreement which is the condition under which all participants in the interaction may pursue their own plans.

From our discussion of Habermas's theory of Communicative Action we have seen that his basic contention in respect of a moral epistemology is that claims to normative rightness can be discursively redeemed, that is, grounded in truth through a process of rational, co-operative discourse. Where do the truth correlates of these claims to normative-rightness lie? We are told that their existence is presupposed in discourse and that we are to look to the stock of 'facticity' in the Lifeworld which,[66] 'In phenomenological terms ... comprises that vast stock of taken for granted definitions and understandings of the world that give coherence and direction to our everyday actions and interactions.' The Lifeworld is the reference point for our normative claims to justification announced in our moral-practical pronouncements, protestations, agreements or disagreements. It is the background against which our criticisable validity claims can be assessed. It is clear, therefore, that we cannot hope for certainty or truth in a conventional epistemological sense in our search for grounding of these claims. We may, however, with the rich, if imperfect, resources of our history of hermeneutic experience in the Lifeworld, plus the 'quasi-transcendentally' grounded, formal principles of rational discourse as our universally presupposed rule book, strive to produce consensus over normative issues. This consensus is to serve as a criterion of truth in these matters.

We have seen how Habermas wishes to present his theory of universal prgamatics as a valid grounding for critique which obviates the alleged defects of an abstract (i.e. non-historical) rationalism or thoroughgoing transcendentalism. Habermas also wants to avoid duplicating the mistake of non-immanently introducing some notion of Reason or human essence equivalent to the Hegelian posit of the Absolute. However, he does want to provide a priori justification for his claims, scope for empirical testability of these claims, *and* furnish us with a criterion of normative-moral validity – that is, a *formal* criterion of validity through rational consensus. Despite the comprehensiveness and innovation of these ideas I think that there are some very traditional epistemological problems within the corpus of the Habermasian project. I will consider them in three stages.

1. I will consider some immediate problems which arise from the attempt to operationalise empirically the theory of discursive will formation and show that there is no escape from the problem of theory-loaded observation at the empirical level.
2. This brings us back to the need for an a priori justification of the theory in the attempt to save the 'reconstructivist' programme from vacuity. Here I examine Habermas's critique of Hegel and the allegedly illegitimate posit of a notion of the Absolute in the attempt to provide epistemological foundations.
3. I want to look at Habermas's suggested replacement of Hegel's conception of the Absolute, and Kant's transcendental ego, by a theory of the social subject derived from the concept of discourse. Here there are serious difficulties inherent in the notion of a consensus theory of truth, and with the theory of argumentation on which it rests.

THE IDEA OF GENUINE CONSENSUS

If we accept Habermas's analysis of the presuppositions and implications of language use, after first accepting that language is a fundamental category of society, we must then accept that a form of social organisation which inhibits or represses communication – that is, seeks to destroy the conditions under which the essential intersubjectivity of society can realise its full, unifying potential – is an irrational, pathological form of organisation. The problem reduces, therefore, to identifying if and when we have reached a genuine consensus as opposed to an ideological one – for as Lukes has clearly shown, observable disagreement is not an essential feature of the existence of manipulated, power-backed, sectional interest-serving, social regulation.[67] In other words, what would be the normative *content* of an undistorted discourse (or what Habermas used to refer to as an 'ideal-speech situation') as opposed to the *form* of it? It must be said that Habermas does not now employ this phrase, and I have avoided it as far as possible. The logic of Communicative Action and 'unrestrained consensus', however, remains unchanged. Lukes's remarks are, therefore, perfectly relevant. Lukes notes that Habermas says:[68]

> ... only communicative ethics guarantees the generality of admissible norms and the autonomy of acting subjects, solely through the discursive redeemability of the validity claims with which norms appear. That is, generality is guaranteed in that the only norms that may claim generality are those on which everyone affected agrees (or would agree) without constraint if they enter (or were to enter into) a process of discursive will-formation.

Lukes is concerned to discover just how this assertion can claim to have any validity as an empirical hypothesis. Habermas admits that,[69] ' ... a direct confirmation of this hypothesis would be possible only in the form of a practical discourse among the very individuals or groups involved'. This, of, course would require some prior knowledge of what kind of claims ought to attract consensus on the basis that we have some knowledge of what interests are suppressed in conditions of systematically distorted communication. Thus we require a:[70]

> '... model of the suppression of generalizable interests' which serves as a 'counterfactually projected reconstruction' specifying of all the actors in question which of their interests are generalizable', how they would interpret their needs, and which norms they would accept as justified under conditions of unconstrained communication.

Lukes's perfectly fair point is that real individuals who have been moulded in suppressive ideological environments may well exhibit desires and wants which they perceive to be consonant with, or constitutive of, their interests, yet which conflict with the hypothetically postulated conception of 'generalisable' interests. In this case the hypothesis is saved from disconfirmation by the conclusion that the discourse under observation is systematically distorted. If, on the other hand, we posit ideally rational agents in discourse:[71]

> ... the whole argument turns on the nature of those agents and the constraints set by the conditions. If these together are such that the appropriate answer is necessarily reached, then the counterfactual hypothesis emerges as vindicated but only because it has been so formulated that it must do so. Ideally rational people in an ideal speech situation cannot but reach a rational consensus.

As might be expected, this problem is not overcome by introducing Piagetian or Kholbergian criteria into the operational content of the hypothesis. This line of criticism springs from the formalism of

Habermas's theory of universal pragmatics. Moral validity is conceived as that which springs from consensus in the process of undistorted communication. We cannot, therefore, specify the content of the consensus prior to its being achieved. But this leaves us with the problem of being unable to identify when the consensus was truly unconstrained. Paradoxically, if we knew what the outcome of a free and co-operative consensus would be, there would be no need to have the debate in the first place, for any debate which contradicted it would be designated as systematically distorted. The 'quasi'-transcendentality, therefore, of the theory of universal pragmatics is empirically unoperationalisable. And if it *were* operationalisable it would not need to be operationalised – we would require no empirical justification for a theory which we already knew to be true a priori. Can it be known a priori?

A FIRST PHILOSOPHY?

Habermas holds that Hegel correctly identified the defects of a Kantian critique of knowledge, in that the transcendental foundations of Kant's system were themselves the product of earlier stages of cognitive development. These stages culminated in the specifically Cartesian conception of radical doubt. In other words, Habermas holds that Hegel was right to point to the unacknowledged assumptions which underpinned the transcendental orientation to the scope and limits of knowledge. Habermas, therefore, is basically in agreement that epistemology must be a reconstructive programme of analysis which logs the development of categories through a process of determinate negation in the development of mind. His dissatisfaction with Hegel, then, is not aimed at the general historicist approach to a first philosophy. Rather it is focused upon Hegel's inconsistency in appropriating the fundamental concepts of objective spirit in the explication of its essence. Hegel, it is alleged, conjures from nowhere the essential structure of *Geist* – the Absolute – thus destroying the reconstructivist nature of the historical enterprise by introducing a speculative, non-immanent conception. This serves as an arbitrary ontological assumption on which he then constructs an interpretative framework which, in turn, serves as a theory of historical development. For, after all, if Hegel is right about the nature of *Geist* in its contentless, yet potentially dynamic, primeval form, then everything else he says about it must be true; for we are starting with the truth from which all reality stems, and to which it must return.

The valid objection which Habermas makes is that we are entitled to ask how Hegel knows what he claims to know about the essence of history. The answer which Hegel gives is contained in the Phenomenology of Mind, which, by its very title, gives us a clue to the inadequacy of the reply. That is, Hegel, through reflection on his own thought processes, claims an insight into the nature of its workings. That thought is bound by logical principles of development, which constantly strive to overcome contradiction in order to produce a systematic closure in the attempt fully to explain the phenomena which it takes as its object, is unquestionable. To ask whether or not this process truly mirrors the nature of its object, however, is the central problem of epistemology. That is, the subject/object dichotomy – the alienation of thought from the world – still remains a live issue despite, for the sake of argument, the accepted validity of the phenomenological analysis of thought. Hegel attempts to overcome the impasse by interpreting this epistemological problem as an answer in itself. That is, this unanswerable question is not a question at all. It is interpreted as an ontological fact. For Hegel, there is no self-contained subject and no discrete sphere of objectivity – no separate worlds of ego and non-ego – there is just *Geist*: reality striving to overcome its inherent tension of contentless *Angst* in order to come to know itself. Reality is mind. It is pure thought thinking about itself and its goal is to come to realise this through the resolution of the contradictions which it must posit in order to come into being as substance from pure form. This drama is played out in corporeal form in and through history where the individual and society symbolise the fundamental polarities of being: the particular and the universal; the finite and the infinite. The former is posited as the fundamental antithesis to the Absolute, a contradiction which must eventually be reconciled with its *universal* essence. Hegel, however, does not tell us how he knows all this.

Habermas's critique of Hegel simply points to this inadequacy at the root of the Dialectical Philosophy. However, Habermas accepts the general validity of the historicist or reconstructivist approach. We must remember that the general criticism of Kant is that this feature of his critique is absent. So, Hegel, it seems, is right to attempt to reconstruct the developmental stages of Mind; Kant is wrong not to do so. But Hegel is allegedly wrong to posit the Absolute in the fashion that he does. How, then, do we attempt to reconstruct the development of Mind, or Reason, without positing the motor of its structured dynamic, its essence – or, in Aristotelian parlance, the *logos* which expresses its purpose or *telos*?

The first thing that we must note is that the concept of development through determinate negation, the very conception of the possibility of reconstruction in the Habermasian sense, or the very notion of evolutionary history, obliges us to posit an end to be achieved. In turn we are obliged to posit an object, the essential nature of which must be compatible with this end, indeed *productive of it*, which is assumed to be the content of the developmental process. The nature of the essence of the object will condition the nature of its processes of development. If we are to suggest that historical analysis has a part to play in epistemology, it is important that we get these presuppositions of explanation in the right order. This is essentially what Michael Schmidt asks us to consider in his penetrating critique of Habermas's concept of evolution.[72] This evolutionary epistemology, we must remember, is the basis of the Habermasian theory of universal pragmatics. This theory is supposed to avoid any non-immanent preconceptions, but, as I will try to explain, historical or reconstructivist approaches to epistemology cannot achieve this categorial self-sufficiency.

Hegel did not start with a concept of the Absolute which then led him to deduce its necessary processes. He started with the phenomenon of the idea of a here-and-now-self with questions about its relationship to that which was not-self; questions which had been unsatisfactorily dealt with by previous selves, and which had inspired those who followed their lead to attempt to correct their mistakes by identifying contradictions and synthesising new answers: that is, trying to create new ideas about the world from something which was held to be important or essential about old ideas about the world. Furthermore, there was held to be something more encompassing, less flawed about these new ideas. All of this implies, as we have clearly noted, a presupposition not only of a temporal continuum in which a process of development may take place but of the ability to identify and track an object through this continuum. Thus the idea of a developmental history of *anything* cannot be held to spring from some presuppositionless void.

In other words, if there is a here-and-now of Reason-now-constituted, this implies the existence of prior stages, which must, in turn, admit of the possibility of *identifying* these prior stages, in terms of essential characteristics, *as* prior stages. That is, prior stages of Reason which link to preceding and succeeding stages of development. Thus, from the phenomenological point of departure of Reason-here-and-now, we are claiming that it is possible to identify its prior stages, and the nature of the contradictions or pregnant tensions within it, which brought about its determinate metamorphosis. That each stage of Reason can be *identified* as a stage of Reason, or that each stage of a particular object, can indeed be identified as a stage in the development of that particular object, presupposes that the object has throughout the process an essential attribute or number of attributes which carry the potential for development, and that the inquirer has knowledge of these attributes. In the case of a reconstruction of the development of Reason, the unquestionably artificial circumscription of a particular epochal paradigm of thought quite obviously presupposes a clear understanding of what is a constant attribute of thought and what are transient, epiphenomenal, destined-to-be-determinately-negated aspects of thought. This is only possible if we know what the goal of the developmental process of thought is supposed to be – for relevant phenomena can be identified only on the basis that they play a significant part in bringing about the end state.

Quite simply, the particular proposition, say, 'The ultimate meaning and purpose of the world is revealed to us in the organisation of nature', may be an aspect of Reason which is condemned to the graveyard of history as Reason develops along its inexorable path. But the form of the proposition *per se*, and the *conception of the direction of this inexorable path* must be imputed and assumed to be in evidence at each and every stage of epochal development. Some permanent, essential feature or features of thought must be held to be in evidence if we are to be able to identify thought at all. Quite obviously, these assumptions are required to make historical or reconstructivist analysis possible – they cannot be *historical* discoveries.

This is true, of course, at the synchronic level. Such presuppositions underpin the assertion that there exist contemporaneous, yet radically distinct, systems of cognition. Therefore, the cultural relativist, who wishes to assert the paradigmatic localisation of not only cosmologies and value-systems but of basic logical systems, falls foul of this unavoidable requirement to assume prior knowledge of the identifying constants of Reason. Hollis gave us a clue to this in his analysis of the conditions under which different logical systems might be encountered.[73] Thus Hegel is not to be criticised for positing the Absolute as the essence of Mind. Its 'absoluteness', in some form, is an unavoidable entailment of the concept of Mind as an evolving entity. It is necessarily the case, therefore, that a reconstructivist approach to the critique of Reason must posit a core of rationality which must be present at each stage of development in order that identification of discrete stages of development may be cognitively apprehended and, more fundamentally, that the concept of development can be coherently espoused. What, after all, is supposed to be developing?

These reflections do, of course, leave scope for arguments as to the precise nature of this essence of reason. But, epistemologically, there is absolutely no room for debate about its essential existence in *some* form. The point is that the essential information we seek is logically prior to historical analysis – it is a presupposition of the possibility of a historical investigation of anything. The quarry is, as Strawson has succinctly put it, the search for ... a core of human thinking which has no history'.[74]

Habermas's solution to this problem is one which attempts to provide a non-transcendental, historically immanent, yet a priori valid grounding for a reconstructivist theory of Reason. Unlike Hegel who posits a priori the genesis of Reason and then charts its inexorable course, Habermas suggests that it is possible to identify the *telos* of Reason by a transcendental analysis of Reason-now-constituted. His theory of Communicative Action admits that Reason is a developing entity, and that Reason-as-we-now-know-it is but a stage in this historical process. According to Habermas, the essential categories of contemporary Reason can be adduced by reflexive analysis of its presuppositions. These are not, however, as Kant would have claimed, to be taken as universal categories; that is, features of Reason having *a*historical and trans-historical validity, but as categories which characterise the modern mind. Thus these categories of rationality are to be seen to have *quasi*-transcendental status. However, these categories of rationality are to feature as the validating structure underpinning emancipatory claims. They are to serve as the content of a hypothesis which suggests that the goal of Reason, laid bare in communication, is egalitarian emancipation. This claim may then be subjected to a historic-empirical, reconstructivist investigation – a critical sociology – which will be the final arbiter of its validity. In other words, we are to be able to synthesise epistemological categories which allow us to ground a theory of substantive rationality. This makes possible the social-scientific critique of social and political organisation with a rational, practical intent; a theory of society which supplies the missing components from Weber's sociology and Marx's theory of praxis. But the irony is obvious: if the quite unhistorical, Kantian-style reflexive critique of here-and-now-Reason correctly yields these morally critical categories, what is the point of employing them as the explanatory basis of an historical sociology – *an interpretive scheme* – which can but confirm the 'hypothesis' that history has always been leading us towards this emancipatory consciousness?

THE NEED FOR FOUNDATIONS

The conceptual framework of these historical investigations informed by this 'quasi-transcendental' analysis can *but* confirm the 'hypothesis'. This does not mean that the claim which constitutes this 'hypothesis' is false or uniformative. It does mean, however, that our *historical* analysis, if accurate, will be transcendentally grounded. In other words, if Reason is what Hegel says it is, we would need Kant's categories to find this out. This logical result is not a cue to embrace paradox and mystery, it is a simple *reductio ad absurdum* of the possibility of a non-transcendental, historicist epistemology. A transcendental grounding of the appropriate categories of such a reconstruction are the point of departure for such an enterprise and thus Habermas cannot coherently claim to have presented a radically innovative epistemological alternative to Kant. In fact what Habermas does do – or must do to be successful – is to replace the Hegelian conception of the Absolute with a Kantian conception of the Absolute. The Habermasian 'Absolute' of which we speak is nothing more nor less than an ethically loaded theory of the historical subject. Habermas attempts to substitute a *dialogical* conception of the social subject for the *monological* transcendental ego; a social subject formed in the historical and social processes of communication, as opposed to a ready made thinking-thing. Our analysis of his theory of truth, however, to which we will attend immediately, points to problems with this project.

CONSENSUS AS A CRITERION OF TRUTH

Professor Pettit has observed that Habermas's conception of social justice invites a question which was of considerable interest to the ancients. In Plato's *Euthyphro* the question is raised as to whether the Gods will something because it is good, or whether it is good because they will it.[75] In Habermas, the parallel is whether a claim secures rational consensus because it is true, or whether it is true because it secures rational consensus. The problem we might face is that, given, for the sake of argument, that we could reasonably stipulate the counterfactual conditions of undistorted communication, could we rely on the normative prescriptions which it produced? Might not some forms of normative regulation ensue from consensus which had the effect of undermining the institution of the communicative forum itself? And might we not know this prior to discussion? If this is so, the theory of universal pragmatics based on consensus loses coherence.

Pettit notes that it is crucial that Habermas preserves the relationship between truth and argument. This is irrefutable in that Habermas's whole project rests upon a theory of argumentation. Habermas says: 'We call those statements true for which we are able to argue.'[76] Pettit says:[77]

> On the basis of this consideration he rejects the assimilation of truth either to the subjective experience of certainty or to correspondence with objective fact. The first move would break the connection between truth and argument because certainty is a private experience ... [the second], assimilation to correspondence ... [,breaks the link] ... because ... the facts in correspondence with which truth allegedly consists must be admitted to be transcendent and inaccessible entities: they are not identifiable after all with the events and objects which form the data of our experience.

Pettit takes this to entail the possibility of two options for Habermas: to adopt the operational account of truth via methodological procedure – e.g. verificationism – and this, as is made clear in *Knowledge and Human Interests*, is unacceptable to him. He therefore must adopt what Pettit calls the sociological approach:[78] 'This says that truth is that property which belongs to propositions and theories that are capable of commanding consensus.' He quotes Habermas:[79]

> I may ascribe a predicate to an object if and only if every other individual who could enter into discussion with me would ascribe the same predicate to the same object. In order to distinguish true from false statements, I refer to the judgment of others – in fact to

> the judgment of all others with whom I could ever undertake a discussion (among whom I include counterfactually all the partners in discussion that I could find if my life history were co-extensive with the history of mankind). The condition for the truth of statements is the potential agreement of all others. Every other person would have to be able to convince himself that I ascribed the predicate 'p' correctly to the object *x* and would have to be able then to agree with me. Truth means the promise of achieving a rational consensus.

With regard to Plato's profound enquiry we may now assume a technical interest. Both the methodological and sociological criteria of truth may be construed in ways which parallel the criterion of 'the Good' in our initial enquiry into the role of consensus:

1. Analytical: truth consists in the ability to command consensus; i.e. true because it commands consensus. (Methodologically, true because it passes the verification tests.)
2. Non-analytical: truth consists in the property which accounts for the consensus; i.e. commands consensus because it is true. (Methodologically, passes the tests because it is true).

Pettit thinks that there is good reason to infer that Habermas wishes his sociological theory of truth to be construed non-analytically. This is the property of a proposition which offers reasons which move people to give this proposition their assent. Habermas says:[80]

> The truth of a proposition stated in discourse means that everybody can be persuaded by reasons to recognize the truth claim of the statement as being justified.'

This truth consists in the inherent reasonableness of the statement, in its 'warranted assertability'. Thus Pettit concludes:[81] 'The property is not defined by the ability of the proposition to command consensus but serves rather to explain that ability.' This is not a novel conception. It is C. S. Peirce's notion that:[82] 'The opinion which is fated to be agreed to by all who investigate is what we mean by the truth.'

What is novel about Habermas's approach, however, is the specification of the consensus which Pettit identifies as having two stages. The first is that the type of discursive argument which a claim must be able to survive must be radical in the sense that every level of validity from first order observation to the assumptions of the conceptual scheme upon which the observation rests must be open to question. This is uncontentious. But Pettit notes that the second stage is not only contentious but 'obscure'. This stage specifies the formal properties which guarantee the 'interrogative space' which allows the radical freedom of movement between argument levels specified in stage one. These are, of course, the formal requirements of the communicative forum or ideal-speech situation. They are summed up, by Pettit as[83]

> ... the general symmetry requirement ... that participants enjoy a fair distribution of chances to speak; more specifically they mean that each participant can open or continue any line of discussion, that each can put forward any assertion or call any into question, that the participants are equally free in their relations with one another to express their most intimate feelings, and that they are equally free to make demands on each other and offer each other help.

Pettit, quite rightly, questions both the need and the efficacy of bringing about such a situation. He points out that no amount of democratisation of the debate will ensure the interrogative space demanded in stage one. If the participants are lazy there will not be much movement between argument levels or dedicated pursuit of deep assumptions. But Pettit is not particularly concerned about this insistence on the democratic, co-operative format. He wants to know why Habermas feels the need to go into such matters:[84]

> Is it not enough to know that truth is that property which would cause a proposition to be accepted by anyone, even when the proposition is subjected to radical interrogation? Why does one have to be told how to ensure that the interrogation is radical in the case where a number of people open discussison with one another, rather than each thinking the matter out on his own?

Pettit offers an illuminating distinction at this point between two conceptions of consensus. One form of consensus he terms distributive; the other collective:[85]

> A proposition admits of distributive consensus if and only if each person assents to it, whether or not after discussion with others and whether or not in awareness of what others think.
>
> A proposition admits of collective consensus ... if the people involved discuss it as a group and come to an unanimous decision about it.

What Pettit finds troubling is that Habermas conceives of truth on a basis which would admit of distributive consensus and then introduces redundant specifications of the ideal speech situation to supplement it. Pettit says:[86]

> Only the first step in Habermas's specification of his theory of truth is to the point; to be rational a person's assent must indeed be able to stand the test of radical argument. There is no reason to say that the assent must be forthcoming as a part of collective consensus achieved in an ideal speech situation; it may coincide with the judgment that would appear on such an occasion, but that is neither here nor there. The discourse in which Habermas says that

> questions of truth are raised is normally an interpersonal affair and it may be this which leads him to put a collective construction on the consensus required by his theory. But, as Habermas himself admits, discourse may also be internalized, it may only involve a single thinking subject.

At what point may discourse only involve a single thinking subject? Habermas rejects this Cartesian doctrine of the monological model of consciousness and we have devoted much time to explicating his view on the matter in this chapter. I think that the project of universal pragmatics runs into very serious difficulties here in that there is a systemic inconsistency between Habermas's conception of the dialogical or communicative subject derived from his theory of argumentation, and the objectivity requirements of his theory of truth. I think that resolution of this issue is the key to the major problem in Habermas's social theory. It also points to a possible solution to a more general problem of social theory in any form: that is, how do we simultaneously make sense of society and preserve the integrity of the concept of the individual?

8

Isolation, Communication and Co-operation

We have seen that there are problems with the Habermasian programme of universal pragmatics at the epistemological, empirical and normative-critical levels of the theory. I think that the problems can be solved, but it requires a wholesale reconstruction of the approach to the concept of a critical sociology. I have already said that I think that a transcendental, or dialectically-necessary, approach to the analysis of practical reason is the key to the resolution of the epistemological problems of a critical social science. I also think that Gewirth's methodology achieves logical necessity in this analysis. However, Gewirth's solution, which concludes this work, requires the acceptance of a *monological* subject. Presenting Gewirth's argument is not too difficult, but preparing the ground for its acceptance is. I think that much of the problem lies with the understandable reluctance, on the part of theorists who wish to criticise the present organisation of society, to concede to the claims of a methodological, or more accurately an epistemological, *individualism*. This word has some unwholesome connotations and is often received as an indication that the worst aspects of libertarian propaganda are about to follow. The implicit assumption is that any understanding of society premised upon a conception of the isolated individual as the basic unit of analysis must rule out the possibility of grounding a critique of bourgeois or possessive individualism. This is not so. Gewirth does employ the notion of an isolated 'thinking thing' to derive his moral principle but, as Beyleveld and Brownsword say, in commenting upon MacIntyre's charge of 'egocentricity' against Gewirth's conception of rights:[1]

> [Gewirth's conception of agency] is not a presumption of individualistic as against communitarian motivation ... Gewirth's concept of agency is not 'egocentric'; it is not a concept that applies only to agents in societies that attach supreme importance to individuals. No assumption is made that agents value their purposes competitively against the purposes of others, or that they do not identify their purposes with group or community values, or even that they do

not conceive of their individual selfs as subordinate to the identity of some group or community.

If this is true, those of us who wish to argue for the collective and co-operative organisation of social life have little to fear from an individualist conception of rationality. This chapter, then, in pressing further critical points against the Habermasian programme of universal pragmatics, is not inspired by the desire to proselytise on behalf of libertarian notions of the individual at the expense of theories of social co-operation. Rather, it aims to clear up the epistemological mess created by the attempt to transcend individual reason and elevate pragmatics, and procedurally supervised consensus, to the position of arbiters of moral truth.

There are, as we have seen, three main components of the Habermasian programme: a pragmatist/hermeneuticist epitemology; a theory of the communicative or dialogical subject; and a procedural/consensus theory of validity for normative-moral claims. We have seen that these systemic components exhibit complex interrelations and condition each other at all levels of analysis. I want to argue for a rejection of all three and a reinstatement, in direct opposition, of a rationalist epistemology, a theory of the transcendental subject, and dialectical-necessity as the criterion of apodictic truth for normative-moral claims. We can present the general features of the Habermasian system as follows:

1. The foundation of the whole system is the general pragmatist notion common to Marx, Nietzsche, Peirce, Dewey through to Quine and on to Post-Modern thought, that human interests condition interpretations of phenomena. This fuels the hermeneutic drive to conceive of conflicts of meaning and explanation as conflicts of interest. The corollary is to conceive of the solution to intellectual conflict as the harmonisation of interest.
2. The task of even abstractly conceiving of a harmonisation of interests within the framework of the Cartesian subject – an isolated 'thinking thing' – appears so daunting that the idea of an essential unity of consciousness which can avoid the Cartesian problem becomes a matter of urgency for the pragmatist system. Solutions lie within the whole, problems lie within the individual; to solve the problem of the validation of consciousness, therefore, Pragmatism locates rationality in the whole.
3. However, knowledge is required by and for individuals. Universalisable validity must be a product of universalisable interest-orientation. Thus individuals may participate in argument procedurally designed to exclude any sectional-interest interpretations/explanations/justifications. This *procedure* can but secure consensus. Consensus is the sign of genuine decentred rationality as opposed to a subject-centred distortion which is merely 'the product of division and unsurpation'.[2]

The procedural or consensus theory of truth is then a product of the Pragmatism in (1) and the anti-Cartesianism of (2). In fact, consensus criteria make no sense other than in a pragmatist/hermeneuticist scheme which has already set up the requisite ontologies of Lifeworld and communicative/social subject. We have rehearsed a fairly comprehensive argument against the attempt to square the notion of the consensus theory with a non-relativist conception of normative rationality. We must turn, therefore, to the elements of the theory which have made this disappointment unavoidable.

RECONSIDERATION OF CATEGORIES

Let us consider Habermas's contention that the orthodox or 'scientific' Marxist conception of the category of labour as the grounding for a critical sociology is too narrow to provide a theory of rational emancipation.The suggestion is that the orthodoxy deals only with the instrumental-technical relations of man to nature and whose *telos* is one of technical mastery or control. Habermas sees this fundamental human interest in material reproduction as being the basis of a universal need or interest-perspective which, in its historical reconstruction, shows us how the epistemological categories of theoretical discourse – the rationality of the natural sciences – have developed into modern positivistic conceptions of experimental, technologically pragmatic methodologies which eschew the intrusion of value-considerations into the sphere of genuine science. This missing normative-moral dimension from the sphere of what is sanctified as 'genuine' science is contained in the underdeveloped – or, rather, systematically repressed – interest-perspective of emancipation. This cognitive relation is a relation not simply to the natural world but to the world of man *in* nature, and, in particular, to the relations of identity and legitimate expectations between labouring language users. Thus normative-moral discourse is grounded in the interest-perspective which is identified as a presupposition of the fact of language use. Language implies the category of communication.

Labour and Communication, for Habermas, thus appear as distinct categories with distinct teleologies which may be cognitively apprehended at the empirical level through a reconstructivist methodology informed by an understanding of the *telos* of these fundamental activities. Epistemologically, we were referred to the consensus theory of truth which grounds itself in relation to distinct ontologies – domains of facticity. These object domains are hermeneutic products, not *dingen-an-sich* beyond the grasp of the subject. In this way, Habermas suggests that the subject-object separation or alienation is resolved by putting consciousness back in touch with its object; for the object domain, as we have noted, is constituted by consciousness in a process of historical-practical development. Consensus as a criterion of truth suggests an epistemology wholly based on a conception of generalisable interests. These genuine interests according to Habermas, provide a rational perspective through socially unified agreement about the way the world is or ought to be, rather than sectional, power-play-legitimated pronouncements about it.

What we must note first is that although Habermas makes a firm distinction between Labour and Communication – where only the latter is held to bear an emancipatory *telos* – both labour and communication are *practical* categories. The traditional division between theoretical-descriptive and practical-prescriptive modes of reason do not feature as part of the Habermasian constitution thesis or, for him, as legitimate epistemological distinctions. *All* knowledge, for Habermas, is the product of practical activity which seeks to resolve the problems of the human condition. Yet the traditional Kantian conception of the dichotomy between theoretical and practical reason is reformulated by Habermas quite sharply in his epistemology. So sharply, in fact, that the category of Labour as a practical dimension of species-being plays no part in the validating interest-perspective of normative-moral or emancipatory claims to truth. I think there is confusion and error here. In attempting to create dichotomous *interest*-perspectives as the foundation for an epistemology of emancipatory hermeneutics, the Habermasian programme has lost sight of the generic, unifying category of all social action, namely, purposivity. This category subsumes both labour and communication. Thus the schismatic construct of interest categories in labour and communication loses purchase on the real nucleus of social action. In short, whether we are discussing 'real, living, labouring individuals', bureaucrats, social scientists or communicators, we are concerned with *agency* and *agents* capable of reasoning theoretically and practically in some form. This nucleus of social action is, then, a category so fundamental that it is presupposed by the very concept of an interest or a need, even if such an interest or need happens to be universal. In our discussion of Weber we saw that the concept of social action presupposed all manner of assumptions about the world and the possibility of intervention in it. Thus it should be perfectly obvious that the 'categories of labour and communication not only appear further up the theoretical ladder than the concept of purposive social action, but that there is a mountain of metatheoretical analysis underpinning the very concept of employing a means to an end. To suggest that the even more rarified notions of, on the one hand, ends which must be pursued by all, and, on the other, ends which are pursued by some at the expense of others, are to serve as *epistemological foundations* is simply not plausible or possible. It will be instructive to press these points further in relation to Habermas's theory of argumentation. We must bear in mind that it is from the idea of argumentation that he derives his category of communicative action and his theory of the social subject – a subject which he suggests is made whole *through* intersubjectivity.

LABOURERS AND COMMUNICATORS

Habermas accepts the force of the argument which seeks to expand the Marxian conception of the category of labour into a richer, morally charged conception of human potential. Indeed, this is what Habermas has done by showing that society cannot reproduce itself simply by transforming and controlling the external world – normative expectations and regulations must be *intersubjectively* instituted in the world of interpersonal relations. But a brief glance at the 'Preface to a Contribution and Critique of Political Economy' would provide us with the opportunity of interpreting Marx in a way which showed that his conception of Labour already entailed the complex intersubjectivity which Habermas wishes to reserve solely for the realm of Communication.[3] The bottom line of Habermas's critique is that the fact of labour does not have teleological implications which can be reflexively reconstructed to provide the theoretical grounding for a theory of generalisable interests. In short, the fact of labour does not announce the moral nature of humanity. I think this is wrong, and that if we pursue this matter we will be able to find out where the mistake lies.

It seems that we must ask some simple questions. First, can a thing which cannot communicate in the Habermasian sense labour in the Marxian sense? The answer is no. Secondly, does the capacity to communicate presuppose the social/historical constitution of reason – that is, does it presuppose the *dialogical* nature of consciousness? The answer is no. Thirdly, even if we accept the validity of a Habermasian conception of an evolution of consciousness structures reducible to an interactive base of economic and linguistic forces of development, does this prove or presuppose the historicity of reason? Again, the answer is no, unless we accept that what passes for reason is reason – and this we clearly cannot do if we are to construct a critical theory of society. Fourthly, and most importantly, we must think carefully about the following point: in respect of fundamental competences, do I need these capacities to get *into* an argument, or to get out of one? In other words, can a thing which, prior to a communicative interaction, is held to be incapable of understanding what a resolution of an argument entails, get into an argument in the first place? If the answer to this last question is no, then the inference from the theory of argumentation from which the action category of Communication is derived is absurd. If I am right about these issues, then there are interesting consequences for social theory. I shall try to substantiate these claims.

By Communicative Action, Habermas means the activity of reaching understanding. Intersubjectivity is a presupposition of this particular form of practical action. Technically, it is the giving and taking of claims and justificatory reasons which are assumed to be discursively redeemable, that is, assumed to be grounded in truth. This pronouncement does not rest easily with the post-structuralist forms of hermeneutic analysis, as will be noted instantly by readers of contemporary texts. Nevertheless, we cannot accept the validity of this category of action as a component of a typology of social action, *and* simultaneously hold to a post-structuralist conception of language which denies the implications for objectivity which attend the independent existence of the sphere of the signified. I do not have the opportunity on this occasion to enter into a detailed review and critique of the body of literature which seeks to deny this claim.[4] Nor is it necessary for me to do so. Whatever the status of these analyses, I intend only to make a logical point about the conception of the subject which Habermas must adopt.

We are interested in the logic of the claim which suggests that we must reject the individual subject *because* of the nature of communication. The post-structuralist position in respect of the constitution of discourse may throw some light on the problem and can be conveniently summarised as follows. Sturrock says of anti-rationalists such as Foucault, Derrida, Lacan etc:[5]

> So there is a common ideology at work here: of dissolution, of disbelief in the ego. The self, in the traditional sense, would appear to such as Foucault as a 'theological' notion, a false transcendence. All these thinkers are against authority and against metaphysics. They do not wish to transcend what they see, in pursuit of some hidden meaning which would 'explain' everything; they do not believe that everything can be explained. Nor do they hold with teleological interpretations of history.

He goes on to say:[6]

> To revert for a moment to the linguistic plane: what these ... thinkers have very influentially done is to advance the claims of the signifier above those of the signified. The signifier is what we can be sure of, it is material, the signified is an open question.

We cannot, of course, include Habermas in this neo-structuralist/Post-Modern camp. For it is the case that Habermas, whilst rejecting the Kantian conception of the transcendental ego and its Cartesian foundations in the conception of the isolated 'thinking thing', and of Hegel's conception of the Absolute, is emphatic in his rejection of the endless indeterminacy which is the consequence of the Post-Modern edifice of hermeneutic analysis. Habermas quite plainly states that criticisable validity claims must be assumed to be redeemable in truth through certain procedures, although these procedures reject the objectivating myths of orthodox epistemology. Thus Habermas walks a tightrope between transcendentalism and modern hermeneutic theory. It seems, however, that a middle way is impossible here. Initially, it will be seen to be impossible on the basis of the continued systemic coherence of the Habermasian programme for social theory; and secondly, and more importantly, on the basis of the possibility of coherence of any programme of social theory. This basic issue of thought and language can be dealt with swiftly and satisfactorily, at least for those who have accepted the basic contentions formulated in the early chapters of this book.

SIGN AND SIGNIFIED

If we accept language as a presupposition of society, as we do, we must unpack the implications of this conception if we are to present an expanded analysis of this notion which gives us an understanding of the role of intersubjectivity through discourse and its normative-moral implications for practical rationality. Language is a system of signs. Signs are arbitrary tokens which can be conventionally institutionalised between language users. If they are not tokens of something, then they are not signs – noises or marks on paper or sand or stones, or movements, are not signs. When Post-Modernists say that the sign is 'material', we must remember that it is the *intensional* analysis of the sign which allows us to conceive of its *extension* as a particular material object class.

The analysis of language does not depart from the concept of a sign. The concept of a sign rests upon the understanding of something to be signified. Something cannot be signified without a sign, but there can be things to be signified in the absence of signs. If signs are being swapped then we have discourse, even though this may not be rational discourse; if signs are being swapped then we have intersubjectivity – by definition – even though this intersubjectivity may be incomplete from the point of view of one or another participant in the sign-swapping interaction. Thus we can characterise intersubjectivity as the recognition that signs are in play – not necessarily that they are successfully interpreted – and this characterisation presupposes an understanding of a sphere of the signified to be conveyed. The material form of the sign is not an empirical indicator which suffices for the essential identification of the sign – the sign is identified on the basis of an assumption made by a prospective communicator. Whether or not the sphere of the signified is simply a tragic fiction, and whether or not the aporias of language are endless looping roads leading nowhere, I must make the distinction between signs and the signified – i.e. language and thought – and if I understand this distinction I must give priority to thought as the source of meaning – i.e. the source of the sign. Thus the theory of meaning must be *semantic* rather than semiotic.

INTERSUBJECTIVITY AND ASSUMPTIONS ABOUT SIGNS

If signs are in evidence, then there must be assumed to be thought. Phenomenologically speaking, this is a *dialectical* and not an *assertoric* claim. I can offer signs to a plant, or a dustbin or a typewriter but unless these objects have a conception of something to be signified – something other than a sign – and a conception of the difference between noises or marks and signs, then there is no intersubjectivity, even though my offering the sign presupposes the possibility If we posit the realm of the signified we must concede, as anti-rationalists from Nietzsche to Derrida point out so clearly, that this meaningful subjectivity, by its very nature, (a) *intends* an objective world, (b) structures representations into forms of '*belief that* ... ', (c) behoves us to choose between truth and falsity, and (d) by virtue of this, forces us into assertion and denial. In short, it can only produce an objectivating discourse structured by the propositional form, conditioned by the canons of logical consistency.[7] So when we talk of the sign giver, the language user, the potential communicator, we must remember that the sign implies all these objectivating categories and consequently we must live within the epistemological confines of these implications if we wish to talk about signs and truth. Post-Modernism is fully aware of the transcendental picture which takes shape behind the orthodox model of language and subjectivity. But it characterises the necessity of the implications, including the implied subject, as mere internal myth-making. The choice, then is between the transcendental subject or no subject. Habermas sees a third option: reject the logocentric subject, but opt for a kind of quantum phenomenal subject – one that pops in and out of existence at certain levels of communicative activity.

The theory of argumentation which Habermas uses is supposed to demonstrate the essentially interactive synthesis of communicative action as being something produced by at least two proto-egos in a unifying interaction of consciousness. This is the focus of my criticism in that this *dialogical* theory of consciousness suggests that, in so far as *validatable* discourse is concerned, we must initially conceive of the isolated social subject as a partial, incomplete ego, bereft of the capacity to synthesise the categories of critical validity but which, in interaction with other such partial egos, becomes whole in the act of communication. This is in contra-distinction to a *monological* conception of the ego, in which consciousness is complete in form alone, and develops through its own internal dialectic of reflection to synthesise the fundamental validating categories of its own existence as reason. This latter description covers Kant's conception of the subject and Hegel's *Geist* – not because these conceptions are in any great detail similar, but because the operation of reason as critique is held by both of them to occur *internally*, that is, *inside* Spirit and *inside* the transcendental subject. With Habermas, we need two to perform the activity of critique. Our criticism turns on this point: what kind of thing can be party to an argument? Can an ego argue with itself: that is, can we have a *monological* conception of an ego, whether it be Hegel's *Geist* or Kant's transcendental ego? We are not asking whether Hegel or Kant were right about their conceptions, but simply whether or not what they suggested is logically possible. If it is then they at least hold out a possible option for a theory of the subject. But can we furnish a theory of the social subject by way of a theory of communication which does not presuppose egos which are already fully capable of critical communication? If we cannot then this suggested alternative is doomed from its inception.

We must consider, therefore, the following argument. If critical intersubjectivity – that is, the capacity to understand assertions and denials, to check, to validate, to accept or reject – is produced through argument, then it cannot exist *prior* to argument. Intersubjectivity is the condition whereby two potential communicators forge a common conception in the sphere of the signified via signs. In other words, they each transform the private world of 'things significant' into 'things to be signified' via a public world of signs – they transform that which is accessible only to them into that which is accessible, in principle, to all. Critical intersubjectivity is allegedly produced in the process of acknowledging that attempting genuinely to communicate presupposes the existence of consensually redeemable, criticisable validity claims which are implicit in the basic act of potentially successful communication.

ARGUMENT, AGREEMENT AND DISAGREEMENT

To argue is to offer justifications for, or alternatives to, certain claims to truth. It presupposes a capacity to identify such claims *per se*, some conception of a criterion of validity for certain claims and thus some conception of what should warrant asset or dissent from a claim. In other words, the capacity to argue presupposes an understanding of what is entailed by the phenomenon of agreement or disagreement – and this, as Habermas rightly points out, is as applicable to moral discourse as it is to instrumental-technical discourse. Now, logically, that is, ideal-typically, for it to be possible for X and Y to argue is, as we noted in Chapter 7, to assert that they are in agreement – at least on the following points:

1. X understands Y.
2. X recognises the incompatibility of Y's views with his own.
3. X realises that 'incompatibility' means 'impossibility of both X's and Y's views being simultaneously true'.
4. Thus, in view of (3), X recognises that 'truth' must be an external quality and not a function of subjective belief. (Clearly, if it was a function of subjective belief both views could simultaneously be true and, hence, disagreement would be impossible.)

5. Both parties to a disagreement cannot possibly disagree over the issues 1–5.

Thus we require at least two parties who are equipped with sign giving and receiving capacities prior to any interaction which attempts to dispute the implied relations between signs and complicated combination of signs. This fundamental competence is a complex affair. We must remember that we have just discussed the implication of meaning and objectivating subjectivity which springs from the concept of the sign. Together with this we must note that to be a sign giver and recogniser is not simply to be capable of differentiating signs from non-signs – for every moment of my experience is a sign for me – it is that I must be able to differentiate sign givers and recognisers from non-sign givers and recognisers if I am to consider the possibility of giving signs. I must know what it is to take signs in my own private world and it may be that the realm of the signified is forever locked within me, for it is solely a product of my interpretations. If a dead leaf is a sign for me I must have a conception of the signified prior to my recognition of it as a sign. But I do not need to assume that the object which is significant for me is, by virtue of this fact, simultaneously a sign giver or taker.

SIGN TAKERS AND SIGN GIVERS

Furthermore, I do not need to ever have given a sign in order to recognise signs; I may simply be a sign taker. I cannot, as a sign taker, be bereft of the concept of language, for I recognise the relationship between sign and signified and between sign and sign; that is, I recognise that there are different significations produced when I acknowledge different configurations of signs. Thus I must have my own conception of language. For if I could only recognise one sign, I could not have a differentiated conception of the sphere of the signified and, hence, *no* conception of the sphere of the signified. So, as a sign taker I am a language user But this does not mean that I have to give signs – even though I must be *capable* of being a sign giver if I am a language user. From my point of view as a sign taker, therefore, Wittgenstein notwithstanding,[8] I can be a fully fledged language user with my own private language even though I do not give signs, i.e. do not use my understanding of the sign system to reciprocate my understanding of what is signified back to the objects which, for me, signify it. Under what conditions, then, would I attempt to utilise my understanding of a sign system to represent that which is signified to me to something which was not me? Whatever may prompt me to attempt this ambitious feat, I would have no possible reason to try unless I had reason to assume or, in the absence of this, could at least hold out the hope, that there were other things which were not simply significant to me, but that I could be significant to them. Thus, assuming that I hold out this hope and launch my career as a sign giver, I must fervently cherish the further hope that my sign system is compatible with theirs. If I give signs and, in return, receive signs with which I am familiar in contexts which I expect – I have good reason to celebrate my success in that I could reason inductively that this is too much of a coincidence to be a coincidence. From here I make the inductively rational assumption that somehow my sign system is broadly the same as that of other things which I tried mine out on in very simple ways. The simple point is that intersubjectivity is a possibility which I cannot rule out from the moment I differentiate signs – and that I can differentiate signs is a precondition of recognising signs at all. That there may be circumstances which contingently force me to attempt to achieve intersubjectivity is not a fact which miraculously brings about the conditions under which it is possible – although such circumstances might well induce those for whom it is already possible to rapidly cultivate a proficiency in this activity.

What we have now, then, is this: isolated sign takers with private language capacities implying the isolated subject and, thus, isolated subjectivity. This subjectivity cannot but *intend* the objective world – the true/false world. This isolated ego has no option but to structure its sign giving in the form of criticisable validity claims. What, then, is missing? According to Habermas, it is the capacity to understand what such claims entail in terms of justification in the face of non-acceptance. Let us not forget that we have got to this point with a *monological* subject – in fact Habermas's theory implies these competences – remember: we have to get into the argument before we can get out of it. Why, then, should parties to argument suddenly realise that the propositions which they find to be in contention are to be redeemed through consensus *when this option is ruled out by the objectivating sujectivity which is required to get them into the argument in the first place.* Just what is supposed to occur in the interaction? If, as is assumed by Habermas, communicators understand the difference between propositional forms, and even if they are not-reflexively aware of the implications of stating that something is the case, and all the epistemological and ontological baggage which comes with it, argument cannot make them aware of it – for the simple reason that unless this baggage was already part of the potential communicator's deep structure of competence he or she would not recognise an argument (or an agreement) in the first place. For argument and agreement are about something which is or is not the case; and we may refer to the conditions for disagreement (1) – (5) mentioned above. In other words, critical intersubjectivity and its ontological presuppositions are logically prior to the concept of argumentation. Thus the dialogical conception of the subject derived from the analysis of argumentation is necessarily false. My capacity for critical communication is guaranteed by my recognition of the sign. What I need to exercise this capacity successfully is another thing which thinks *like me*. I do no have to wait until one appears to be suddenly endowed with this capacity. Indeed, if I did not have this capacity I would never recognise such a thing if it did appear. In fact I never will be sure that one has appeared – this possibility remains an assumption which I simply can never revise. The problem of 'Other Minds' remains a live issue – but only for *Other* Minds. Intersubjectivity and the redeemability of criticizable validity claims is *my* problem because it is *my* idea.

PURPOSIVITY, INTERSUBJECTIVITY AND LABOUR

I asked whether or not a thing which could not communicate (by which we mean a thing which does not have the capacity to communicate) could labour in the Marxian sense of the word. To begin with, we may ask if labour in this sense is an empirical phenomenon. How do we know it when we see it? This issue is not seen as a problem for the Marxist theory of society – it is a Marxian presupposition of society. It is axiomatic that mortal humanity must interact with the material world to secure its continuation. Thus on the basis of this uncontentious claim, there is no problem with the operational criteria of the concept of Labour. We could say that when we see people engaging in activity which seeks to transform their world into useful items conducive to their basic requirements of subsistence and after this for their comfort or recreation, then we are witnessing the activity of labour. Hunting animals, building shelters, making clothes or cooking food can be conceptualised as labour in the sense of meeting these material requirements of continued existence of the human species. Why, then, do we not hold out the hope for spiders that we do for labouring humanity when we see these creatures intricately weaving a shelter-cum-tool-cum-weapon-cum-larder with a geometrical and ergonomic expertise of staggering proportions – precisely to fulfil the subsistence and reproduction requirements just listed?

Marx is perfectly clear on the essence of the distinction and, as is well known, had no difficulty distinguishing architects from bees (or spiders):[9]

> ... what distinguishes the worst of architects from the best of bees is namely this. The architect will construct in his imagination that which he will ultimately erect in reality. At the end of every labour process we get that which existed in the consciousness of the labourer at its commencement.

Thus the *fundamental* presupposition of society is not Labour conceived of as material reproduction, neither is it language, it is *purposive consciousness*, and given the inevitability of interrelations of the labour process, *the potential intersubjectivity of purposively rational beings and the normative implications contained therein.* The important point we can make here in respect of the debate concerning the social/communicative/dialogical versus the individual subject is this: the Marxian conception of the relationship between knowledge and social labour departs from the fact that any member of the human species cannot rationally deny that his own continuance depends on successful interaction with the natural world in the process of labour. Labour cannot be performed without entering into relations with others. Thus the interest perspective of Labour implies social co-operation even from the point of view of one who merely wishes to secure his own existence. The idea is that proper thinking cannot be done individually.

But this does not imply the rejection of the individual subject *even if we accept the interest-perspective of labour as an epistemological category.* For, even if we did, the notion of co-operative labour as a precondition of existence is a *transcendental result of the analysis of the conditions of practical success of the individual agent.* We cannot split the notion of labourer from communicator, thus reason, and the possibility of its practical application *together with the assumption that the nature and categories of this phenomenon of my experience is communicable*, is the fundamental assumption, the point of departure, for social theory. Thus the concept of society is immanent in the individual. We cannot have labourers or language users without presupposing this conception of the individual agent and all the potential faculties of critical communication which go with the conditions for agency. We do not need a conception of agency to have a history of the insect or to understand what insects do. We do need a conception of the agent to distinguish, *in essential terms*, the spider from the subject of social theory. Habermas's distinction between the interest perspectives of Labour and Language leads us down the wrong tracks. One implies the other and both rest upon a more fundamental conception which gives us a unitary interest perspective. But the construction of epistemology in the context of an interest perspective (i.e. a Pragmatist epitemology) is not the issue – the conditions of having an interest perspective *at all* transcend this debate. Thus needs and perspectives are not the issue. Our point of departure must be the conditions of *agency*.

To conclude these reflections I want to make some attempt to pre-empt what may be a remaining objection. Given that we must construct epistemological foundations from the viewpoint of the isolated subject, and given that the principles of substantive practical rationality are to be adduced from the transcendental analysis of the presuppositions of agency, how are we to universalise any result without an appeal to social consensus? I have suggested that this problem lies at the root of the rejection of the notion of the individual for critical social theory. Nowhere is the allure of this device more clearly in evidence than in a more recent statement of Habermas's continued adherence to the theory of

Communicative Action. Speaking of the domination of cognitive-instrumental discourse over the repressed normative-moral potential of practical reason he says:[10]

> The ... contemporaneity and interdependence of the two processes can only be grasped if the false alternative set up by Max Weber, with his opposition between substantive and formal rationality, is overcome. Its underlying assumption is that the disenchantment of religious metaphysical world views robs rationality, along with the contents of tradition of all substantive connotations and thereby strips it of its power to have a structure forming influence on the lifeworld beyond the purposive-rational organization of means.

This, then, is the familiar problem to which, as we know equally well, he counterposes his proposed solution in consensus. The following quotation is nothing new, but, in the light of our critique of the communicative subject, the problem of validation of normative-moral claims takes on a new and clearer meaning for us. He says:[11]

> If ... not just constative but also regulative and expressive speech acts can be connected with validity claims and accepted as valid or rejected as invalid, the basic, ontological framework of the philosophy of consciousness ... proves to be too narrow. The 'world' to which subjects can relate with their representations or propositions was hitherto conceived of as the totality of objects or existing states of affairs. The objective world is considered the correlative of all true assertoric sentences. But if normative rightness and subjective truthfulness are introduced as validity claims analogous to truth, 'worlds' analogous to the world of facts have to be postulated ... The legacy of logocentrism is still noticeable in the terminological difficulty of expanding the ontological concept of 'world' in this way.

More traditional schools of analytical philosophy have posed this question in a more traditional way: can there be truth correlates for moral propositions? It is a little disappointing to find out that it was only this problem which was causing all the trouble. But if we can free ourselves from this ontological mode of thought, we can face the issue with some degree of confidence. We may as well ask what are the truth correlates of logical or metatheoretical propositions, or indeed any non-empirical proposition. My remarks in Chapter 1 and our discussions of Finnis's notion of 'self-evidence' may at last be of some help to us here. We do not have to postulate worlds of facts corresponding to the propositional content of claims which express necessary presuppositions of deductive, theoretical or practical reasoning. If theoretical reason is possible only on the assumption that there is an external world independent of my beliefs, then the proposition 'There is an external world' is not an *ontological* claim – or if it is intended as one it is unsupportable. It is an *epistemological* claim which cannot rationally be denied from the point of view of one who reasons theoretically. If we can identify similarly irrefutable assumptions concerning practical reason, from the point of view of one who attempts to engage in it, and these assumptions have other-regarding consequences for the regulation of our actions, then we will have epistemological grounds for practical-moral claims. It is possible to couch these claims in an ontological language by noting that we have in a sense ontologised reason by taking it as its own object in our investigations. Against arguments which deny propositional status to moral claims *because* they have no 'correspondence correlate' this line of argument could be adopted. It is unnecessary, however, because empricist-based objections like this cannot even theorise the intelligibility of the non-empirical claims which underpin their own analyses.[12] Ontology is not relevant to the problem before us: the question is whether or not any substantive practical precepts can be shown to be *dialectically-necessary*.

9

Purposivity and Morality

In this concluding chapter I want to do my best to argue for a defence of Alan Gewirth's claim to have derived a moral principle with determinate content from the premises of bare instrumental reason. If he is right, then I think that we have said enough to show that the methodological problem of reconciling substantive rationality with objectivity can be overcome. It is easy to become over-enthusiastic about one's own areas of interest, but I think it can be said that, potentially, this is of enormous significance. As far as I can see, incorporating the substance of a genuinely successful foundational argument for ethical objectivity is the only way in which social science can aspire to be anything other than the vehicle of institutional ideologies.

It is important that genuine attempts to make progress towards the resolution of epistemological problems are given careful scrutiny. Gewirth's efforts do deserve our best attentions, but I have little space here to do justice to his work. However, those who are unfamiliar with it, or those who had not considered it in relation to the methodology of the social sciences, may benefit from this short contribution. Fortunately, the time of writing coincides with the publication of Beyleveld's massive and scrupulous explication, analysis and defence of Gewirth. For those who see some merit in my general thesis concerning the requirement of a moral basis for concept formation in social science, accept that such a foundation can be provided only through a dialectically-necessary analysis of practical reason, and can see the possibility of this in my presentation of Gewirth's argument, I can do no more than refer them to Beyleveld's comprehensive treatment of all extant English language objections to it.[1] This being said, I intend to begin by letting Gewirth speak for himself in the presentation of the three stages[2] of the argument, and then offer defences to what I consider to be interesting objections to each stage.

Gewirth is clear about the issues which constitute the central problems of moral philosophy. It appears from our foregoing analyses that these questions are also the central problems of concept formation in social science. Gewirth reduces them to three areas of concern. They are:[3]

> ... the authoritative question: Why should one be moral, in the sense of accepting, as supremely authoritative or obligatory for one's actions the requirement of furthering or favorably considering the important interests of other persons, especially when these conflict with one's own interests? ... the distributive question: Whose interests other than his own should the agent favorably consider in action? ... [and] the substantive question: Of which interests should favorable account be taken?

The apparent intractability of these issues lies in a more general problem of intellectual endeavour itself. Gewirth says that conflicting answers can be given to these three questions on the basis of arguments which appear not to contain logical or empirical errors.This situation leads to the acceptance of moral scepticism as a rational position despite the existence of paradox. If moral scepticism is to be avoided, therefore, and in the absence of empirical techniques to determine these issues one way or another, there must be some correspondence-correlate or independent variable which 'determines the truth or at least the correctness of moral judgments'.[4]

Gewirth maintains that the solution to this problem can be found through an analysis of the concept of agency and the dialectically-necessary imperatives which become binding on an agent on pain of contradicting itself as an agent. An agent, or prospective purposive agent (PPA), is a being which sees itself as acting voluntarily (without force or compulsion) in order to achieve certain desired ends or purposes of its own.[5] Further, the agent must regard its purposes as 'good' in the (not necessarily moral) sense of their being goals which are[6]

> ... worth aiming at or pursuing; for if he did not so regard it he would not unforcedly choose to move from quiesence or non-action to action with a view to achieving the goal. This conception of worth constitutes a valuing on the part of the agent; he regards the object of his action as having at least sufficient value to merit his acting to attain it, ...

Thus:

> ... the primary ... basis of judging something to be good is precisely its connection with one's pro-attitude or positive interest or desire whereby one regards the object as worthy of pursuit.

Gewirth adds:[8]

> So long as this wanting is not a case of forced choice ... it constitutes a valuing on the part of the agent so that, to this extent, he regards the purpose or object of his action as good ...

This condition of agency (together with the notion of 'conative normality')[9] is the fundamental premise in Gewirth's argument. It has not escaped criticism,[10] yet we have said quite a lot, especially in our discussion of Hollis, that supports a voluntaristic conception of the agent as a fundamental presupposition of social science. This conception withstands the *noumenal* possibility of a universal determinism in that a simple determinism allied to material causation is epistemologically untenable if a demarcation between the natural and the social spheres is to be conceptually appropriated on the level of explanation. Furthermore, determinism notwithstanding, this conception of agency is still accurate from the standpoint of the agent. This standpoint is the central feature of the dialectically-necessary method employed by Gewirth.[11]

Thus, as with the concept of communication, this conception of agency is an unavoidable assumption of the epistemology of social science. However, we can take this opportunity to argue for the basic premise of voluntary agency (i.e. at least a partial freedom from determinism, or at least the logical possibility of it) as a substantive issue. In the context of the dialectically-necessary method employed by Gewirth, it is important that we can show that deductive reason is not only obligatory in all practical and theoretical discourse, but free of paradox in its self-referential application. I promised, in Chapter 6 *supra*, to present a fuller account of the meta-logical justification for deductive reason – an account which did not simply rest on an appeal to self-evidence. It is convenient here, then, to examine not only the nature of the extra-logical justification of logic itself but also the argument for freewill as against determinism which, in its Kantian form, relies on the production of contradiction consequent to the assumption of determinism on the part of a rational being. This contradiction suffices to prove the apodictic validity of the assumption of free will. In other words, determinism is held to be self-refuting. But if self-refutation depends on logical consistency, and logical consistency itself is in contention, then is not the appeal to contradiction as a refutation viciously circular or question-begging? We may examine, then, an argument which draws these issues together and questions not only the assumption of free will, but of any attempt to provide sound arguments for *any* position in the face of the mere *possibility* of determinism.

THE LOGIC OF VOLUNTARISM

In Mark Bernstein's paper 'Involutional Determinism' (and George Myro's reply, 'Are There Black Holes in Logic?') published as 'Justification and Determinism: an Exchange'[12] the issues of determinism/free will, notions of justification and the validity of the logical device of pointing to the 'self-refuting' nature of arguments are drawn together. This is understandable in that the problem of free will in Kant is seen to be overcome by the apparently self-refuting nature of the assumption that our reasoning is determined. The apparent self-refutation of determinism is held to provide a justification for the assumption of, though not a proof of the truth of, free will. Bernstein wants to argue that the idea of self-refuting arguments (e.g. the argument *for* determinism from the point of view of one who reasons practically, or denials of logic etc.) or, more precisely, the idea that we can refute arguments by pointing to their self-refuting properties, is based upon question-begging premises. Free of this logical check, he goes on from here to explore the consequences of the assumption that determinism is true. The results as he presents them are quite startling; however, I am not really concerned with these implications, but rather his remarks about the illegitimacy of the application of logical principles alleged to characterise arguments like Kant's (*for* free will) and other transcendental or, as we now may say with some confidence, dialectically-necessary arguments. His paper and Myro's reply provide a stimulating occasion to rehearse some arguments in defence of the assumption of voluntariness in Gewirth, and to supplement my critique of empiricist/pragmatist and Post-Modern rejections of logic as 'circular' (intended to mean question-begging and, hence, invalid or uninteresting) in Chapter 1 *supra*, and my arguments against Finnis in respect of his remarks about the question-begging nature of deductive reason in Chapter 4 *supra*. I do not reproduce Myro's reply, which is extremely lively and subtly illuminating. But, although I lack Myro's delicate touch, I hope that I can make some contribution to the substance of the exchange.

Bernstein understands determinism as the thesis that all events are caused in the sense of transitive material causation as described in our discussion of Hollis in Chapter 5 *supra*. While remaining neutral as to the substantive issue, Bernstein suggests that arguments which have assumed this thesis to be true result in the denial of free actions, including the actions of intending meanings and giving reasons and justifications for arguments. He goes on to say that rebuttals of the determinist claim have been unsatisfactory or fallacious in that they have 'tended to leave the nature of the relationship between reasons and actions quite mysterious'.[13] He wants to focus on one such category of attempted rebuttal, that of the 'self-defeating' or 'self-refuting' argument.[14] He suggests that this logical gambit, although at least as old as Sextus Empiricus, owes its modern origin to Kant, 'at least as it applies to the Free Will/Determinism issue'[15] He quotes Kant thus:[16]

> ... we cannot conceive of a reason which consciously responds to a bidding from the outside with respect to its judgments, for then the subject would attribute the determination of its power of judgment not to reason but to impulse. Reason must regard itself as the author of its principles, independently of foreign influences; consequently,

> as practical reason or as the will of a rational being, it must regard itself as free.

Bernstein argues, rightly, that Kant's presentation of the alleged 'self-refutation' of the assumption of determinism does not rule out the actual possibility of determinism being true. *If*, then, as is admittedly possible, determinism is true, we would have no choice but to *think* that the refutation of determinism were true. But then this result, likewise, would not be a genuine thought, but merely the next stage in the[17]

> ... involutional cycle ... [which] does not stop here, for this last claim (as well as this one) fall[s] prey to the same line of reasoning. Thus it seems, determinedly, that the notions of truth and validity are devoid of content. Even worse, similar reasoning leads to this nihilistic conclusion concerning all of our concepts (or at least so I am determined to think).

We are on the slide here, but the brakes can be applied. The regress must be halted by showing that the self-refutation of the assumption of determinism really is a once-and-for-all justification of, or at least the requirement to *assume*, the thesis of free will. But Bernstein thinks that the attempt to nail this disconcerting problem by labelling it as self-refuting simply begs the question; not just against determinism, but in general. Descartes and Wittgenstein are drawn into the debate, but he starts with, and I shall confine myself to, a classical sceptic, Pyrrho, who has been 'credited with the pronouncement that nothing is true'. Bernstein says:[18]

> This might, at first, appear to lack paradox and simply be a self-refuting claim. For if nothing is true, then 'nothing is true' is not true, and therefore (assuming a two-valued logic), some statements are true. But further inspection shows this rebuttal spurious, for *it begs the very question at issue*. For in trying to show the falsity of Pyrrho's claim, we are assuming the truth of 'if nothing is true, then "nothing is true" is not true.' [my emphasis]

But this is wholly inaccurate. 'Begging the question', or the *petitio principii*, is indeed a logical fallacy, but we do not have one here. The identification of an instance of begging the question licenses us to reject an argument as rationally uncompelling because an 'argument' which begs the question is not an argument – it is a simple assertion of a claim lacking any material or logical support. If, for instance, one is called upon to defend, through argument, the thesis of revealed truth, and one 'argues', as did Barth, that it is revealed to us that revelation is truth, one begs the question by *assuming arbitrarily* – that is, without adducing *justification*, the truth of revelation, and then presenting, purely as a display, this mere assertion in the form of an argument by affecting to infer (albeit soundly) that, if revelation is true, then revelation is true.

Now how does Bernstein's example demonstrate a similar fallacy in the critical response to Pyrrho's claim? To describe accurately the rejection of Pyrrho's claim as a begging of the question it would have to be the case that one had assumed what one wished to prove against Pyrrho, namely, the falsity of the claim 'nothing is true' (i.e. to have assumed that 'something was true'). On the basis of this assumption, one would simply declare that Pyrrho's claim was incompatible with this arbitrary assumption and thus must be rejected. This would indeed be perverse argumentation. But is this what is taking place in the rejection of allegedly self-refuting arguments? Clearly it is not: Pyrrho's claim is held to be self-refuting by pointing out the following.

1. 'Nothing is true' is equivalent to 'I know something to be true, namely, that nothing is true'.
2. (1) is equivalent to 'something is true and nothing is true'.
3. (1) implies (2), (2) is contradictory, therefore (1) must be false.

The above is a pristine example of an *argumentum reductio ad absurdum.* The *reductio* principle states that a proposition which implies a contradiction must be regarded as false. This brings us to the point where we have to contend with Bernstein's failure to grasp the difference between valid argumentation and the principles upon which such argumentation rests. For then he says:[19] '*Equivalently*, in attempting to show Pyrrho mistaken, we are assuming the validity of the *reductio* form of argument' [my emphasis]. Well, of course we are assuming the validity of this principle, and, what is more, we are assuming the validity of the elemental basis of this compound principle. We shall let Bernstein state it:[20]

> Or, *what comes [to] much* ... [the] same point[21] we might charge Pyrrho with involvement in a self-contradiction, for he seems committed to both (a) and (b)
>
> (a) nothing is true
>
> (b) it's true that nothing is true.
>
> But the reply is analogous to the one above; this argument *clearly begs the question by assuming the truth of the Law of Contradiction.* [my emphasis]

Responding to this problem is not logically demanding. It is a thankless task, however, for several reasons. One is that, if the proponent of the purported paradox conceives the object of the exercise as being the preservation of a puzzle and not the resolution of a logical problem, then the mental effort required to articulate a solution to the puzzle to the satisfaction of its proponent, if indeed this is possible, is simply a waste of time and energy. Another is that the conclusions of arguments which defend logical principles, even when true, contain less useful information than is already present in their premises. In a sense this renders the exercise futile, in that such argument cannot produce conviction in the mind of one who is in want of it. This is probably why some have been quick to interpret such arguments as question-begging. This is not a wise move, however, for arguments *against* logical principles result in conclusions which utilise the very principles which they seek to refute, and yet, in spite of this, always turn out to be false. I hope to make this clear in the following remarks.

We are not concerned with gratuitous puzzle-making in regard to Mark Bernstein's contribution and thus we can be assured of his good faith. In view of this we can expect agreement on the fact that the issues raised are *meta-logical* and thus *ultimately* foundational. We must, therefore, also expect agreement on the fact that we cannot coherently discuss the validity of arguments in respect of their conformity to logical principles if these principles themselves are the subject of scrutiny. If we are to 'bracket' the validity of logical principles in order to scrutinise them, then parties to such an enterprise must take responsibility for the reflexive difficulties which are likely to arise in the course of the analysis. One such responsibility is to recognise and accept that an argument which seeks to criticise the status of certain logical principles cannot employ those same principles as part of a successful critique. Another is to realise that demands for justification cannot coherently be made in conjunction with the thesis that justification is impossible, and, further, that if one is to claim that (any) justification is impossible, then one can expect to face a request for a justification of *this* claim. Only on these grounds is it possible to proceed. It seems that my remarks concerning the futility of defending logical principles are already vindicated. However, capitulation to mere assertion is the only alternative and this is not the honourable option.

Bernstein wants to expose certain attempts at refutation as question-begging. We have seen that he is wrong to characterise the refutation of Pyrrho as such. But let us forget that for a moment. Suppose that it *was* an instance of question-begging or *petitio principii*. What does he find objectionable about this kind of 'argument'? Why does he think that this form of reasoning has no force? Is it because it relies upon an assumption which itself requires justification? If this is not his objection then he has no business invoking the fallacy of begging-the-question, for this is its *only* logical application. Thus we can be sure that it is his objection. In which case, if we are to call into question logical principles themselves – as Bernstein does – then his argument entails that *all* arguments are question-begging, because it is a fact – and one that Bernstein shows quite clearly – that *all* arguments rest upon logical principles. Are we, then, to concur with Bernstein in this regard and thus, infer that *his* arguments are question-begging? Certainly not, for this would be to plunge quite unnecessarily into what George Myro refers to as 'Bernstein's Whirlpool'.On the contrary, we are to go back to the mutually agreed and unavoidable observation that this is a *meta-logical* issue and that we (and this includes Bernstein) cannot settle meta-logical issues by recourse to logical principles – although we may articulate some meta-logical conclusions through *reflection* on logical principles. We *can* show that Bernstein is guilty of contradiction. Contradiction is final, and thus the policy of mutually assured destruction need not be implemented.

The contradiction that would have dragged us into the whirlpool is the claim that an argument which rests upon the Law of Contradiction (i.e. *any* argument) is question-begging and thus invalid. The contradiction here is not immediately obvious, but let us note that Bernstein regards begging the question, *pointing out* that someone is begging the question, the assumption of and application of the *reductio* principle and the application of the Law of Contradiction *as one and the same illegitimate move.* This is simply to assert that all and any arguments are invalid because all logical principles are invalid. If the quotations above are examined it can be seen that this is exactly what is going on: Bernstein says that begging the question is *equivalent* to the assumption of the *reductio* principle, and that this latter 'comes [to] much [the] same point' as accusing someone of contradicting themselves.

What we have to make very clear here is that to accuse someone of begging the question is not to employ a *reductio* argument against them; it is not to accuse them of contradiction; it is not even to accuse them of stating a falsehood; it is, depending upon the context of the exchange, either to refuse to accept their attempt to refute *your* claim/argument as being necessarily compelling, or to refuse to accept *their* claim/argument as being necessarily compelling, on the basis that they have arbitrarily – *without justification* – assumed the truth or falsity of *the very question at issue.* The concept of justification is the crux of the matter. For it can *never* be true that a person begs the question by assuming the validity of the Law of Contradiction, or by employing the *reductio* in argument or by pointing out that someone else is begging the question. Because begging the question can only occur when one has failed to provide a justification for a premise, and this state of affairs can only be brought to light when the evaluator of an argument is capable of identifying the absence of justification – in other words, when the evaluator of an argument understands what it means to provide such a justification.

To justify a claim is simply to provide a rationally adequate reason for its acceptance. In other words, to justify Q is to show that if P is true then Q is true, and that P is indeed true. To accuse someone rightly of begging the question is to point out to them that what they seek to prove (Q) depends upon the truth of some proposition (P) and that they have failed to show that P is true. It does not mean that Q is false, it just means that we are not rationally bound to accept Q as being true. Now this does not prove the truth of any principle of logic. However, it does prove beyond any doubt that anyone who wants to accuse someone of begging the question has already accepted the validity of the principle we have just employed, namely, *modus ponens*, and that, therefore, whatever the *exact* relationship is, they have accepted the Law of Contradiction which so obviously underpins it.[22] Finally, they must therefore agree that it would be impossible for them ever intelligibly to accuse a person of begging the question when the question at issue is the validity of the Law of Contradiction (and, hence, the Law of Identity, and hence, the *reductio*, and hence *modus tollens*). To assume that these principles are valid *and* employ them to suggest that they are invalid is a contradiction.

Has this exercise been worthwhile? We have certainly not provided an argument to prove the truth of the logical principles at issue. We have, however, synthesised the *meta-logical* maxim that these principles must be assumed to be valid for *any* argument. This obviously renders contradictory any argument which attempts to invalidate them. We have, then, made some progress; we have proved that accusations of question-begging, or vicious circularity, cannot be intelligibly employed against the foundational principles of logic. Free from confusion concerning what is and what is not question-begging, let us return to the argument for freedom in the face of the possibility of a universal determinism.

Why not put Kant's argument this way: to *know* that determinism was true would be to arrive at rationally justified belief that this state of affairs was the case. Thus the belief that determinism was true would be a product of rational autonomy. This event (our coming to this belief state) would, however, like any other event, be a product of (heteronomous) causality. Thus we would have a belief state that was both the product of freedom and not the product of freedom. If this is a contradiction, which prima facie, it appears to be, then we have a rapid and sure refutation of the assumption of determinism: if the above is a contradiction then the assumption which implies it must be false. That assumption is the thesis of determinism, hence it must be false. But we will grant that there is enough in the argument to determinism to give its seemingly contradictory corollary the status of paradox. It is only genuinely paradoxical if the proposition which produces the contradiction – in this case the assumption that everything, including our reasoning, is determined – *is logically unavoidable*. Is this genuinely paradoxical? Well, it is if the possibility of the formulation 'knowing that we are determined' is allowed to go unchecked.

The point is, as Kant says, that reason is the author of its own principles. The notion of determinism – let us not forget – is intelligible only when we have understood the notion of causality. Where does the notion of causality come from? In Kant it is a transcendental result of reflection upon the possibility of empirical knowledge. Although we must assume that causality operates in the world, its status is purely hypothetical: if knowledge of an external world (itself a hypothesis of the possibility of experience) is possible, then causality must be assumed to operate within it if experience is to be intelligible. Determinism, i.e. the persistence of an all-pervasive causality, is thus a notion which is intelligible to us through rational reflection on the possibility of knowledge. If reason is right, this does not entail that causality exists in a world external to our consciousness, it entails that reason has the power correctly to identify the elements (categories) of its own structure. And this is to say only that we cannot *but* experience the *world of objects* (but not necessarily subjects) in terms of (material) causality. This is the only sense in which the assumption of the *truth* of causality and, hence, determinism, makes sense. To ask, therefore, whether reason itself is determined (for this is what is entailed by asking if *everything* is determined) is to ask whether or not a category which we must accept is produced by the understanding to explain the *nature* of understanding, can itself produce the understanding. There is no need to ask if (a) it is rational to assume that reason explains the phenomenon of causality – to be rational is to explain the world in terms of causality. Thus it is pointless asking (b) whether causality explains the phenomenon of reasoning – it obviously does not. To ask (c) if causality operates upon reason is equivalent to asking (d) does causality exist in the world independently of reason?

We know that we would require reason to allow us to answer (d) because we know that (a) is certainly true and (b) is certainly false. We know that (c) and therefore (d) are unknowable. Thus we know that (a) cannot be refuted; (b) is ruled out; (c) and (d) could never be the subject of any rational inquiry or never be known to have the slightest bearing on our understanding, experience or explanation of the world; (a) is a statement of freedom and rational autonomy. In the face of this, how do we contrive to make an interesting discussion out of the free will/determinism debate? Answer: we assume something that we know already to be ruled out as a rational option (i.e. illegitimately attempt to manufacture a paradox) and chart its weird consequences. The involutional cycle, if not our propensity for manufacturing puzzles, stops here.

This being said, we are in a fairly secure position, in respect of the assumption of voluntary agency, to present Gewirth's argument to the supreme moral principle, the principle of generic consistency (PGC). Gewirth says:[23] 'Addressed to every actual or prospective agent, the PGC says: "Act in accord with the generic rights of your recipients as well as of yourself."' We must bear in mind that[24]

> Throughout, the argument proceeds from within the conative standpoint of the rational agent who is concerned to secure or maintain the proximate necessary conditions of his successful agency, while at the same time he acknowledges the general requirements of deductive and inductive reason.

I quote Gewirth for reasons of maximum brevity and absolute accuracy. I choose his 1988 paper, 'The Justification of Morality', rather than *Reason and Morality*, simply because the more recent exposition of his work benefits from the attention to detail which is induced by ten years of scholarly criticism. The argument, however, has not changed since its original formulation of 1978. In fact the majority of Gewirth's replies to criticism take the form of reiterations of his detailed substantiations of the main argument in *Reason and Morality*. It is the form rather than the substance of the argument to the PGC which Gewirth is concerned to refine ten years on. The exposition below, therefore, and Gewirth's acknowledgement of persisting objections give us what Gewirth at least regards as the core of the issue, and we may note that these surviving elements have enjoyed scrupulous attention.

THE ARGUMENT TO THE PRINCIPLE OF GENERIC CONSISTENCY (PGC)

Gewirth says:[25]

> The argument undertakes to establish two main theses. The first is that every actual or prospective agent logically must accept that he or she has rights to freedom and well-being. The second is that the agent logically must also accept that all other actual or prospective agents have the same rights he claims for himself, so that he must act toward other persons with favorable consideration for their freedom and well-being as well as his own, even in circumstances where his own interests will be more effectively advanced by other sorts of actions.

Thesis 1[26]

> Since every agent acts for the sake of achieving purposes which he regards has having some goodness or value, at least for himself, and since his having freedom and well-being is the proximate necessary condition of such achievement, every agent has to accept (1) 'My freedom and well-being are necessary goods.' Hence, he also has to accept (2) 'I must have freedom and well-being.' This 'must' – judgment follows from (1) because of two interrelated aspects of the 'must'. On the one hand, it reflects the factual relation of means–end necessity that the having of freedom and well-being bears to all successful action. On the other hand, it reflects the practical prescriptiveness of the agent's conative attitude toward his purpose fulfilment so that he advocates or endorses his having freedom and well-being.
>
> Now by virtue of accepting (2), every agent has to accept (3) 'I have rights to freedom and well-being.' For, if he rejects (3) then,

because of the correlativity of claim-rights and strict 'oughts,' he also has to reject (4) 'All other persons ought at least to refrain from removing or interfering with my freedom and well-being.' By rejecting (4), he has to accept (5) 'Other persons may (i.e. it is permissible that other persons) remove or interfere with my freedom and well-being.' And by accepting (5) he has to accept (6) 'I may not (i.e. it is permissible that I not) have freedom and well-being.' But (6) contradicts (2). Since every agent has to accept (2), he must reject (6). And since (6) follows from the denial of (3), every agent must reject that denial, so that he logically must accept (3) 'I have rights to freedom and well-being'

Thesis 2[27]

Since the necessary and sufficient reason for which the agent claims these rights is that he is a prospective agent, he must accept (7) 'I have rights to freedom and well-being because I am a prospective agent.' Hence, by universalization, he must also accept (8) 'All other prospective agents have rights to freedom and well-being.' Now this is a moral judgment, because it requires the agent to take favorable account of the interests of all other prospective agents. And (8), in turn, logically requires the agent to accept (9) 'I ought to act in accord with the generic rights of all other agents as well as of myself.' Since all other agents are the actual or potential recipients of the original agent's action, (9) is equivalent to the PGC. Thus the PGC has been given a rational justification of the sort indicated above: any agent who rejects it contradicts himself.

PRELIMINARY OBJECTIONS

I will first deal with what Gewirth has chosen to list as the four main preliminary objections to the argument before going on to select other criticisms which I consider to be of concern to the integrational problems of social science and moral theory. I merely paraphrase the objections and quote Gewirth's replies to these preliminary points, again with reference to his 1988 paper.

1. *Does the argument imply that whatever an agent holds he must have, he therefore has a right to?*[28]

The reply to this objection is that since the argument is based on reason, its 'must' is restricted to the truly necessary goods of action, so that contingent, dispensable goods do not meet the conditions of this 'must'.[29]

2. *Rights are not established because an agent may accept the 'ought' of step (4) without accepting the 'rights' of step (3). Oughts may be upheld for reasons other than being correlative to rights, e.g. on utilitarian grounds.*[30]

> The reply is that any such other grounds for the 'ought' would remove from it the directly personal prudential basis which the argument shows it must have because of its exclusive initial concern with the agent's own needs of agency. Thus the 'ought' is not upheld on general utilitarian grounds or on other grounds not primarily related to its beneficiary, as something which he must hold is due or owed to himself by virtue of its being required for all his purposive actions.[30]

3. *The amoralist or adeonticist, rejecting all 'rights talk' outright, does not embroil himself in the 'may' judgments or permissibility issues ensuing from his rejection of the 'ought' judgment in step* (4)[32]

> The reply is that no agent can rationally reject either a self-directed or an other-directed 'ought' judgment. For if his life or some other aspect of his basic well-being is threatened, and he thinks that the only way he can ward off this threat is by doing *X*, which is in his power, then he will say or think 'I ought to do *X*.' Hence, he must also accept 'I ought to be free to do *X*', which is equivalent to the other-directed 'ought' – judgment, 'Other persons ought to refrain from interfering with my doing *X*.' Thus, even an amoralist must accept 'ought' judgments and their correlative rights-judgments, as well as judgments about what is permissible.[33]

4. *An agent may claim generic rights for himself on necessary and sufficient grounds less extensive than the property of agency and accept the logical extension of such a claim without recognising the validity of the claim in all prospective agents.*[34]

> The reply is that if any agent were to hold that he has the generic rights on the basis of his having some less extensive property or description (such as being white or capitalist or having some proper name) this would commit him to the possibility that, if he were to lack this property, he would not have the generic rights. But we saw, in the argument for the first main thesis, that every agent logically must hold that he does have the generic rights. Hence, to avoid self-contradiction, the agent must accept that the necessary and sufficient reason for which he has the generic rights cannot be anything less extensive than his being a prospective agent.[35]

The objections and replies above are offered more as further exposition and bolstering of the main structure of the argument. I want to go on now to examine some interesting points which have been raised against this careful presentation of the argument.

PROBLEMS WITH GEWIRTH

As with all important philosophical developments, there is a large body of critical literature devoted to Gewirth's argument. Moreover, as is to be expected, these criticisms are not uniform in the sense that they target a particular stage of Gewirth's argument as being particularly problematic. Some, as we have noted, question the assumption of 'agency' *per se*[36] some the assumption of a conative disposition of the agent;[37] others question the analytic and, hence, allegedly tautological or trivially definitional status of the argument.[38] There is criticism of the propriety of adducing truths from the dialectically-necessary method.[39] I feel, however, that the substantial groundwork of investigation and logical analysis we have undertaken earlier in relation to the epistemology of the social sciences, and given that we have responded fully to objections to a voluntaristic conception of agency, permits us to dispense with a detailed account of most of these objections. Let us proceed to the second stage of the argument – the claiming of rights to freedom and well-being.

I think that this a part of the argument – which is a very simple piece of reasoning as Gewirth presents it – which can be justifiably held to require detailed elucidation. This is the stage from (2) 'I must have freedom and well-being' to the derivation from it, (3) 'I have rights to freedom and well-being'. This is the stage which troubles writers such as Bond, McMahon, Hare, Golding, Singer and others to the extent that some of these writers have held that the concepts which are involved in this inference are not only 'mysterious' but 'nonsensical' and 'unintelligible'.[40] The alleged inadequacy of the argument is held to centre on the concept of a prudential right. This is absolutely pivotal for the derivation of the moral force of the PGC from the non-moral, that is, non-other-regarding premises of the rationality of prudential rights claims. In essence the point of the collective criticism in this regard focuses upon the alleged equivocation involved in claiming that an agent must not only recognise his own obligation to defend his freedom and well-being for the sake of his own interests but that he must also consider that others are obliged at least to refrain from interference with them, and that they must accept this obligation for reasons which are unconnected with their interests.

R. M. HARE: WEAK RIGHTS/NO RIGHTS?

R. M. Hare's article 'Do Agents Have to be Moralists?' is a convenient point of departure for the debate.[41] The problem and, I suggest the solution appear within the criticism itself. The steps in the argument which Hare is concerned to clarify are (a) the move from the recognition of freedom and well-being as necessary goods to the suggested corollary of the requirement to claim rights to these necessary goods. I shall label this as Hare's 'weak rights' thesis (WRT); and (b) the move from claiming rights to freedom and well-being to according these rights to all agents, which I shall label as Hare's 'no universalisation' thesis (NUT)

Hare says:[42]

> I shall be concentrating on the two steps in the middle: 'hence he must claim rights to freedom and well-being; hence he must accord the same rights to all agents...' I shall argue that the first of these steps is only valid in a somewhat weak sense of 'rights', if such a sense exists, in which a right-claim is not necessarily universalizable (i.e. in which we may claim a right without being thereby committed to extend it to others who have the same reasons for claiming it as we have). If there is no such sense, then the step is invalid. But even if there is such a sense, it is not that which is required in order to make the next step valid, viz. 'hence he must accord the same rights to all agents who have the same reasons for claiming them as he has'. In short, Gewirth is guilty of a fallacy of equivocation.

Gewirth asserts that the recognition of the necessary goods of freedom and well-being imposes a logical obligation, a strict 'ought', on the agent to claim a right to them. Claiming a right to his freedom and well-being is equivalent to claiming that others ought not to interfere with his freedom and well-being. To deny this is equivalent to accepting the permissibility of interference and hence, accepting the cessation of prospective agency. Hare thinks that this step is invalid. He says:[43]

> Let us admit, for the sake of argument that the agent must *want* his purpose to be achieved (at any rate want it *ceteris paribus*), and that if one wants the purpose to be achieved, one must *want* whatever is a necessary condition for its achievement. But does it follow that one must therefore think that other persons *ought* to supply these necessary conditions, by refraining from interfering? Can I not want something, without thinking that I ought to have it?

This objection, prima facie, has been dealt with in Gewirth's preliminary defences. Of course, it is the case that I can want something without thinking that I 'ought' to have it, in the sense that this is equivalent to my claiming a right to it. But here we must note that it is not a matter of my wanting my freedom and well-being in the way that I may want a new red bicycle. It is that whatever I want or desire, there are things which I must value independently of my wants or desires.

If I want to be a great sprinter, or even a moderately successful one, I must value the means for achieving this goal. (It is worth noting that Gewirth's argument extends to those agents whose values may be considered as 'obviously' [popularly] perverse, e.g. rapists, robbers, child molesters, drug barons etc. My example is chosen merely for the sake of taste.) One aspect of the means is that I must get up in the morning and train in all weathers. I detest having to do this yet, because of my ultimate goal, I take drastic action to make sure that I wake up in the morning, to make sure that I am not locked in my house, and to prevent people detaining me on my way to the training ground. A million other examples would suffice, but, if nothing else we have shown an equivocation here in Hare's use of the word 'want'. It can be cleared up by noting the following formulations: 'I want to be a sprinter/have a new bike/play chess with my friend on the other side of town', *therefore,* I must want the basic requirements of freedom to pursue this/these goal(s)'. More generally, we can say, 'If I want anything, then I *must* want the wherewithal to get it'. The types of wanting, however, are not identical: 'I want X because I like it' does not entail 'I like everything which I need to do to secure X'. However, 'I want X and getting X entails doing Y' does entail 'I *must* make sure I do Y or abandon my quest for X'.

My wanting X, therefore, is conditional upon my own criterion of what is 'good' in the sense in which Gewirth clearly defines it in his exposition *supra*. The sense in which I must consider the wherewhithal to achieve X as 'good' is a logical obligation stemming from my criterion of goodness in the above sense. It is equivalent to 'I strictly ought to value my freedom and well-being according to my criterion of 'good'. I am only released *rationally* from this obligation on relinquishing my criterion of 'goodness'. But this strict obligation to defend my freedom and well-being is immediately reinstated by an alternative criterion of 'goodness' I may adopt, and I must adopt some criterion of 'goodness;' or relinquish my prospects of agency – this, of course, is the sanction of pain of contradiction at the foundation of Gewirth's argument.

Hare's criticism rests upon a misunderstanding of the nature of the agent's obligation to defend his freedom and well-being. The obligation, the 'ought;' in question here is what Gewirth calls a prudential 'ought'. This simply means that the requirement to perform an action is brought about by recognition of ones own interests, as opposed to a moral 'ought', which is an obligation to act in recognition of the interest of others. Hare suggests that the 'ought' which obliges an agent to claim rights to his freedom and well-being cannot be prudential, as Gewirth insists, because;[44]

> ... when I say *other persons* prudentially ought to do something, I must mean that they ought to do it in *their* own interest; I cannot mean that they ought to do it in *my* interest. So the step from the perhaps true premise that the agent wants something to the conclusion that *he* prudentially ought to seek it (and whatever is a necessary condition for it) may be all right; but this does not entitle us to conclude that he must think that other people prudentially ought to give it him; for it would not be true that they ought, and there would

> be no reason why he should think so, if to give it him would not be (and were known by him not to be) in *their* interests.

But the simple reply to this is that the agent does not claim a right to his freedom and well-being on the basis that co-operation and respect from others is in *their* interests. He does not claim that others prudentially ought to value *his* freedom and well-being. He claims that they ought to respect (in the sense of taking care not to damage) his freedom and well-being because it is necessarily in *his* .[45] Clearly, any other claim to rights would not be prudential, but moral, and therefore question-begging. This is precisely Gewirth's point. It may be worthwhile to remind ourselves that this claim is dialectically required from the agent's standpoint. *Assertorically,* Hare is quite right to say that[46]

> Other people do not automatically have *obligations* to supply what the agent prudentially ought to seek; there is no *requirement* on them to supply it (the prudential requirements are all on *him*, not on them); and he is not warranted in censuring *them*, only himself if he fails to get what he needs through his own (prudential) fault.

This is an extremely interesting observation because it forcefully makes the point for Gewirth's argument. The agent certainly must censure himself severely if he fails to take steps to get what he needs for his prudential well-being. So much so that he must recognise that he acts irrationally if he does not seek to secure his prudential necessities – his freedom and well-being. And if he recognises that he must secure these necessities on pain of relinquishing his status as an agent – i.e. that this is a strict *duty*, then he must demand the freedom to perform his duty. But Hare seems to think that the agent must also realise that others are justified in taking no notice of this demand. This is Hare's WRT in its most rational form. Hare's NUT follows as a corollary of WRT for it is clear why Hare refuses to admit the universal scope of such rights claims. His WRT can be presented as the position whereby the agent recognises his right to his freedom and well-being on the basis that they are necessary goods but that this stems from his own prudential interests. Thus, his right is grounded in his own interests. He may extend this right to others and, hence, recognise a duty to them *only* if he introduces the optional, unsubstantiated and irreducibly moral premise that the interests of others should be treated on a basis of equity with his own. Hence, according to Hare, the universalisation step in Gewirth's argument is in fact an egalitarian premise which seeks to ground his egalitarian conclusion embodied in the PGC. I think that this debate is the central area of concern in Gewirth's project – what is the nature and scope of prudential rights; is the notion even intelligible?

FURTHER OBJECTIONS TO PRUDENTIAL RIGHTS

McMahon pursues the theme of alleged equivocation in Gewirth's attempt to universalise dialectically-necessary claims of prudential right and thereby turn them into moral rights. His approach is to argue that there is a profound distinction between 'oughts' of evaluation and action-guiding 'oughts'. An 'ought' of evaluation (OE)[47] ... reports the existence of sufficient reason, from some point of view, for regarding a particular event or state of affairs as desirable. [e.g.] ("There ought to be fewer clouds in the sky.")' An 'ought' of rationality or action-guiding 'ought' (OAG):[48] '... reports the existence of nonmoral (typically prudential) reasons for action sufficient to warrant the performance of some action by an agent. [e.g.] ("You ought to exercise regularly.")'. McMahon holds that Gewirth's derivation of (4) 'All other persons ought at least to refrain from removing or interfering with my freedom and well-being', from (1) 'My freedom and well-being are necessary goods' is invalid in that the only sort of 'ought' judgment that (1) can logically authorise is OE and that such an 'ought' does not furnish sufficient reasons for action for others with regard to the requirements of my freedom and well-being. McMahon states that 'ought' judgments which are evaluative occur only in instances where OAGs would be out of place. McMahon, then, thinks that (1) 'My freedom and well-being are necessary goods' refers to goods or a 'good-judgment' that licenses only an ought of desirability analogous to the remark about clouds in the sky. But Gewirth replies:[49]

> McMahon's construal of (1) as containing or authorizing only the 'ought' of evaluation is mistaken. For on this construal the agent's statement that his freedom and well-being are necessary goods would simply report the existence of these qualities as 'desirable', but with no practical advocacy or conative commitment on his part to ensuring his continued possession of them. But on the contrary, ... the agent's statement (1) of the necessary goodness of his having freedom and well-being is equivalent to the 'must'-statement (2) 'I must have freedom and well-being', and this is regarded by him as prescriptive for the conduct of other persons. For in holding that he *must* have freedom and well-being, the agent implicitly *demands* of other persons that they at least not interfere with his having what he needs to have in order to be an agent and not to have general chances of success in fulfilling his purposes. Hence he regards both (1) ['My freedom and well-being are necessary goods'] and (2) 'I must have my freedom as well-being'] as action-guiding for others because of this prescriptive component.

The ambiguity of McMahon's notion of a sufficient reason for action should be mentioned here. Gewirth notes that 'There is a sufficient reason for A to do X' may be taken to mean (a) 'A acknowledges that there is sufficient reason to do X' or (b) 'From someone's point of view there is sufficient reason for A to do X'. It is on the basis of construing the notion of an OAG in the form of (a) above that McMahon criticises the conception of prudential rights and, hence, universalisation of rights in Gewirth's argument. Gewirth, however, insists on emphasising that his argument focuses upon the agent's reasons for claiming rights, not on the *addressee's* reasons for honouring the claims.[50]

McMahon, in effect, denies the coherence of prudential rights in the above sense. He says:[51]

> It remains mysterious how an agent's judgment that his freedom and well-being are necessarily good could justify him in concluding that other agents have a non prudential reason to contribute to the maintenance of these conditions.

Gewirth insists in his reply to this criticism that the reasons given to the addressee of the rights appear as personally prudential (for the addressor) and thus not prudentially binding on the addressee. Yet the addressee, though not accepting the reason given, can still recognise it as a reason for action. Gewirth says:[52]

> Now it is clear that right-claims make sense even when there is no having of reasons in the personal sense. For example, when slaves say to their masters, 'We have a right to be free, so you ought to free us,' this makes sense even when the masters do not accept the reasons on which the slaves base their claims.

Is there, however, as McMahon suggests, in the impersonal sense of 'having a reason', as in the case exemplified by the slaves' assumption that a non-prudential reason for action has a justificatory force for their masters, an implicit *moral* assumption that there are certain general reasons which, in principle, are acceptable to all rational persons? If this is so, says Gewirth,[53] '... then McMahon would be correct in saying that what I call prudential rights are really moral ones, because of the requirement of generally acceptable justificatory reasons.' Gewirth, however, is perfectly clear on this matter. He insists that it is sufficient for the intelligibility of a right-claim that[54]

> ... the agent has his *own* sufficient reasons for urging his rights against other persons, ... Of course, the agent must also assume that his addressees understand his claim; but they will understand it, at least in the first instance, as reflecting his own needs or purposes, not theirs nor any more general system of rules.

RADICALISING THE DEBATE ON REASONS

I think it is at this point that pursuing the debate becomes futile on less than an epistemological level. There must be a more forceful reformulation of the *dialectical* inference from 'I must have my freedom and well-being' to 'I have rights to my freedom and well-being', to settle the matter one way or the other. We must remember that it is this step which, when universalised, licenses the jump for the prudential to the moral.

Perhaps, therefore, the question should be put, 'Who is to decide what is a good reason for anything?' We must bear in mind that we have devoted much time to showing that the concept of society is a concept which is immanent in the individual, and that precisely what constitutes an individual is an epistemological question. The phenomenology of self is the starting point for cognitive appropriation of the categories of experience – including the experience of acknowledging the existence of other selves. Thought is one such category and coherence is a defining feature of it. Now if I am to have an understanding of what constitutes a good reason for a particular action or a good reason for making a particular inference, I must have an understanding of what a reason for anything is. This competence is not, as we have clearly seen in our critical analysis of Habermas's conception of the category of communication, something which requires the assistance or presence of other communicators – or other things like me. Thus what constitutes a good reason *per se* is not something I can hope to glean from others. If I am not capable of recognising a good reason when I see one in my transcendental isolation, I will not be brought to this stage of competence by a postulated other, precisely because others like me only exist as a product of my interpretation of what another (mind) could be like. Any putative signs which I took to be on offer would have to be processed in terms of my rational categories. Thus there could be no debate and subsequent enlightenment about the constitution of such categories. It follows therefore, that if Gewirth's argument is to be of any help to us in our quest for a methodologically efficacious conception of substantive rationality, it must cohere with this fundamental conception of the subject.

Normative (instrumental or moral) discourse requires capacities for the rational understanding of normative categories on the part of individuals. The conception of the individual is necessary for the conception of others who may be party to discourse. This much is mere reiteration of previous discussion. The conception of a right, therefore, is not some mysterious dialogical product of history and society, it must be a reflexively obtainable concept immanent in the conceptual structures of practical reason which constitutes the practical dimension of the transcendental ego. Gewirth's analogy of intellectual rights (the justification of inferences), with other rights-claims, forcefully makes this point. Prudential rights, therefore, arise from the fundamental competence to recognise the justification of an inference and are merely substitution instances of other valid inferences within the rational competence of the subject. As we are obliged to take our point of departure from the phenomenology of the individual ego to formulate epistemological categories, it becomes obvious that the application of epistemological categories to the sphere of normative phenomena originate in, and, hence, must be applicable to, the individual ego. We know nothing of others in this ultimately basic sense and, hence, can learn nothing from them in this ultimately basic sense.

PRUDENTIAL RIGHTS AS PRIMARY RIGHTS

Thus, if rights are intelligible at all, prudential rights are primary, for if the individual cannot formulate the concept of a right in terms of its own interests, there can be no possibility of it recognising them in others. As with intersubjectivity, rights are, in this dialectical sense, *my* idea. Consequently, even in the absence of others and even in the absence of my acknowledgement of the existence of others, the fundamental capacity to recognise a reason or a justification – irreducible notions – for an action or an inference must be assumed to exist if it is to exist at all.

Now within the dialectical reconstruction of the individual agent as presented by Gewirth, there is no implied acknowledgement of the existence of others, nor need there be, prior to the claim of right to freedom and well-being. If the step of the agent's claiming rights to his freedom and well-being is valid, it must be validly derived from the preceding premises which make no reference to the actual or possible social location of the individual agent. Thus, whatever constitutes the justification for claiming these prudential rights, such justification cannot in any way be connected with the existence of others and, *a fortiori*, cannot be connected with whatever others consider to constitute justifications. It remains only to show that prudential rights claims make sense from the standpoint of hypothetically isolated agent abstracted from history and society. If this is possible, then consideration of what constitutes an action-guiding reason cannot be referred to the acceptance or otherwise of hypothetical others and their hypothetical interests.

We know that the common usage of the term 'right' is generally defined in terms of the correlative conceptions of entitlement or due to an individual, and thus an obligation or duty on the part of another. This is not merely a convention of use, it is a conceptual result of the employment of the notion of an entitlement, right or justification. It is, therefore, obviously a mistake to suppose that in cases where no others exist, talk of entitlement or right ceases to imply a notion of duty or obligation owed.[55] The isolated agent recognises that he acts irrationally if he does not defend his freedom and well-being. In other words he recognises a duty to defend them imposed by reason – he is logically obliged, required, it is incumbent upon him on pain of relinquishing his prospective agency to defend them. Thus it follows that in his isolation he has quite coherently acknowledged this overriding prudential *duty*. There can be no notion of morality (in the sense of other-regarding reasons) in this recognition of duty, for there are simply no others to regard.

The isolated agent recognises this duty to defend his freedom and well-being because he is a prospective agent. He then contemplates what it would be like if there were others like him: that is, if there were other prospective agents. Because they must be hypothesised in his own image he would recognise that they, too, had overriding duties to defend their freedom and well-being – for precisely the same reasons as he – for there only are *his* reasons. The isolated agent would not have to worry about the possibility of disagreement over this matter of prudential duties. The isolated agent would know – it is otiose to say know a priori – that these posited others, should they appear, would, on pain of contradicting themselves as agents, acknowledge these duties.

MY DUTY TO OBLIGE OTHERS TO REFRAIN

Now, from the first-person perspective, how can I claim to be logically justified in defending my freedom and well-being, and necessarily expect the agreement of another rational agent to this justification, and consider that another rational agent has no obligation to refrain from interfering with them? I realise that he is not obliged to refrain from interfering with my freedom and well-being on pain of relinquishing his own agency. But I must *oblige* him not to interfere on pain of relinquishing *mine*. I must take a stand equivalent to the following:

> *I oblige all agents to refrain from interfering with my freedom and well-being on pain of severe censure or even physical harm, on the basis that I am charged with the overriding duty of protecting them.*

I would claim this rule to have obligatory force on the sovereign authority of the logic of (prudential) practical reason. In other words, I would claim the right to posit the rule. This is equivalent to claiming the right to put others under an obligation. From my point of view, therefore, they have this obligation. It becomes obvious that this is equivalent to claiming rights to my freedom and well-being. The arguments from Hare, McMahon etc. against the notion of prudential rights are in fact arguments which suggest that others might not recognise the sovereignty of the authority which licensed the rule. This is utterly irrelevant – *I must*. And this is all Gewirth needs to prove.

FROM THE PRUDENTIAL TO THE MORAL

From my point of view, as a Prospective Purposive Agent (PPA), I have these rights to freedom and well-being. Now if I have these rights *because* I am a PPA, is it not necessarily the case that I must assent to a very simple piece of logic, namely, that if I have these rights in virtue of a certain property, then anything else which has this property also has these rights?

Before discussing the profound implications of this *logical* point, let us remind ourselves that we are dealing with the rudiments of the predicate calculus, and not the justification of rights. We are asking whether or not the following sequent is valid:

$$(1)\ \exists x\ (xF \rightarrow xG) \rightarrow (x)\ (xF \rightarrow xG).$$

If it is, then all substitution instances of it are valid; e.g.

$$(2)\ \exists x\ (xPPA \rightarrow xRFWB) \rightarrow (x)\ (xPPA \rightarrow xRFWB).$$

Now if (1) is read as the simple theorem that 'if there is an x such that if x has F then it has G, then for all x, if x has F then x has G', then the simple substitution instance (2) is uncontroversial and uncontestable for it merely puts 'being a PPA' and 'having rights to freedom and well-being' in place of F and G. If, as a PPA, I must assent to this stage of the argument by virtue of the logical principle of universalisation (LPU) as presented in (1), then it amounts to my acceptance of duties to other PPAs on the basis that I have acknowledged that they, too, by virtue of being PPAs, have rights to their freedom and well-being. The move from the prudential (stage 2): 'I must claim rights to my freedom and well-being', which is equivalent to 'I must consider that I have rights to freedom and well-being', to the moral (the other-regarding dimension of practical rationality) (stage 3): 'I must consider that all PPAs have rights to their freedom and well-being', is achieved by the LPU and the correlativity of rights and duties – not by any assumption that I ought to recognise my predicament in others and sympathise by extending consideration to them.

The LPU is not contentious in itself. However, the content of the proposition which results from it has attracted some attention. Several writers have objected to the claim that the inference in the universalisation stage results in the logical necessity of accepting the PGC – even if stage (2) is assumed to be valid.[56] Their objection is that all stage (2) gives us is the inference that all PPAs must claim rights to *their* freedom and well-being, but that this simply means that any particular PPA must hold that all other PPAs must claim rights to theirs. Critics have claimed that to arrive at the PGC, however, which states that all PPAs must act in accordance with those rights claims, an auxiliary (and fatally question-begging) assumption must be introduced: i.e. something of the form, 'I must take favourable account of PPAO's (i.e. another PPA's) freedom and well-being and PPAO must take favourable account of my freedom and well-being.' This is very similar to the objections to the notion of prudential rights. However, there is a subtle difference.

There is substantial agreement that, if stage (2) is valid, the logical principle of universalisation (LPU) allows us to get from: 'I am a PPA therefore *I* must consider I have a right to *my* freedom and well-being', to:

'[I must accept that] All other PPAs must consider *they* have rights to *their* freedom and well-being.' The PGC, however, requires that we can validly infer that: 'I am a PPA therefore *I* must consider that other PPAs have rights to their freedom and well-Being.'

In dealing with this point Beyleveld says that the PGC can be secured if it is possible to show *prior to universalisation*, i.e at stage (2) that a PPA must claim rights to freedom and well-being *because it is a PPA*. If this is possible, then it can be demonstrated, without any additional assumptions, that any and all PPAs must acknowledge the right to freedom and well-being of any and all other PPAs *because* these others are PPAs. Beyleveld says that writers who have objected to stage (3) have largely ignored the argument in Gewirth which makes this crucial point. Gewirth calls it 'the argument from the sufficiency of agency' (ASA).[57] Enthusiasts may consult these primary sources but I am determined to keep to a bare minimum in my treatment of stage (3). I will try to explain the problem as I see it – bearing in mind that we are assuming that stage (2) is valid.

The objection arises because it appears that at stage (2) it is necessary that a PPA claim rights to freedom and well-being by virtue of having purposes, but, so the objection goes, because of the ambiguity of the formulation, 'I must claim rights to my freedom and well-being because I am a PPA', the sufficiency of the claim may be interpreted as being based on something more specific than just the having of generic purposes – e.g. some particular purpose or attribute. This is essentially the substance of Richard Friedman's objection.[58] If this is sound, then it seems that the result of universalisation will only require a PPA to acknowledge the right of, and thus a corresponding duty to, another PPA which claims a right on the basis of an identical specific property, purpose or attribute. In other words, to get to the PGC we have to show that the property of agency itself – simply being a PPA – is not only a necessary condition of claiming a right to freedom and well-being but that it is a *sufficient* condition. If this is possible, then the universalisation of the rights-claim requires a PPA to recognise the right claimed in the case of all claimants who are simply PPAs – regardless of the specificity of their purposes or attributes. In other words, we must show that it is the following which is being universalised in stage 3: 'I am a PPA → [I am a PPA → I must consider that I have rights to freedom and well-being]' Again, we can do no better than quote Gewirth on the matter:[59]

> The agent's description of himself as a prospective purposive agent is both a necessary and a sufficient condition of the justifying reason he must adduce for his claim to have the generic rights. That it is a necessary condition can be seen from the fact that every agent performs his actions by virtue of having purposes whose fulfilment he regards as good. And it is because freedom and well-being are

> required for such purposive actions that every agent claims the right to these generic features of action. If agents had no purposes, they would not claim any rights to act or to have freedom and well-being. The justifying reason for every agent's claim to generic rights must hence refer to a description of him involving the purposes for which he acts: that he is a prospective agent who has purposes he wants to fulfil.
>
> This description of the agent is also a sufficient condition of the justifying reason he must adduce for his having the generic rights. If the agent were to maintain that this reason must add some qualifying restriction to this description, and must hence be less general than his simply being a prospective purposive agent, then he could be shown to contradict himself. Let us designate by the letter D such a more restrictive description. Examples of D would include, 'My name is Wordsworth Donisthorpe,' 'I am highly intelligent (or benevolent)', and other descriptions like those mentioned earlier. Now let us ask the agent whether, while being an agent, he would still hold that he has the rights of freedom and well-being even if he were not D. If he answers yes, then he contradicts his assertion that he has these rights only insofar as he is D. He would hence have to admit that he is mistaken in restricting his justificatory description to D. But if he answers no, that is, if he says that while being an agent he would not hold that he has these rights if he were not D, then he can be shown to contradict himself with regard to the generic features of action. For, as we have seen, it is necessarily true of every agent both that he requires freedom and well-being in order to act and that he hence implicitly claims the right to have freedom and well-being. For an agent not to claim these rights, at least implicitly, would mean that he does not act for purpose he regards as good at all and that he does not regard the necessary conditions of his actions as necessary goods. But this in turn would mean that he is not an agent, which contradicts the initial assumption. Thus, to avoid contradicting himself the agent must admit that he would hold that he has the rights of freedom and well-being even if he were not D, and hence that the description or sufficient reason for which he claims these rights is not anything less general or more restrictive than that he is a prospective agent who has purposes he wants to fulfil.

This is certainly a powerful *reductio* of the objection to the universalisation stage. If it is successful, which seems incontrovertible, it means that any agent must recognise the right of any other to defend its freedom and well-being. This being so it follows that, from the point of view of all and any agents, all and any agents therefore have these rights. It is *assertorically* the case, therefore, that all agents must acknowledge that it is necessarily the case that they must act in accordance with the generic rights of the recipients of their actions. If this argument is valid, which it appears to be,and its premises inescapable, which, from the point of view of the agent (including social scientists), they are, then this approach would succeed in establishing the logical necessity of a basic moral principle upon which all moral considerations must rest.

The application of Gewirth's principle to concrete situations is a complex affair. It involves the explication of observance of the PGC in the context of basic, non-subtractive and additive goods; i.e. those features of agency which are indispensable for the maintenance and improvement of prospective agency.[60] The acceptance of the general principle, however, is not, once the step to claiming rights in line with the ASA is granted. Furthermore, we are not concerned here with the application and implications of the principle, for the long trek through Weber, Finnis, Hollis, Habermas and Gewirth was undertaken solely to demonstrate the conceptual necessity of the relationship between practical reason and moral reason, and the implications of this for the methodology of social science. In short, if I reason practically I reason morally. If I attempt to reason practically and contradict the moral obligations imposed upon me by the presuppositions of my practical precepts, then I cannot be said to be acting reasonably. That the social scientist must attempt to construct models of social action in a framework of means and ends, i.e. on the basis of a conception of practical rationality in some form, it follows that any concept of social action appropriate to the task must include this moral component.

Epilogue: Principle and Method

My intentions at the outset were to show two things:

1. Social Scientists must make moral judgments in formulating their basic explanatory concepts.
2. The scientific determination of moral judgments is possible.

The discovery that practical reason brings society into being, and that practical reason can be shown to be constituted by moral categories, brings us to the realisation that the sociological enterprise is a quest to make moral sense of the social world with a scientific intent.

The immediate implication of this realisation is that social science is a morally critical enterprise. Its general concepts, through which we strive to grasp complex phenomena are, or should be, charged with a moral content; not through the delusions of partisanship, but in the name of objectivity itself.

Thus our conceptions of law, democracy, power, etc. must be constructed from, as Finnis says, the practically reasonable point of view; and, as Gewirth has demonstrated, this is *necessarily* a moral point of view. I am content to conclude, therefore, that at very least we must admit that a positivist non-cognitivism, or hermeneutic relativism are antithetical to the conception of social science. In view of this I offer suggestions for some (even newer) Rules of Sociological Method:

1. An object of investigation must be delineated by a prima facie analysis resulting in an agreed referent which does not, in any arbitrary way, prejudge the nature of the object to be investigated.
2. This basic referent must be ideal-typically modelled as a practical enterprise from the non-arbitrary vantage point of practical rationality.
3. The dialectically-necessary principles of practical rationality must be applied to the objective context of action to provide the perspective of the idealised agent.
4. This ideal-typical (substantively rational) perspective constitutes an essential definition of a practical phenomenon.
5. This essential conception provides a non-arbitrary framework for

empirical analysis of social phenomena – i.e. empirical research in the social sciences appears as the morally critical enterprise of judging the conformity of normative actuality to normative rationality.

Notes

Introduction

1. Unger, R. M., *Law in Modern Society* (Free Press, New York, 1976), p. 53.
2. Ibid.
3. Ibid., p. 49.

Chapter 1

1. Confusion may ensue from the proliferating vocabulary in the social sciences concerning issues of value: 'normative', 'value-judgment', 'value-laden', 'evaluative', 'ethical', 'moral' etc. I have found it useful to use Weber's distinction between formal and substantive rationality (see chap. 3 *infra*) in explicating the problem of the intrusion of values into concept formation. Briefly, a value-judgment is made when a judgment of the rationality of *ends in themselves* is asserted. To say that an end is intrinsically rational is to say that a rational person ought categorically to pursue it. This is in contradistinction to the purely formal judgment of the instrumental rationality of employing efficacious means to the achievement of any *given* end. Thus for most purposes the term 'substantive rationality' will suffice to replace 'value-judgment' etc. However, moral reason may be distinguished *within* substantive reason in that, on the one hand, there may be prudentially rational ends which are categorical and thus substantively rational, or, on the other, the intention may be to assert the intrinsic desirability of some aesthetic experience. Following Gewirth (*Reason and Morality*, University of Chicago Press, Chicago, 1978, p. 1), we can point out that moral reason, however, is essentially other-regarding (see chap. 6 *infra*). Other-regarding imperatives must be epistemologically grounded if social science is to claim objectivity; thus the term 'moral' is more accurately used in criticising the shortcomings of social science. The word 'normative', however, need not be connected to discussion of value or morality. A normative statement is one which implies, assumes or explicitly propounds some standard of correctness by which to evaluate an activity or an object. Thus 'stainless steel is the best material for the job' is a normative statement. So, too, is 'one ought to use stainless steel if one wishes to do the job well'. The word 'normative' is used by all manner of authors connected or loosely connected with the social sciences and philosophy to mean 'value-laden'. If I use it in

any ambiguous context, it will be qualified by a suffix: e.g. normative-instrumental, normative-moral etc. Finally, I am happy to use the words 'moral' and 'ethical' interchangeably. A moral theory, an ethical theory, a theory of Natural Law, or a theory of substantive rationality with other-regarding imperatives, if successful, all entail the resolution of the same problem and so there is little point in making a fuss about which phrase is used.

2. I have in mind e.g. the positivism of Auguste Comte and J. S. Mill (cf. *A System of Logic*, Ballantyne Press, Edinburgh, 1884 and the appendix on Comte) in general, and Book 6 'The Logic of the Moral Sciences' in particular. Also Durkheim's exhortations in *The Rules of Sociological Method* and *The Division of Labour in Society*. The general point is well made by Giddens, A., *Durkheim* (Fontana Press, London, 1978) chaps. 1 and 2., pp. 21-49. Cf. also Benton, T., *The Philosophical Foundations of the Three Sociologies* (Routledge & Kegan Paul, London, 1977), chaps. 1, 2 and 3.
3. Cf. e.g. Weber, M., *The Methodology of the Social Sciences* (Free Press, New York, 1949).
4. I refer to the Nietzschean and Heideggerian influences which, through Foucault and Derrida, characterise Post-Modern texts. The kind of thing I have in mind is described well by Rorty in Rorty, R. *Consequences of Pragmatism* (Harvester Press, Brighton, 1982), intro. xvii-xliv. Also cf. Thomas McCarthy's introduction to Habermas, J., *The Philosophical Discourse of Modernity* (F. Lawrence trans., Polity Press, Cambridge, 1987), pp. viii-xvii.
5. Arguing for a divergence of methodological approach from the natural sciences does not imply that all is well with the so-called 'hard' empirical disciplines. A positivist account of natural science not only fails to provide us with a workable sociology it also fails to account for the rationality of natural science. Ted Benton, in *The Philosophical Foundations of the Three Sociologies* (see note 2 *supra*) makes this plain.
6. I refer to Durkheim's *Division of Labour in Society* (Macmillan, New York, 1933), and Unger, R., *Law in Modern Society* (Free Press, New York, 1976). Here, at p. 47, Unger says that 'Each society reveals through its law the innermost secrets of the manner in which it holds men together.'
7. I originally couched the argument in straightforwardly jurisprudential terms in my doctoral thesis, *Towards an Integrated Theory of Natural Law* (University of Sheffield, 1990). By 'Natural Law' I mean an objectivist theory of the ethical foundations of legal authority and obligation. The kind of *secular* theory I have in mind is set out in Beyleveld, D. and Brownsword, R. *Law as a Moral Judgment* (Sweet and Maxwell, London, 1986), cf. pp. 1–32.
8. This is not just a simple statement of a commitment to some form of 'structuralism' or 'structural determinism' or 'system theory'. I hope that my discussion of Martin Hollis in chap. 5 *infra* makes this clear.
9. Vulgar relativism is the kind of faith in immediate tangibility which characterises common-sensical views of the world: e.g. 'seeing is believing' *but* politics/morality/aesthetics is a 'matter of opinion', 'I know what I like' etc. The fact/value distinction is really an empiricist

doctrine of empirical verifiability and is most clearly expressed in Logical Positivism. By 'relativism', given the rejection of the empiricist theory of direct observation, I mean the position which holds that conceptual frameworks condition our interpretation of phenomena, and that it is impossible to choose (rationally) between competing frameworks.

10. See note 4 *supra*.
11. The issues are about the nature of the 'knowing' subject and the nature of language. There are hundreds of texts which address these issues from a Post-Modern or neo-structuralist perspective. It would be crass to suggest that they were a homogeneous mass of undifferentiated repetition, but it would be similarly unwise to imagine that there is no basic common ground – notwithstanding the claims of authors who do not wish to be 'processed ' or 'pigeonholed'. Norris, C., *Deconstruction – Theory and Practice* (Methuen, New York, 1982) is a clear account of the fundamentals of Post-Modern approaches to philosophy, social science and literature.
12. This is an important point. It concerns the meta-logical justification of logic itself. If this is possible it must be done without assuming the validity of the logical principles themselves. If we have to start from logic, then this would appear to be unavoidably question-begging. The solution is to distinguish between types of circularity. One type is vicious and logically fallacious (or at least argumentatively uncompelling); the other is genuinely epistemological, in that it is an analysis based upon reflection on the conditions of intelligible experience. The principles which are synthesised by this transcendental method (in a Kantian sense), or what amounts to the same thing, dialectically necessary method (in a Gewirthian sense), achieve apodictic validity not by proving *assertorically* the truth of logic or theoretical or practical principles, but by showing that such principles must, from the viewpoint of the arguer, the inquirer or the pursuer of purposes, be *necessarily assumed to be true*. This is very different from showing that such principles are *in fact* true – very different because this is *in fact* impossible.
13. This interpretation is, I think, accurate in respect of Kant given his distinction between phenomena and noumena. The phenomenal categories apply solely to phenomena whilst 'things-in-themselves', or *noumena*, are beyond the grasp of reason. Thus if truth is understood as some correspondence between the semantic content of our understanding and these ultimately 'real' (independent of all constituting powers of cognition) 'things', we cannot say that reason gives us truth. But to regard what Kant offers as somehow second best is a very curious way to look at the problem. It presents this idea of 'absolute knowing' as being the ultimate quest of philosophical endeavour. But this relationship between the mind and these un-understandable 'objects' is quite odd. It has nothing to do with the idea of knowledge. In fact it is doubtful if the idea makes any sense at all. It is a form of understanding without understanding. Descartes seems to be clear on this matter.

    > if . . . we can never have any reason to doubt that of the truth of which we have persuaded ourselves, there is nothing more to

> inquire about; we have all the certainty that can reasonably be desired. ... What is it to us if someone should feign that the very thing of whose truth we are so firmly persuaded appears false to the eyes of God or of the Angels and that hence, speaking absolutely, it is false? Why should we concern ourselves with this absolute falsity, since we by no means believe in it or even have the least suspicion of it? For we are supposing a belief or a conviction so strong that nothing can remove it, and this conviction is in every respect the same as certitude. (As quoted from *Oeuvres de Descartes* VII, 145 [Latin]; 113–14 [French] in Frankfurt, H. G., 'Descartes Validation of Reason' in Willis Doney (ed.), *Descartes* (Macmillan, London, 1970), pp. 225–226

14. This is particularly important. The idea of dialectic is, of course, at least as old as the memory of Socrates. What Socrates did could be described as a *dialectically contingent* method of reasoning. That is, from any particular claim he would draw out entailments, some of which were embarrassing to his opponents, or even contradicted their initial claims. In Gewirth, we find a similarly dialectical method in that his aim is to draw out the implications of certain claims and refer them to their origins in respect of their consistency. However, Gewirth calls his approach to moral philosophy a dialectically *necessary* method in that it proceeds from claims which *necessarily must be made*. For instance, Gewirth holds that one cannot deny that one is an agent, and that from this unavoidable claim we can draw out a logically irrefutable principle of practical reason with moral content. Similarly, Habermas wants to analyse the dialectic of communication in respect of its moral implications for institutional design.
15. Hume can be credited with this view and its subsequent popularity. It is known as 'Hume's Fork'. Cf. Hume, D., *Enquiries* etc. (L. A. Selby-Bigge [ed.], third edn., Clarendon Press, Oxford, 1975) section IV, paras 20, 21, pp. 25, 26. Logical Positivism resurrected it and A. J. Ayer popularised it in *Language Truth and Logic* (Pelican, 1971).
16. Cf. Pap, A., *Semantics and Necessary Truth* (Yale University Press, New Haven, 1958), chap. 7, pp. 162 ff.
17. Cf. e.g. Gayatri Spivak's preface to Derrida, J., *Of Grammatology* (Johns Hopkins University Press, Baltimore, 1976) for an excellent presentation of the interpretation of *logos* in Rousseau, Nietzsche and Derrida.
18. Gewirth, in *Reason and Morality* (University of Chicago Press, Chicago, 1978), pp. 22–3, regards reason as the ultimate justificatory standard. By 'reason' he means adherence to the canons of deductive and inductive logic because 'they respectively achieve logical necessity and reflect what is empirically ineluctable ... and are the only sure ways of avoiding arbitrariness and attaining objectivity.' He goes on to say:

> It is indeed the case that there have ... been historical demands that reason itself in turn pass various justificatory tests set by religious faith, aesthetic rapture, and so forth. But the very scrutiny to determine whether these tests are passed must itself make use of reason. For example, salient powers of

reason must be used in order to check whether the products of logical and empirical rationality are consistent with propositions upheld on the basis of faith, or whether the use of reason is compatible with the experiencing of aesthetic feelings, and the like. Thus any attack on reason or any claim to supersede it by some other human power or criterion must rely on reason to justify its claims.

19. Cf. Goudge, T. A., *The Thought of C. S. Peirce* (Dover Publications, New York, 1969), pp. 11–15. Here Goudge quotes Peirce as saying: 'thinking, as cerebration, is no doubt subject to the general laws of nervous action'. This is also a view shared by Quine.
20. Cf. e.g. 'Two Dogmas of Empiricism', in Quine, W. V. O., *From a Logical Point of View* (second edn, Harvard University Press, Massachusetts, 1980). That 'all principles are (pragmatically) revisable' is a statement which must be held by a Pragmatist epistemology, is to be expected. Cognition is a practical tool as far as Pragmatists are concerned, and, they allege, it is our practical requirements which explain cognition, and not the other way round. Thus, logic, although of great service in the past, must not outstay its welcome. If, as it is alleged, modern quantum mechanics finds the intrusion of basic logical principles such as the principle of noncontradiction (or the Law of Contradiction), and the Law of Excluded Middle, to be getting in the way of their objectives – i.e. to 'explain' phenomena which 'appear' to contradict the laws of logic, then the tail must not be allowed to wag the dog, and logic must go.

   Of this view Beyleveld says:

   > 1. The principle of noncontradiction, in stating that a statement and its denial cannot be true *of the same set of circumstances*, is a principle presupposed in our assumed ability to delineate different classes of objects, and in our practice of denying that any statement is true. Anyone who says that the principle of noncontradiction is not a law of thought presupposes this principle by making such a statement. Anyone who asserts that there are alternative principles of consistency to this principle presupposes that thee are different principles of consistency, and in so doing relies upon the principle of noncontradiction as a more fundamental principle of consistency.
   >
   > 2. It is sometimes suggested (see, e.g. Quine [op. cit.] that the ultimate reason for entrenchment of the principle of noncontradiction in our thinking is that it is useful in ordering our experience, and that counterexperience could lead us to give it up. I disagree, and for two reason: (*a*) being able to form the notion of a 'counterexperience' presupposes the principle of noncontradiction, and (*b*) being able to infer that an experience is a counterexperience presupposes the principle of noncontradiction (as well as that of *modus ponens* [at the very least]). [Beyleveld, D., *The Dialectical Necessity of Morality* (University of Chicago Press, Chicago, 1991), p. 331.

21. Cf. Popper, K., *Conjectures and Refutations* (Routledge & Kegan Paul, London, 1963), pp. 97–9. Popper notes that Cardinal

Bellarmino, unlike Berkeley, was not concerned with the validity of the instrumentalist epistemology which he used in his capacity as an inquisitor. Bellarmino wrote:

> Galileo will act prudently ... if he will speak hypothetically, *ex suppositione* ... to say that we give a better account of the appearances by supposing the earth to be moving, and the sun at rest, than we could if we used eccentrics and epicycles is to speak properly, there is no danger in that, and it is all that the mathematician requires. (op. cit., p. 98, n. 2).

Popper says:

> Later certain Pragmatists based their whole philosophy upon the view that the idea of 'pure' knowledge was a mistake; that there could be no knowledge in any other sense but in the sense of *instrumental* knowledge; that knowledge was power and that truth was usefulness. ... Today the view of physical science founded by Osiander, Cardinal Bellarmino, and Bishop Berkeley has won the battle without another shot being fired. Without any further debate over the philosophical issue, without producing any new argument, the *instrumentalist view* ... has become an accepted dogma. (op. cit. p. 99).

22. The point is obvious: prediction and control of the natural world is simply one aspect of the Will to Power merging into the Will to Truth in the verificationist methodologies of Positivist theories of science. The critique of technology appears as the critique of instrumental reason in the work of the Frankfurt School, e.g. Horkheimer, M. and Adorno, T., (trans. J. Cumming), *Dialectic of Enlightenment* (Seaburg, New York, 1972). This current of domination is seen to be contained in the idea of Enlightenment itself. Marxism itself is seen as part of the continuum of dominant instrumental discourse. In line with this Habermas rejects the category of labour in Marxism as an emancipatory perspective and replaces it with communication (see chap. 7 *infra*). Foucault's relationship with the Western Marxist critique is interesting. As Mark Poster explains in *Foucault, Marxism and History* (Polity Press, Cambridge, 1984), chap. 1, pp. 10 ff., Foucault's post-structuralism understands Weber's, Horkheimer's, Adorno's, Marcuse' and Lukacs' critique of bureaucratic/instrumental/technological rationality, but sees this critique as still rooted in the ideology of Reason itself. The critique of technological rationality is in fact the point of contact between Post- or Western Marxisms and Post-Modernisms.
23. See note 25 *infra.*
24. Thomas McCarthy (introduction) to Habermans, J., *The Philosophical Discourse of Modernity* (Polity Press, Cambridge, 1987), pp. viii–ix.
25. Cf. Habermas, J., *The Philosophical Discourse of Modernity* (op. cit.) lecture XII, pp. 336 *et seq.* Habermas says:

> The variations of a critique of reason with reckless disregard for its own foundations are related to one another ... They are guided by normative intuitions that go beyond what they can accommodate in terms of the indirectly affirmed 'other of reason'. Whether modernity is described as a constellation of

> life that it reified and used, or as one that is technologically manipulated, or as one that is totalitarian, rife with power, homogenized, imprisoned – the denunciations are constantly inspired by a special sensitivity for complex injuries and subtle violations. Inscribed in this sensitivity is the picture of an undamaged intersubjectivity that the young Hegel first projected as an ethical totality.

26. Foucault's work is most important in this regard. *The Order of Things: An Archeology of the Human Sciences* (1973) and *Madness and Civilisation* (1973) are central texts. Cf. also 'The Critique of Reason as an Unmasking of the Human Sciences' Michel Foucault, in Habermas, J. (op. cit.), pp. 238–65.
27. I think this is a permissible reading of Nietzsche. Cf. e.g. Mugge, M., *M. A. Nietzsche* (Dodge Publishing, New York, 1914), pp. 46 ff.; Danto, A. C., *Nietzsche as Philosopher* (Macmillan, New York, 1967), pp. 72–5, 76, 226–8. Habermas, J., 'The Entry into Postmodernity: Nietzsche as a Turning Point', in Habermas, J., (op. cit.), p. 83 ff. Also cf. Nietzsche, F. *Beyond Good and Evil* (T. N. Foulis, Edinburgh, 1909), chap. 1 ['Prejudices of Philosophers'] and Spivak's preface to Derrida, J., *Of Grammatology* (op. cit.) Also Norris, C., *Deconstruction* (Methuen, New York, 1982), chap. 4 and esp. p. 61, where Norris says of Nietzsche's views on the Greek foundations of modern thought:

    > Behind all the big guns of reason and morality is a fundamental will to persuade which craftily disguises its workings by imputing them always to the adversary camp. Truth is simply the honorific title assumed by an argument which has got the upper hand – and kept it – in this war of competing persuasions.

28. Derrida's deconstructionist project attempts to mount a critique of phonocentricism by showing that the sign is endowed with a magical reality only through the mythical 'presence' of the knowing subject. (Cf. preface to his *Of Grammatology*, op. cit.) Habermas says:

    > Adorno's 'negative dialectics' and Derrida's 'deconstruction' can be seen as different answers to the same problem. The totalizing self-critique of reason gets caught in a performative contradiction since subject-centered reason can be convicted of being authoritarian in nature only by having recourse to its own tools. (Habermas, J., [op. cit.], p. 185).

29. I have more to say on this important point in chap. 6 *infra* in respect of Finnis' arguments concerning the 'circularity' of defences of deductive reasoning. Also in chap. 9 (*re* Bernstein) I discuss the concept of contradiction and *petitio principii* and offer a meta-logical analysis of the validity of logical principles which cannot be said to be question begging.
30. Cf. e.g. Lukes, S., *Power: a Radical View* (Macmillan, London, 1974). Here Lukes shows quite clearly that the concept of power in any sociologically relevant sense requires a supporting theory of *real interest* unless all consensus is to be assumed to be genuine consensus. Also Habermas's essay, 'On Levelling the Genre Distinction between Philosophy and Literature', in Habermas, J. (op. cit.), pp. 185–210. Also see note 21 *supra*.

31. Cf. Macintyre, A., *After Virtue* (Duckworth, London, 1985), chap. 2, provides a good discussison of the pervasiveness of emotivist thought. Macintyre says:

    > ... since emotivism fails precisely as a theory of the *meaning* of moral expressions, analytical philosophers by and large rejected emotivism. Yet emotivism did not die and it is important to note how often in widely different modern philosophical contexts something very like emotivism's attempted reduction of morality to personal preference continually recurs in the writings of those who do not think of themselves as emotivists.

32. For example, Habermas is indebted to Steven Toulmin for his analysis of argumentation which forms the basis of Habermas's Theory of Communicative Action. He explains that

    > Toulmin criticizes absolutist views that base theoretical knowledge, moral-practical insight, and aesthetic evaluation on deductively conclusive arguments or empirically compelling evidence. To the extent that arguments are conclusive in the sense of logical inference, they do not bring anything new to light; and to the extent that they have any substantive content at all, they rest on insights and needs that can be variously interpreted in terms of changing frameworks or 'languages', and that, therefore, do not provide any ultimate foundations.

    This is a restatement of the Logical Empiricist doctrine that analytic truth is vacuous or tautological – mixed in with a non-positivist critique of theory neutrality plus a dash of incommensurability theory.
33. E.g. as in Parsonian functionalist accounts of the family. Cf. Bilton *et al. Introductory Sociology* (Second edn, Macmillan, London, 1981), chap. 7, for a range of references and examples.
34. E.g. as in Marxist accounts of the nuclear family. See note 33 (esp. pp. 282 ff.).
35. Cf. e.g. excerpts from Fuller, Hart, Finnis etc., in Lloyd and Freeman, M. D. A., *Lloyd's Introduction to Jurisprudence* (Stevens and Sons, London, 1985), pp. 127 ff.
36. On this confusing point see chaps 1 and 2 *infra*. The issue is whether or not the 'ideal-type' is an empirical generalisation based on the statistical frequency of features or practices common to what are regarded as similar institutions, or whether the ideal-type is a rational model of an enterprise from some point of view which transcends all contingent opinion.
37. See chap. 3 *infra*.
38. Cf. Finnis, J., *Natural Law and Natural Rights* (Clarendon Press, Oxford, 1980), chaps 1 and 2.

Chapter 2

1. Cf. Guy Oakes's introductory essay to Weber, M., *Roscher and Knies: The Logical Problems of Historical Economics*. (Free Press, New York, 1975), esp. pp. 24-39. Cf. also Collingwood, R. G. *The Idea of History* (Oxford University Press, London, 1966), pp. 165 ff. An extended account of the issues dealt with in this chapter is to be

found in Toddington, S. W., *Towards an Integrated Theory of Natural Law* (Ph.D.thesis, University of Sheffield, 1990), chap. 1.

2. Cf. Weber, M., *The Methodology of the Social Sciences* (Free Press, New York, 1949).
3. See note 1.
4. The counterpart to the methodological theses of the German schools is to be found in the work of J. S. Mill. Guy Oakes summarises what I will call the 'Unitarian' or positivist thesis of scientific method:

    > There are no distinctive features of the socio-cultural phenomena. All phenomena are 'natural' phenomena, the possible objects of laws of nature. The methods of the natural sciences have universal prescriptive application. It follows that there are no methods of investigation peculiar to the socio-cultural domain.

    He goes on to say

    > At the time Weber wrote his monograph, it was perhaps John Stuart Mill who had provided the clearest and most uncompromising statement of this position. It is found in the famous Book VI of *A System of Logic* entitled *On the Logic of the Moral Sciences*. This text acquired much influence after its translation into German. The term 'moral science' was the source of the unfortunate German expression *Geisteswissenschaft – science of mind.* (Oakes, G., in Weber, *Roscher and Knies* (op. cit.), p. 21.

5. The nomological scheme of explanation (e.g. Mill), or something like it, is shown to be at the root of Roscher's (and others') scheme of explanation of history and culture. Particularly, the notion of the *Volksgeist* is seen to be the explanatory equivalent of the notion of the universal 'laws' which are alleged to underpin empirical regularities in the positivist scheme of explanation. CF. Weber, *Roscher and Knies* (op. cit.), pp. 59–69.
6. Cf. Weber, M., *Roscher and Knies* (op. cit.), pp. 60–1.
7. This is, of course, a central issue in the philosophy of natural science. A good discussion of it can be found in Benton, T. The Philosophical Foundations of the Three Sociologies (Routledge & Kegan Paul, London 1978), chap. 3.
8. Cf. Weber, M., *Roscher and Knies*, (op. cit.), pp. 60–2.
9. Cf. Oakes, G. in Weber, M., *Roscher and Knies*, (op. cit.), pp. 21–2; see note 4 *supra*. Mill's original discussions can be found in a *A System of Logic* (Ballantyne Press, Edinburgh, 1884), E.g. pp. 106, 107, 108, 122, 186, 205, 206, 207, 208.
10. See note 1.
11. Cf. Weber, M. *Roscher and Knies* (op. cit.), pp. 55–61.
12. Ibid., p. 59.
13. Ibid., p. 5.
14. Ibid., p. 59.
15. Cf. ibid., p. 61 ff.
16. Cf. ibid., p. 61.
17. Ibid.
18. Ibid., p. 62.

19. On this important point cf. Weber, M., *Roscher and Knies* (op. cit.), pp. 55–63, esp. pp. 61–3.
20. Cf. ibid., p. 57.
21. Cf. pp. 63, 64.
22. Cf. ibid., pp. 95–7.
23. Ibid., p. 96.
24. Ibid., pp. 96, 97.
25. Cf. ibid., p. 97.
26. Ibid., p. 98.
27. Ibid., p. 98.
28. Cf. ibid., pp. 101 ff.
29. Ibid., p. 102.
30. Ibid.
31. See my introductory remarks to chap. 3 *infra*, where I discuss the prima facie coherence of the 'value-neutral' ideal-type and the notion of value-relevance.
32. Weber, M., *Roscher and Knies* (op. cit.), p. 104.
33. Cf.(3) ibid., p. 120.
34. Cf. ibid., p. 121.
35. Ibid.
36. Cf. ibid., pp. 122, 123.
37. Cf. ibid., p. 123.
38. Ibid.
39. Ibid., p. 185.
40. Ibid., p. 186, 187.
41. Ibid., pp. 187, 188.
42. Ibid., p. 188.
43. Ibid.
44. Cf. ibid.
45. Cf. Oakes's remarks in his introduction to Weber, M., *Roscher and Knies* (op. cit.), p. 39.

Chapter 3

1. Weber, M., *The Methodology of the Social Sciences* (Free Press, New York 1949).
2. Cf. Weber, M., *Roscher and Knies: The Logical Problems of Historical Economics* (Free Press, New York, 1975), pp. 102–4.
3. Cf. Beyleveld, D., *The Epistemological Foundations of Sociological Theory* (Ph.D. thesis, University of East Anglia, 1975), pp. 174–81.
4. Beyleveld, D., (op. cit.), p. 174.
5. Weber, M., *The Methodology of the Social Sciences* (op. cit.), p. 89.
6. Weber, M., *Roscher and Knies* (op. cit.), p. 72.
7. Beyleveld, D. (op. cit.), p. 183.
8. Brubaker, R., *The Limits of Rationality* (George Allen and Unwin, London, 1984).
9. Perhaps Brubaker's book should be called 'The Limits of *Verstehen*'? It is Weber's methodology which is causing the problem.
10. Brubaker, R., (op. cit.), p. 50.
11. Ibid., p. 50.
12. Ibid., p. 51.
13. This will be made clearer as we progress; however, my view is that

Wertrationalität is rationality conditioned by the employment of efficacious means to the achievement of ends, and so is *Zweckrationalität*. With the latter, however, there is a greater degree of calculation *en route*. The end of the action, though, is still constituted by an ultimate value. Weber characterises modernity as an epoch in which calculation and control are ubiquitous – abundant in our practices – and in this sense, dominant. I cannot see any deeper distinction than this quantitative one which would warrant a typological dichotomy. See note 16 *infra*, and the corresponding quotation from Brubaker. I am grateful to Roger Brownsword and William Outhwaite for drawing my attention to this issue.
14. Brubaker, R. (op. cit.), p. 54.
15. Ibid., p. 36.
16. Ibid., pp. 36, 37.
17. Outhwaite, W., *Concept Formation in Social Science* (Routledge & Kegan Paul, London, 1983), p. 131.
18. Ibid.
19. Ibid.
20. Ibid.
21. Ibid.
22. I take it that non-cognitivism in ethics implies relativism in ethics. If ethical/moral beliefs cannot be the object of scientific or rational justification, then all ethical/moral beliefs are on a par in the sense that none is more, or less, rational than any other. This is one sense of relativism. Another is that, in this case, the only way ethical/moral beliefs can be explained is by reference to some contingent set of circumstances. These beliefs can then be said to have some explanation relative to these circumstances.
23. Löwith, K., *Max Weber and Karl Marx* (Allen and Unwin, London, 1982). See note 6, chap. 4 *infra*.
24. Outhwaite, W. (op. cit.), p. 132.
25. Ibid., p. 131.
26. Ibid., p. 132.
27. Ibid., p. 133
28. Ibid.
29. Ibid.
30. Cf. Weber, M., *The Methodology of the Social Sciences* (op. cit.).
31. Brubaker, R., *The Limits of Rationality* (op. cit.), p. 93.
32. Ibid., p. 93.
33. Ibid., p. 94.
34. Ibid., p. 95.
35. Ibid.
36. Ibid.
37. Ibid.
38. Ibid., p. 97.
39. Ibid., p. 98.
40. Ibid., p. 101.
41. Cf. Benton, T., *The Philosophical Foundations of the Three Sociologies* (Routledge & Kegan Paul, London, 1977), p. 113.
42. Cf. Macintyre, A., After Virtue (second edn., Duckworths, 1985), chap. 2.

43. Cf. Weber, M., *Roscher and Knies* (op. cit.), pp. 98-101.
44. Cf. Book 6 of J. S. Mill's *A System of Logic*, (Ballantyne Press, Edinburgh, 1884).
45. See note 6 of chap. 4 *infra*.
46. This is the contention of John Finnis in chap. 1, of *Natural Law and Natural Rights*. See chap. 4 *infra*.

Chapter 4

1. Finnis, J., *Natural Law and Natural Rights* (Clarendon Press, Oxford, 1980).
2. Ibid., chaps 1 and 2.
3. Legal Positivism does not share the straightforward methodological philosophies of the 'Unitarian' scheme outlined by J. S. Mill in his *System of Logic*. That John Austin, one of the most influential of Legal Positivists, should have been so closely involved with Mill as both colleague and teacher is odd, in that we do not see Austin's approach to legal phenomena modelled on Mill's uncompromising nomological method of explanation. What we do see in the positivist tradition in jurisprudence is the assumption that to understand law and government, as a technique, is possible only if one first sets aside the question of *legitimacy*. This assumption is question-begging (and I use this phrase with great care in view of our discussions of the *petitio principii* elsewhere) against the Natural Lawyer in that it implies that there is a phenomenon, law, which can be examined in its essential detail apart from its context and content of legitimacy – i.e. its moral rationality. But the Natural Law thesis is precisely that there cannot be such a phenomenon. That the aims of Austinian Positivism rest upon this begging of the question is clear from Cotterrell's account – Cf. Cotterrell, R., *The Politics of Jurisprudence* (Butterworths, London, 1989), pp. 57–9 – where we note that law is clearly defined, by Austin, as an expression of power. If law is defined as an expression of power only contingently connected with legitimacy or morality, then there is little point in trying to argue that it is *necessarily* connected with legitimacy or morality.

   My remarks concerning the pseudo-positivism of Hart are meant to suggest that Hart cannot criticise Austin for failure to attend to the *practical point* of compliance with rules, as he clearly does in his discussion of the methodological necessity of adopting the 'internal point of view' – (cf. Hart, H. L. A., *The Concept of Law* [Clarendon Press, Oxford, 1961], e.g. p. 96) and arbitrarily rule out the possibility that practical reason can have moral implications. This is doubly important in understanding Hart: Hart attempts to justify and distinguish legal obligation, moral obligation and obligation under threat of illegitimate power. Thus he must provide a practical reconstruction from the internal point of view (an ideal-type) of legal obligation – which must be a categorical obligation, not simply a prudential choice to avoid punishment, harm or some other sanction – but which cannot be a moral obligation. This sails so close to the wind in regard to a Natural Law thesis that its claim to be 'positivist' consists simply in denying any necessary connection between law and morality. This is an arbitrary choice of nomenclature and of little importance. It is the implications of the *actual* methodological assumptions involved that are of sole concern.

4. See note 3 *supra* where I explain that the point is that it will be seen to be logically impossible to mix interpretive explanations in social science with an assumption of nomological backing e.g. role determinism. (See chap. 5 *infra):* and likewise impossible to talk about rational explanation (in terms of a practically reasonable point of view) which does not involve moral judgment. Hart attempts to do this.
5. We have discussed this at length in chap. 2 *supra*. Weber's views are to be found in Weber, M., *Roscher and Knies: The Logical Problems of Historical Economics* (Free Press, New York, 1975), pp. 186, 187.
6. When Weber talks about value-freedom he assumes that the task of the social scientist, or, as we noted in ch. 3 *supra,* the remit of the moral philosopher, is simply to trace the implications of fundamental value-choices unambiguously given. In this way we build a rational-type or ideal model of a particular enterprise which serves us as a definition and datum line for empirical evaluations (see chap. 2 *supra*). But who give them to whom? Who formulates the unambiguous goals of capitalism, or Protestantism, or the prison system or the welfare state? We cannot accept the common-sense view of the aims of any enterprise, for, clearly, we may simply be jotting down error, delusion, wishful thinking or a successfully inculcated ideology. We can focus on this problem by considering Giddens's account of the ideal type:

   > An ideal type is constructed by the abstraction and combination of an indefinite number of elements which although found in reality, are rarely or never discovered in this specific form. Thus the characteristics of the 'Calvinist Ethic' which Weber analyses in *The Protestant Ethic* are taken from the writings of various historical figures, and involve those components of Calvinist doctrines *which Weber identifies as of particular importance in relation to the formation of the capitalist spirit.* [my emphasis] (Giddens, A., *Capitalism and Modern Social Theory* (Cambridge University Press, Cambridge, 1971), pp. 141, 142.

   Giddens is right; this is what Weber did. In other words, true to his methodological prescriptions as propounded in *Roscher and Knies* concerning the rejection of the nomological method which sought to identify the generic or common features of cultural phenomena with the *essential,* he attempts to construct an ideally rational type. But making judgments about what is essential about religious or economic activities is to make judgments about the ultimate ends of such activities from a point of view which transcends all subjective opinion, or it is simply to make an arbitrary judgment about what is essential. Neither position is consistent with Weber's views on the requirements of objectivity in social science: the first involves a value-judgment; the second is mere assertion.

   The issue becomes even more confused when we note that Weber's methodological doctrines are not always completely understood by those who purport to endorse his views. Informative discussions of the creative business of ideal-type construction in the absence of an essentialist criterion of significance in practical activity can be found in Andreski, S., *The Insights and Errors of Max Weber* (Routledge & Kegan Paul, London, 1984), chaps 2 and 4. In Andreski, S., *Elements of Comparative Sociology* (Weidenfeld and Nicolson, 1984), p. 87, we have laid before us the real problem of not only ideal-type construction but of how we are to make sense of, on the one hand, Weber's remarks in *Roscher and Knies* concerning the need to reject any hope of making sense of history and culture by recourse to the description of common or generic features of phenomena, and, on the other, his (and others') propensity to treat ideal-types as empirical generalisations. Comparative sociologists who might call themselves Weberians seem to have followed their mentor's example faithfully: i.e. they have completely disregarded the metatheoretical arguments presented in *Roscher and Knies* which proved how inadequate attempts such as the following are to appropriate social phenomena:

> ... types should preferably be defined in a way that permits inclusion of several cases: in other words, very narrow as well as very wide definitions should be avoided unless some important considerations make them imperative. The concept of feudalism, for instance, can be made so narrow as to apply only to, say, Northern France in the 13th century, whilst it can also be defined so widely that it will fit all pre-industrial states, neither of these extremes lends itself to subtle theorizing, which calls for a definition which helps to classify pre-industrial polities. Or take 'totalitarianism'. Many definitions have been proposed which fit only Nazi Germany or Soviet Russia, and not even both, whereas it might be more illuminating to have a definition which distils *the common features* of these regimes without pre-judging the question of compatibility or concatenation of these features with other perhaps equally *important* characteristics [my emphasis].

Is it the common features we wish to identify, or the important ones? Or is it that the common features *are* the important ones? If it is the latter, then this straightforwardly contradicts Weber's methodological pronouncements.

But it is not just self-professed Weberians who utilise the notion of the ideal-type. Marx did and Marxists do frequently. Curiously, it is not the error of treating common or generic features as essential features in the construction of the ideal-type which characterises Marxism, it is an unequivocal judgment of what are the most important features of the historical process. We may note that in Marxist orthodoxy the Theory of Surplus Value appears as an ideal-type of one aspect of capitalist relations of production. That is, it appears as a model of the instrumentally rational behaviour of purchasers, of labour power. The emphasis in this model concentrates upon the issue of the equity (or not) of the value of the product in relation to remuneration for the labour expended in creating the value of the product. But the owner/non-owner relationship, or even the rich and multi-faceted phenomenon of work in a capitalist society, or even the conception of ownership, appears as a narrow target of analysis given the complexity of relations in modern society. The assertion that the mechanism of expropriation of surplus value from labour is the *essential* feature of our understanding of production relations is clearly open to dispute. What is required is an argument that shows us why we should adopt this point of view. We may add that as regards the two approaches, i.e. the selection of common features, on the one hand, or selection of *important* features, on the other, only the latter is a sociological approach.

7. See the discussion of formal/substantive rationality in chap. 3 *supra.*
8. Finnis, J. *Natural Law and Natural Rights* (Clarendon Press, Oxford, 1980), pp. 3, 4.
9. Ibid., p. 4.
10. Ibid.
11. Ibid., p. 6.
12. Ibid., p. 7.
13. Cf. ibid.
14. We may recall that in *Roscher and Knies* (op. cit.), Weber rails against the notion of the generic or typical features of history and culture as equating to the *essential.* Weber is right in this but see note 6 *supra* for the confusion which this causes in Weber's supposedly 'value-free' approach.
15. For further references to the standard stuff cf. Golding, M.P., *Philosophy of Law* (Prentice-Hall, New Jersey, 1975), chap. 1 in general, and especially pp. 7–9, and 12 ff. for a discussion of the problem of defining the word 'law' and relating this definition to the social practice. Also cf. Cotterrell, R., 'The Sociological Concept of Law' (*Journal of Law and Society*, 10 (1983), p. 241). Most importantly, cf. Beyleveld, D. and Brownsword, R., *Law as a Moral Judgment* (Sweet and Maxwell, London, 1986), pp. 83–98 and (on Finnis) 98–109.
16. Finnis, J. (op. cit.), p. 10.
17. Ibid.
18. See note 6 *supra.*
19. Cf. Finnis (op. cit.), p. 20, fn. 1.3.
20. Fortenbaugh, W. W., 'Aristotle's Analysis of Friendship: Function and Analogy, Resemblance and Focal Meaning', *Phronesis,* 20 (1975), pp. 61–2.
21. Ibid. p. 52.
22. Ibid. p. 53.
23. Ibid., p. 53, 54.
24. Ibid., p. 55.
25. Ibid.
26. Ibid., p. 56.
27. Ibid., p. 57.
28. Ibid., p. 59.
29. Ibid.
30. Ibid.
31. Finnis, J. (op. cit.), p. 10.
32. Ibid., p. 11.
33. Ibid.

34. Ibid.
35. Beyleveld, D. and Brownsword, R., *Law as a Moral Judgment* (Sweet and Maxwell, London, 1986), p. 118.
36. Ibid., p. 120.
37. Finnis, J. (op. cit.), p. 12.
38. Ibid.
39. Ibid., p. 13.
40. Ibid.

Chapter 5

1. Hollis, M., *Models of Man* (Cambridge University Press, Cambridge, 1977).
2. Ibid., pp. 2, 3.
3. Ibid., p. 7.
4. Ibid., p. 6.
5. Ibid., p. 7.
6. Ibid., p. 9.
7. Ibid., p. 10
8. Ibid., p. 12.
9. Ibid., p. 14.
10. Ibid., p. 47.
11. Ibid., pp. 44, 45.
12. Ibid., p. 46.
13. Ibid., p. 47.
14. Ibid., p. 48.
15. Ibid.
16. Ibid.
17. Ibid., p. 49
18. Ibid., pp. 50, 51.
19. Ibid., p. 51.
20. Ibid., p. 52
21. Cf. Newton Smith, W. H. *The Rationality of Science* (Routledge & Kegan Paul, London, 1981), pp. 44–76, for a discussion and critique. The original source of the falsificationist programme is presented in Popper, K., *Objective Knowledge* (Clarendon Press, Oxford, 1972), pp. 1–29.
22. Hollis, M. (op. cit.), p. 53.
23. Ibid.
24. Ibid. p. 55.
25. As do, for instance, Harre, R. and Madden, E. J. in their *Causal Powers* (Blackwell, Oxford, 1975). Cf. also Bhaskar, R., *Philosophy and the Idea of Freedom* (Blackwell, Oxford, 1991), Vol I.
26. Ibid. p. 57.
27. Ibid. p. 64.
28. Ibid. p. 65 referring to Arthur Pap's *Semantics and Necessary Truth* (Yale University Press , New Haven, 1958).
29. Ibid. p. 65.
30. Ibid.
31. Ibid. pp. 66, 67.
32. Ibid.
33. Ibid.

34. Ibid., p. 70.
35. Ibid.
36. Ibid., p. 73.
37. Ibid., p. 74.
38. Ibid.
39. Hollis, M. (op. cit.), pp. 74, 75, 76.
40. Hollis, M. (op. cit.), p. 75.
41. Ibid., pp. 76, 77.
42. Ibid., p. 77.
43. Ibid., p. 78.
44. Ibid.
45. Ibid.
46. Cf. ibid., p. 81.
47. Ibid., p. 82.
48. Ibid., p. 82.
49. Cf. ibid.
50. Ibid., p. 83.
51. Cf. ibid., p. 82.
52. Ibid., p. 88.
53. Ibid.
54. Ibid.
55. Ibid. p. 89.
56. Ibid., p. 90.
57. Ibid., p. 89.
58. Ibid., p. 90.
59. Ibid., p. 91.
60. Hollis mentions Williams, B., *Problems of the Self;* Wiggins, D., *Locke, Butler and the Stream of consciousness*; also Strawson, P., *Individuals.*, cf. Hollis, M. (op. cit.), p. 91.
61. Ibid., p. 96.
62. Ibid., p. 95.
63. Ibid., pp. 95, 96.
64. Ibid., p. 96.
65. Ibid.
66. John Searle, Speaking on the mind/brain problem in his Reith Lecture broadcast on BBC radio in 1984.
67. Hollis, M. (op. cit.), p. 102.
68. Ibid., p. 103.
69. Ibid., p. 102.
70. Ibid., p. 103.
71. Ibid.
72. Ibid., p. 104.
73. Ibid., p. 105.
74. Cf. ibid., pp. 103–6.
75. Ibid., p. 106.
76. Ibid., p. 122.
77. Ibid., p. 124.
78. Ibid., p. 125.
79. Cf. Ibid., pp. 107–12.
80. Cf. Ibid., p. 112

Chapter 6

1. Hollis says at p. 138 of *Models of Man* 'I do not want to end the chapter in the mists of ethics ... our model of autonomy is an explanatory model.' However, the assertion that the rationality of action can be adduced only by evaluating the rationality of ends is an assertion equivalent to the claim that a theory of substantive rationality is required in order to formulate a concept of social action. It is the equation of substantive rationality and ethics which I have been emphasising throughout this work. Substantive rationality is moral rationality when other-regarding criteria are involved.
2. This is the problem which Habermas seeks to resolve by way of a theory of the *dialogical* or *communicative* subject as opposed to the *monological* or isolated subject of Cartesian analysis, or Kant's transcendental ego. My comments in chaps. 7 and 8 *infra* focus on this problem and argue for an individualist conception. I note that epistemological individualism is confused with bourgeois individualism, and suggest that an antipathy to Cartesian and Kantian concepts of the individual as a basis of ethical theory have been attacked on the basis that this individualism is seen to be antithetical to a rational justification for social co-operation. I do not think that this is the case: in chap. 8 *infra*. I argue that intersubjectivity, and, hence, the idea of society, stem from rational assumptions which must be made, and cannot be revised by individuals.
3. i.e. the thesis that legal phenomena consist, in essence, in nonmoral properties, and can (must) be studied separately from the issues of the moral legitimacy of legal rules and decisions. Cf. e.g. Hart, H. L. A. *The Concept of Law* (Clarendon Press, Oxford, 1961). See also chap. 4 *supra*.
4. Finnis, J., *Natural Law and Natural Rights* (Clarendon Press, Oxford, 1980), p. 59.
5. Ibid., p. 64.
6. Ibid.
7. Ibid.
8. i.e. an action should be performed at time t, if it was not performed at time t, it can never be performed at time t *because* time flows only one way, and the interval t is no longer available. Thus, 'being late' is inferred from the observation that an action is performed at time $(t + n)$ where n is some positive unit of time. *Given* that there is no possibility of $(t - n)$ as an opportunity to perform the action ... etc.
9. Ibid., p. 64.
10. Ibid., p. 65.
11. Ibid., p. 67.
12. Ibid.
13. Ibid., p. 68.
14. Ibid., p. 69.
15. Ibid., p. 68.
16. Here is just a sample:

    As a body of conventions and esoteric conditions the compelling character of logic, such as it is, derives from certain narrowly defined purposes and from custom and institutionalized usage. Its authority is moral and social, and as such it is admirable material for sociological investigation and explanation. In particular, the credibility of logical conventions, just like the everyday practices which deviate from them, will be of an entirely local character.

From Bloor, D. and Barnes, B. in 'Relativism, Rationalism and the Sociology of Knowledge', in M. Hollis and S. Lukes (eds), *Rationality and Relativism* (Basil Blackwell, Oxford, 1982). In addition, see my comments on Bernstein's 'Involutional Determinism; in chap. 9 *infra*: and Pap's discussion of the linguistic theory of the a priori in *Semantics and Necessary Truth* (Yale University Press, New Haven, chap. 7. Also my comments on Hollis in this section and see notes on Russell's 'Theory of Types' in Klein, M. (op. cit.), note 34 *infra*.

17. Evans Pritchard's views on the Azande are well known. Cf. also Dan Sperber's article 'Apparently Irrational Beliefs', in M. Hollis and S. Lukes (eds), (op. cit.), pp. 149–80.
18. Cf. Quine, W. V. O. 'Two Dogmas of Empiricism' in *From A Logical Point of View* (Harvard University Press, Cambridge, Mass. 1980).
19. Thomas Kuhn and Paul Feyerabend spring to mind. Cf., respectively, *The Structure of Scientific Revolutions* (Chicago University Press, Chicago, 1970), and *Science in a Free Society* (New Left Books, London, 1978).
20. Cf. Beyleveld, D. and Brownsword, R., *Law as a Moral Judgment* (Sweet and Maxwell, London, 1986), pp. 115, 116: '...thoroughly reflexive circularity is a virtue and not a vice when attempting to support a priori knowledge claims'.
21. See note 20 *supra*.
22. This issue merits more attention and I attempt to injure severely two birds with one stone by discussing it in relation to the logic of determinism – or, more accurately, the denial of agency – in the final chapter on Gewirth. See chap. 9 *infra*.
23. Hollis, M., 'The Limits of Irrationality', in M. Hollis and S. Lukes (eds), (op. cit.) Also *Models of Man* (op. cit.), pp. 147 ff.
24. See chap. 9 *infra*.
25. Hollis, M., *Models of Man* (op. cit.), p. 147.
26. Ibid., pp. 149, 150.
27. Ibid.
28. Ibid.
29. By this I mean, in the hope of following Kant, that it is intelligible to claim that in a world of 'things-in-themselves', beyond our understanding or possible experience, there may be alternative logics and other forms of reason, contradictory objects, worlds without time or space, etc., but, if there were, we could not have experience of them. Similarly, we may admit that all our thought processes (including these here) are completely determined. But what warrant we would have for entertaining this *noumenal* possibility, or what purpose this assumption could serve, is not apparent to me. See my remarks in chap. 9 *infra*. re: Bernstein's 'Involutional Determinism'.
30. Speaking in defence of the dialectically necessary method. Gewirth makes similar claims for deductive and inductive reason in *Reason and Morality* (University of Chicago Press, Chicago, 1978). See note 18 in chap. 1 *supra*.

31. Finnis, J., (op. cit.), p. 68.
32. Cf. Pap, A., *Semantics and Necessary Truth* (Yale University Press, New Haven, 1958), chap. 7 on 'The Linguistic Theory of the A Priori'. This is an important text – now out of print.
33. Finnis, J., (op. cit.), p. 68.
34. Russell, B. and Whitehead, A. N., *Principia Mathematica*, 3 vols, (Cambridge University Press, New York, 1910-13) (cf. 'The Theory of Types'). Cf. Kline, M., *The Loss of Certainty* (Oxford University Press, New York, 1980), p. 22, who says:

    > Russell and Whitehead wished ... to avoid the paradoxes that arise when a collection of objects is defined that contains itself as a member. The resolution by Russell and Whitehead of this difficulty was to require that 'whatever involves all members of a collection must not itself be a member of the collection'. To carry out this restriction in the *Principia* they introduce the theory of types.

    See also my discussion of Bernstein's 'Involutional determinism' in chap. 9 *infra*.
35. See note 23 supra.
36. Finnis, J. (op. cit.), p. 68.
37. Descartes, in the first meditation, says '... I see so clearly that there are no conclusive signs by means of which one can distinguish clearly between being awake and being asleep ... (Descartes R., *Discourse on Method and the Meditations* [Penguin 1982], p. 97). However, in the sixth meditation he recants:

    > ... I must reject all the doubts of these last few days, ... particularly the general uncertainty about sleep, ... for now I see a very notable difference between the two states in that our memory can never connect our dreams with one another and with the general course of our lives, as it is in the habit of connecting the things which happen to us when we are awake. ... And I must not in any way doubt the truth of these things, if, after having called upon all my senses, my memory and my understanding to examine them, nothing is reported to me by any one of these faculties which conflicts with what is reported to me by the others. (op. cit., p. 168).

    But Descartes speaks of strange dreams with unconnected happenings and strange disappearances. We would not, on the criteria above, be able to distinguish rational (well-connected) dreams from wakeful experience. Testing the connectedness of experience is the point. However, Gewirth says:

    > The method of clearness and distinctness as Descartes develops it ... exhibits no merely psychological or subjective criteria, but rather logical and perceptual ones which the mind is to use in order to ascertain the conformity of its thought with a world external to it. (Gewirth, A., 'Clearness and Distinctness in Descartes', in W. Doney (ed.), *Descartes* (Macmillan, London, 1967), pp. 276, 277.
38. This is surely what Kant meant by phenomena and noumena. Phenomena is not simply appearance in opposition to a noumenal 'reality'. Phenomenal reality is phenomena validated by the

application of science. Science must be conducted within the limits of experience and is conditioned by the categories of the understanding. My grasp of this issue has been greatly increased by Deryck Beyleveld's unpublished paper 'Transcendentalism and Realism'. This paper is essentially a critique of Bhaskar's views and is of some importance in the light of the acknowledgement of Bhaskar's contributions to the philosophy of science, and the publication of his multi-volume work *Philosophy and the Idea of Freedom* (Blackwell, Oxford, 1991). Beyleveld's interpretation of the phenomena/noumena distinction seems to bring Kant and Descartes very close together on the issue of the limits of reason and the expectations of science.

39. Finnis, J., (op. cit)., p. 68.
40. Ibid., p. 68.
41. Cf. Newton-Smith, W. H., *The Rationality of Science* (op. cit.), pp. 44–76 for a full discussion of the issue.
42. For a discussion of this cf. Newton-Smth W. H. (op. cit.), chap. 4.
43. Finnis, J. (op. cit.), p. 68.
44. Cf. Popper, K., *Conjectures and Refutations* (Routledge & Kegan Paul, London, 1963), pp. 33 ff.
45. Finnis, J. (op. cit.), pp. 68, 69.
46. Cf. e.g. Quine, W. V. D. 'Two Dogmas of Empiricism', in *From a Logical Point of View* (Harvard University Press, Cambridge, Mass., 1980), p. 46 (esp. the last paragraph).
47. Finnis says:

    > Nowadays the claim that something is self-evident is commonly misunderstood by philosophers. They think that any such claim either asserts or presupposes that the criterion of the truth of the allegedly self-evident principle, proposition or fact is one's *feeling of certitude* about it. This is indeed a misunderstanding. Self-evident principles such as those I have been discussing are not validated by feelings. On the contrary, they are themselves the criteria whereby we discriminate between feelings, and discount some of our feelings (including feelings of certitude) however intense, as irrational or unwarranted, misleading or delusive. (Finnis, J. [op. cit.], p. 69.)

48. See my discussion of Bernstein's arguments in chap. 9 *infra*.
49. Hume's dictum that we cannot derive an 'ought' from an 'is' is perfectly true if it is interpreted as the claim that we cannot logically infer a categorical imperative from the assumption of a contingent empirical fact. But the kind of facts which we are discussing in this chapter are not contingent, and neither are they empirical. They are necessary and non-tautological, Hume did not recognise the possibility of such statements and so we can be sure he was not talking about these kind of truths when he formulated his 'Law'.
50. In *Reason and Morality* (Chicago University Press, Chicago, 1978), p. 1, Gewirth says:

    > ... a morality is a set of categorically obligatory requirements for action that are addressed at least in part to every actual or prospective agent, and that are concerned with furthering the interests, especially the most important interests, of persons or recipients other than or in addition to the agent or the speaker.

Cf. also Beyleveld, D., *The Dialectical Necessity of Morality* (University of Chicago Press, Chicago, 1991), chap. 9, where he defends Gewirth's argument from accusations that his definition of morality is arbitrary. Beyleveld says, at p. 332, 'Gewirth's definition of morality, though not universally shared, begs no questions: it is used to raise his questions, not to answer them'.

51. Finnis, J. (op. cit.), p. 86.
52. Ibid.
53. Ibid., p. 87.
54. Ibid.
55. Ibid., p. 88
56. Ibid.
57. Ibid.
58. Ibid.
59. Ibid.
60. Ibid., p. 89
61. Ibid., p. 92.
62. Ibid.
63. Ibid., p. 97.
64. Ibid., p. 100.
65. Ibid., p. 101.
66. Ibid.
67. Ibid., p. 102.
68. Ibid., p. 103.
69. Ibid., p. 104.
70. Ibid., p. 105.
72. Ibid.
73. Ibid.
74. Ibid., p. 107.
75. Ibid., p. 106.
76. Ibid., p. 107.
77. Ibid., pp. 109–26.
78. Ibid., p. 126.

Chapter 7

1. Cf. McCarthy, T. translator's introduction to Habermas, J., *The Theory of Communicative Action* (Heinemann, London, 1984) and his comments on Horkheimer, M. and Adorno, T. re: *The Dialectic of Enlightenment*; An interesting discussion of the developments of Western Marxism appears in Poster, M., *Foucault, Marxism and History* (Polity Press, Cambridge, 1984), chap. 1.
2. Cf. Finnis, J., *Natural Law and Natural Rights*, (Clarendon Press, Oxford, 1980), chap. 1.
3. Habermas, J., *The Theory of Communicative Action*, I (Heinemann, London, 1984), p. 7.
4. Cf. Pusey, M., *Jurgen Habermas* (Tavistock, New York, 1987), e.g. p. 75 for a comprehensive explanation of the concept.
5. Habermas, J. (op. cit.), chap. 3.
6. Cf. e.g. Giddens, A., *Capitalism and Modern Social Theory* (Cambridge University Press, Cambridge, 1971), pp. 65 ff.
7. Cf. translator's preface to Habermas, J. (op. cit.), xxii–xxiii.

8. CF. ibid., xxii.
9. Durkheim, E., *The Division of Labour*: cf. Giddens, A. (op. cit.), p. 101.
10. Translator's preface to Habermas, J. (op. cit.), p. xviii.
11. Ibid., p. xviii, xix.
12. Ibid., p. xix.
13. I refer to modern analytical philosophy's attempt to eliminate metaphysics from the theory of meaning. Logical Positivism is a prime example, of course, but Marcuse's analysis of the rise of positivism post Hegel in Marcuse, H., *Reason and Revolution* and Habermas's discussion of the methodologisation of epistemology into pure technique, at the expense of evacuating the subject from the concept of knowledge in *Knowledge and Human Interests*, are the areas of analysis which I have found most informative of the moral effects of our conception of science in modernity.
14. Translator's preface to Habermas, J., (op. cit.), p. xvii–xviii.
15. Cf. Lukács, G., *History and Class Consciousness* (Merlin Press, London, 1968).
16. Outhwaite, W., *Concept Formation in Social Science* (Routledge & Kegan Paul, London, 1983).
17. Held, D. and Thompson, J. B. (eds), *Critical Debates* (Macmillan, London, 1982), p. 222.
18. Ibid., p. 221.
19. Ibid.
20. Ibid.
21. Cf. e..g. Neumann, F., *Behemoth: The Structure and Practice of National Socialism – 1933-1944* (Harper & Row, New York, 1966).
22. Held, D. and Thompson, J. B. (eds) (op. cit.), p. 222.
23. Ibid.
24. Ibid.
25. Ibid.
26. Ibid., p. 223.
27. Habermas has had reservations about the link with Peirce. In 'A Reply to my Critics', in D. Held and J. B. Thompson (eds) (op. cit.), p. 274, he says: 'In the light of the debate set off by Kuhn and Feyerabend, I see that I did in fact place too much confidence in the empiricist theory of science in Knowledge and Human Interests.'
28. The theory of Communicative Action holds communication to be the fundamental emancipatory category of society in opposition to Marx's category of labour.
29. In D. Held and J. B. Thompson (eds) (op. cit.), chaps 1 and 8, respectively, Heller and Giddens take Habermas to task for his allegedly impoverished conception of the Marxist category of labour. Habermas, in 'A Reply to my Critics', in D. Held and B. J. Thompson (eds) (op. cit.), p. 222 says:

    Agnes Heller renews an objection that has been raised from different sides against my separation of the concepts of labour and interaction. Stated briefly, this reservation is directed against the reduction of labour to 'instrumental action'; the idea of labour, of productive activity, of practice – so the argument goes – is thereby robbed of its deeper dimension: the

> 'anthropological significance' of labour is lost. Above all, what is lost is the normative content of creativity and self realization; and without the rationality inherent in this externalization, objectification and appropriation of essential human powers, the concept of alienated labour must also lose its sting. This objection brings Heller to the impressive formulation that in social reproduction there lies a claim to undistorted purposive activity no less than to undamaged communication ... I am not unaware of the weight of tradition to which a humanistic Marxism that began in the name of the philosophy of practice (Praxis) can appeal. Impulses emanating from Heideggerian Marxism of the early Marcuse and from the Husserlian Marxism of the early Sartre were picked up by Karel Kosik and Enno Paci, became fruitful in the Yugoslavian Praxis group and in the Budapest School, and had a broad international influence, as can be seen for instance, in the circle around the American journal Telos ... it is no accident that Heller speaks in this connection of the 'romantic' features of Marx's early writings.... Charles Taylor traces this motif back through romanticism to Humboldt and Schiller ... and above all to Herder ... When Marx borrowed from Romanticism (through Hegel) the expressivist ideal of self formation, transferred aesthetic productivity to the practical working life of the species, conceived social labour as the collective self-realization of the producers, and, against this background, represented the activity of the modern wage labourer at once as alienated and as the modern emancipatory force, he found himself faced with a series of difficulties. These difficulties cannot be overcome by anthropologically elucidating a concept of Praxis ...

Habermas's reasons as to why we cannot read Marx in the expressivist context is less than convincing. He suggests (ibid., p. 225) that a problem lies with the analytic clarification of such a concept but, even assuming that a formulation could be adequately constructed, there would be doubt as to whether '... this paradigmitic mode of activity is as universal as purposive activity and communication'. I can only suggest that this would depend upon how we formulated the concept of labour. If, as Habermas suggests is the case, the reproduction of social structures is impossible without communication, then this would necessarily be a component of the concept of labour as *expressive* of species being. That purposive activity is juxtaposed to labour here as a separate conception of human action is very strange – purposive activity is the fundamental presupposition of historical discourse and as such appears as an undifferentiated *agreed referent* (see chap. 4 *supra* for analysis) – it is *the* universal conception in such matters. Further, citing Honneth (ibid., p. 225), Habermas says:

> ... Honneth traces without illusions a development of industrial labour, which, under the pressure of the imperative to rationalise, has become further removed from the model of the craftsman's activity. Correspondingly, the concept of

labour has been purged of all normative content in industrial sociology and has been discharged from the role of an emancipatory driving force in social philosophy. If we add to this the trend towards shorter working time and towards a corresponding devaluation of the relevance of labour within the life world, then it becomes evident that the historical development of industrial labour is cutting the ground from under the philosophy of Praxis.

But these remarks are very odd. They are historical descriptions which would serve as evidence of the validity of the thesis of alienated labour conceived of as a *denial* of expressive species being. That craftsmanship has been purged from the daily lives of the vast majority of workers by capitalist development does not in any way undermine the thesis that workers are, essentially, frustrated craftspersons. Finally, the fact that modern sociologists and philosophers do not *choose* to conceive of the phenomenon of labour as announcing an emancipatory *telos* says even less about the essential nature of labour than the preceding remarks. If fashions in sociology and philosophy determined the nature of social reality then we would merely have to think utopia to be in it. My point is that, notwithstanding the argument over labour versus communication, might not there be something to say about simply *the having of purposes*?

30. Cf. Habermas, J., *The Theory of Communicative Action*, I (op. cit.), chap. 1, and especially the thesis developed in Habermas, J., *Knowledge and Human Interests* (Heinemann, London, 1972), pp. 1–8.
31. Habermas, J., *The Theory of Communicative Action*, I (op. cit), p. 1.
32. Ibid., pp. 1–2.
33. Ibid., p. 2.
34. Ibid.
35. Ibid., fn. 5, chap. 1.
36. Ibid., pp. 2, 3.
37. Habermas, J., *Knowledge and Human Interests* (op. cit.).
38. Cf. Ibid., pp. 1–8.
39. Outhwaite, W., *Concept Formation in Social Science* (Routledge & Kegan Paul London), p. 68.
40. Ibid.
41. Ibid., p. 69.
42. Ibid.
43. Ibid., p. 70.
44. Ibid., see 'Carnap'.
45. Ibid., p. 71.
46. Ibid., p. 70.
47. Cf. Schmidt, M., *Habermas's Theory of Social Evolution*, in D. Held and J. B. Thompson (eds) (op. cit.) p. 162.
48. Pusey, M., *Jurgen Habermas* (Tavistock, New York, 1987), p. 69.
49. Habermas, J., *The Theory of Communicative Action*, vol. I (op. cit.), p. 10.
50. Ibid.
51. Ibid., p. 11.
52. Ibid.

53. Ibid.
54. Ibid.
55. Ibid., p. 12.
56. Ibid.
57. Ibid.
58. Ibid., p. 13.
59. Ibid., p. 14.
60. Ibid., p. 15.
61. Cf. ibid., pp. 288–95 – quoted in Pusey, M. (op. cit.) p. 77.
62. Pusey, M. (op. cit.), p. 77.
63. Ibid., p. 78.
64. Ibid.
65. Habermas, J., 'A Reply to my Critics' in D. Held and J. B. Thompson (eds) (op. cit.), p. 263.
66. Pusey, M. (op. cit.), p. 58.
67. Cf. Lukes, S., *Power a Radical View* (Macmillan, London, 1974).
68. Lukes, S. 'Of Gods and Demons: Habermas and Practical Reason', in D. Held and J. B. Thompson (eds) (op. cit.), p. 137.
69. Ibid., p. 138.
70. Ibid., p. 138.
71. Ibid., p. 140.
72. Cf. Schmidt, M., in D. Held and J. B. Thompson (eds) (op. cit.), p. 164.
73. Cf. Hollis, M., *Models of Man* (op. cit.), chap. 7.
74. Strawson, P. F., *Individuals* (Methuen, London, 1959), p. 10.
75. Pettit, P., 'Habermas on Truth and Justice', in G. H. R. Parkinson (ed.), *Marx and Marxisms* (Cambridge University Press, Cambridge, 1982), pp. 212, 213.
76. Ibid., p. 211.
77. Ibid.
78. Ibid., p. 212.
79. Ibid.
80. Ibid., p. 213.
81. Ibid.
82. Ibid.
83. Ibid., pp. 214, 215.
84. Ibid., p. 215.
85. Ibid.
86. Ibid., p. 216.

Chapter 8

1. Beyleveld makes these points in addressing remarks made in MacIntyre, A., 'Rights, Practices and Marxism' (*Analyse und Kritik*, 7, (1985), pp. 234–8). Cf. Beyleveld, D., *The Dialectical Necessity of Morality* (University of Chicago Press, Chicago, 1991), p. 448 and *re* Pollis, pp. 156–9.
2. Habermas, J., *The Philosophical Discourse of Modernity* (Polity Press, Cambridge, 1987), p. 315.
3. Marx, K., 'Preface (to a Contribution and Critique of Political Economy' in L. Colletti (ed.), *Marx – Early Writings* (Penguin, Harmondsworth, 1975), pp. 42 ff.

4. Cf. Derrida, J., *Of Grammatology* (Johns Hopkin University Press, Baltimore, 1976), exemplifies the kind of denial of the subject I am talking about.
5. Sturrock, J. (ed.) *Structuralism and Since* (Oxford University Press, Oxford, 1979), p. 15.
6. Ibid.
7. This conception of the subject is not in contention. Post-Modern analyses identify this substratum of meaning and objectivity as an implication of discourse. But they want to say that the necessity of the presupposition of the subject, and the necessity of the assumption of a true/false world, is just a by-product of the sign. I want to say that this conception of subjectivity and the implicit conditions of objectivity and critical discourse are epistemological assumptions which are transcendentally or dialectically obligatory, and thus epistemologically valid. The real point of contention is, again, the *circularity* of the inferences which lead to an understanding of the nature of subjectivity. Post-Modern and Pragmatist writers refuse, as we have noted at length, to admit of any non-vacuous products of circularity or necessity. On this point they are clearly wrong, as we have already shown in our discussions of this issue in Chap. 1 *supra*, of deductive reason in Finnis in chap. 6 *supra*, and as I emphasise in my discussion of Bernstein in chap. 9 *infra*.
8. I refer to Wittgenstein's 'private language/following a rule' argument. Cf. Trigg, R., *Understanding Social Science* (Blackwell, Oxford, 1985), pp. 23–6, for a discussion of this issue.
9. Marx, I., *Capital*, I (Lawrence & Wishart, London, 1977), p. 174. Cf. also Cooley, M., *Architect or Bee? The Human price of Technology* (Langley Technical Services, Slough, 1980), for a profound discussion of the creative agency inherent in the Marxian concept of labour.
10. Habermas, J., *The Philosophical Discourse of Modernity* (Polity Press, Cambridge, 1987), p. 315.
11. Ibid., . 313.
12. In my doctoral thesis, *Towards an Integrated Theory of Natural Law* (University of Sheffield, 1990), chap. 3, I discussed at length the nature of the arguments which denied propositional status to moral/ethical statements. An objection which I found to be common was that no theory of reference could adequately explain the potential truth-value of categorical imperatives for the reason that no notion of correspondence between the semantic content of the statement and the 'world' could plausibly be presented. In particular I looked at the emotivist assumptions about reference and the Logical Empiricism which appeared to inform them. I also devoted considerable time to Bernard Williams's paper, 'The Truth in Relativism', *Proceedings of the Aristotelian Society* (1976), pp. 74–5, 215–88. Williams says that although there are things for moral statements to be true *to* (individuals, groups, 'cultures'), there is nothing for them to be true *of* (i.e. no world of moral facts). In reply I attempted to construct a theory of truth correlates for moral propositions whereby categorical imperatives referred to the principles or laws of practical reason in the same way that logical statements are true

when they describe principles of deductive reason. The principles themselves are transcendentally grounded, or, what amounts to the same thing, dialectically necessary. I see now that this two-tier scheme of dialectical necessity and reference is entirely superfluous. Dialectical necessity is enough. My remarks is that chapter about the proposition as being the *form* of a belief, and that this form always intends a reference to 'reality', are, however, of some interest in the context of a theory of the subject. Beliefs (about anything) are semantic wholes (the content of propositions) which take the form of assertions and denials. We are stuck with this, and as Habermas points out, communicating our beliefs brings with it the implication that these claims (about 'reality') can be redeemed from an investigation of that reality. In the case of a claim which is dialectically-necessary, I am faced with having to claim 'P', recognising that 'if P then Q', and thus being unable to reject (rationally) 'Q'. There is no point worrying about the reference of the terms which comprise 'Q', (e.g. '*x* is the case', '*y* categorically ought to be the case'), the point is whether or not one can avoid the *modus ponens*. If not, then one has to accept that 'Q' is the case – whatever 'being the case' means.

Chapter 9

1. Beyleveld, D., *The Dialectical Necessity of Morality – An Analysis and Defense of Alan Gewirth's Argument to the Principle of Generic Consistency* (University of Chicago Press, Chicago, 1991).
2. The three stages of the argument (not to be confused with the numbered propositions which crop up in the presentation of the argument) are dialectical inferences from the standpoint of the agent which appear in this order:
    1. 'I must value my freedom and well-being'.
    2. 'I must claim rights to my freedom and well-being'.
    3. 'I must acknowledge that all agents have these rights' (i.e. I must acknowledge the necessity of the Principle of Generic Consistency).
3. Gewirth, A., *Reason and Morality* (University of Chicago Press, Chicago, 1978), p. 3.
4. Ibid., p. 7.
5. Cf. ibid., pp. 37, 38.
6. Ibid., p. 49.
7. Ibid., p. 50.
8. Ibid., p. 51.
9. 'Conative normality' is not simply voluntary agency, it is the translation of purposeful thought into action. Cf. Gewirth, A., (op. cit)., p. 90; and Beyleveld, D., (op. cit.), p. 30: a conatively normal person is a being who 'has the self-interested motivations common to most persons and is willing to expend the effort needed to fulfil them … .
10. Cf. Nielsen, K., 'Against Ethical Rationalism; in E. Regis Jnr (ed.), *Gewirth's Ethical Rationalism* (University of Chicago Press, Chicago, 1984), pp. 59–83 (esp. pp. 78, 79); and Beyleveld's reply in Beyleveld, D. (op. cit.), pp. 165, 166.
11. Cf. Beyleveld, D., (op. cit.), pp. 69, 70. Also on contradiction etc. pp. 329–32.

12. Bernstein, M. 'Involutional Determinism', *The Monist,* 71 (3 July 1988), pp. 358–65.
13. Ibid., p. 359.
14. Ibid.
15. Ibid.
16. Ibid.
17. Ibid., p. 361.
18. Ibid., p. 362.
19. Ibid.
20. Ibid., pp. 362, 363.
21. Here the actual text reads: 'or, what comes much to same point, ...'.
22. I am not saying that *modus ponens* implies the Law of Contradiction; this would, I suppose, be to employ *modus ponens* in defence of itself. There are probably two irreducible notions here, that of inference and that of contradiction. But *modus ponens* certainly cannot be employed without the observance of non-contradiction. Obviously, to manipulate two propositions one must understand that these propositions are different from each other and identical with themselves.
23. Gewirth, A. 'The Justification of Morality', *Philosophical Studies,* 53 (1988), pp. 245–62 (p. 245).
24. Ibid., p. 246.
25. Ibid.
26. Ibid., pp. 246, 247.
27. Ibid., p. 247.
28. Ibid., p. 248.
29. Ibid.
30. Ibid.
31. Ibid.
32. Ibid.
33. Ibid. Cf. also Beyleveld, D., (op. cit.), pp. 163–76, where this objection is comprehensively discussed in respect of several authors.
34. Gewirth, A. (op. cit.), p. 248. Cf. also Beyleveld, D., (op. cit.), pp. 244–6, in particular, and chap. 8, in general, for a discussion of the move from the prudential to the moral via universalisation.
35. Gewirth, A. (op. cit.), p. 249.
36. Cf. Beyleveld, D. (op. cit.), pp. 66, 67 (*re* Trigg, R.).
37. See note 9 *supra.*
38. This is the objection which alleges that Gewirth's argument reduces morality to logic: cf. e.g. Beyleveld, D. (op. cit.), pp. 102–5, where he replies to Bond, E. J. 'Gewirth on Reason and Morality', *Metaphilosophy,* 11 (1980), pp. 36–53. Bond's arguments in this regard are to be found at pp. 36, 37. In respect of Bond's *ignorationes scripti* cf. Gewirth's foreword to Beyleveld, D. (op. cit.), p. xvii.
39. This issue is, of course, foundational. Cf. Beyleveld, D. (op. cit.), pp. 110–13, in reply to Adams, E. M., 'Gewirth on Reason and Morality', *Review of Metaphysics,* 33 (1980), pp. 579–92 (590). Cf. also Gewirth, A. (op. cit.), p. 44.
40. Cf. Bond, E. J., 'Gewirth on Reason and Morality' (op. cit.), p. 50; McMahon, C., 'Gewirth's Justification of Morality', *Philosophical Studies,* 50 (1986), pp. 261-81; Hare, R. M., 'Do Agents Have to be

Moralists?' in E. Regis Jnr (ed.), (op. cit.), pp. 53 ff.; Golding, M. P., 'Human Rights', *Nomos*, 23 (1981), p. 171; Singer, M. G., 'On Gewirth's Derivation of the Principle of Generic Consistency', *Ethics*, 95 (1985), pp. 298–90; In defence of this stage cf. Scheuermann, J., 'Gewirth's Concept of Prudential Rights', *The Philosophical Quarterly*, 37 (148) p. 391; and Beyleveld, D. (op. cit.), pp. 201–31. Notably McMahon and Bond are highly sceptical of the notion of prudential rights. See notes 46–54 *infra*.

41. Hare, R. M., 'Do Agents Have to be Moralists?' (op. cit.).
42. Ibid., p. 53.
43. Ibid., p. 54.
44. Ibid.
45. Cf. Beyleveld, D. (op. cit.) pp. 201-31.
46. Hare, R. M., 'Do Agents Have to be Moralists?' (op. cit.), p. 54.
47. McMahon C., 'Gewirth's Justification of Morality' (op. cit.), p. 269.
48. Ibid.
49. Gewirth, A., 'The Justification of Morality' (op. cit.), pp. 250, 251.
50. Ibid., p. 258.
51. McMahon, C. (op. cit.), p. 276.
52. Gewirth, A., 'The Justification of Morality' (op. cit.), p. 259.
53. Ibid.
54. Ibid., p. 260.
55. Beyleveld replies to Golding, MacIntyre and Pollis on this question. The 'Robinson Crusoe' objection to stage 2 of Gewirth's argument as presented by Golding, and Beyleveld's reply, can be found in Beyleveld, D. (op. cit.), pp. 159, 160.
56. Cf. Beyleveld, D. (op. cit.), pp. 257–303.
57. Cf. ibid., pp. 43-6; and Gewirth, A., *Reason and Morality* (op. cit.), pp. 109, 110.
58. Cf. Friedman, R. B., 'The Basis of Human Rights: a Criticism of Gewirth's Theory', in J. R. Pennock and J. W. Chapman (eds), *Nomos* 23: *Human Rights* (1981), pp. 148–57; and Beyleveld, D. (op. cit.), pp. 244–6.
59. Gewirth, A., *Reason and Morality* (op. cit.), pp. 109, 110.
60. Cf. ibid., chap. 4 etc.

Index